MELISSA SANDS

THE SECOND WIFE'S SURVIVAL MANUAL

BERKLEY BOOKS, NEW YORK

THE SECOND WIFE'S
SURVIVAL MANUAL

A Berkley Book / published by arrangement with
the author

PRINTING HISTORY
Berkley edition / May 1982

ISBN: 0-425-05236-2

"He seemed so perfect in the beginning...Now I live with my married man, but the secret thoughts I have cannot be shared with him. I can hardly face them myself."

—*Tulsa, Oklahoma*

"When I was a mistress I knew ecstacy, but I knew agony too. Now the ecstacy isn't so overwhelming anymore. But there isn't any agony. And when I lie in bed watching my husband sleep, I still think all this may be a dream. But it isn't. It's a dream come true!"

—*Lisle, Illinois*

"I can't shake this feeling about my married man. He makes love to me, makes promises, and I wonder does he do the same with her? Once we're married, will he do it with a new woman? Can he ever be trusted?"

—*New Orleans, Louisiana*

"I was ashamed to admit to anyone how jealous I was at first. I wasn't allowed to say it as his mistress. Suddenly as his second wife my jealousy exploded. I had to either beat this green monster or go from second wife to divorcée."

—*Winter Haven, Florida*

"My married man told me everything and I told him everything about me, all the details. After we were married, we came to regret all those confidences. Honesty isn't always the best policy."

—*Deer Park, Illinois*

"When he got his divorce and married me, I thought I had it made. I don't know what happened to us exactly. All I know is that our desire to be near each other has seemed to vanish into thin air."

—*Lindsey, Ohio*

"His kids made me feel like a dirty object. I was referred to as 'her.' After 9 months they began calling me Sandy. After 2 years they actually liked talking to me. And now, you know, I really look forward to their visits!"

—*Belmont, California*

Berkley books by Melissa Sands

THE MAKING OF THE AMERICAN MISTRESS
THE MISTRESS' SURVIVAL MANUAL
THE SECOND WIFE'S SURVIVAL MANUAL

Acknowledgments

In a publishing era of caution and confusion, I am grateful for a publisher like Rena Wolner. Her commitment to subjects of merit is unwavering. I thank her on my behalf as well as for all the people who have been helped.

Since I uttered the word "mistress" publicly, I have met a sea of people heretofore isolated in agony and fear. I owe much of my inspiration to those who have written to me, enlightened me, and inspired us all. Thanks for your contribution. I wish I could write back to each of you, but alas I can only answer a few letters. So many of you must accept this blanket thank you.

I am constantly indebted to my agent, Roslyn Targ, who acts superbly as a buffer for me as well as my bolster. Creativity is at times an agonizing occupation and cannot function without this practical, supportive relationship that Roslyn provides. Roslyn has helped me far more than she realizes.

The finished book owes a debt of gratitude to Linda Healey, my editor. Her insights add polish to my ideas, perspective to my plans, and a logic to my arguments, and reason to some of my strained emotions. I have come to value highly and depend on her criticism. I look forward to benefiting from these again.

I want to mention specific thanks to Diane Glynn for her commitment and Ling Lucas for her enthusiasm and dedication. Our dealings have been periodic and I have never adequately expressed my gratitude.

In the end as in the beginning, Michael, my husband, deserves his due. It is not easy to live with a writer. He must act as my editor, agent, supporter, therapist, cheerleader, etc., etc., etc., and he does so with grace and steadfastness. This book involved reliving old pains we both could have done without. However, even in our pains we share and become closer. Thank you darling.

Thank you all.

Dedication

To my Father who taught me to wish,

to my Mother who taught me to aspire,

to my husband, Michael, who taught me perspective,

with love to you all.

Contents

PART IV   STRATEGIES FOR COPING

Table of Tests

Introduction

Could you go from mistress to wife? Today you are a mistress. You may define your married man as "safe," a "distraction" from your marriage, an "obsession," or "the love of a lifetime." You may feel the frustration suggested by one mistress who wrote me:

"I have something wonderful going with my married man, but it's sad, too. I can't tell anyone how happy he makes me. I want him all to myself. I'm looking for a future. But there's no future in being a mistress." (Marietta, Ohio)

Is there a future in being a mistress? For some, the only future is more of the same. For others, there is a future as that married man's wife. And tomorrow, you, regardless of what you think now, could be one of those mistresses who makes the "Triangle Transition" and goes from mistress to wife! I know, because I was a mistress whose future meant marrying my married man!

I was once a mistress, isolated, madly in love, and in distress. My personal trauma led to my organizing other mistresses in a group called Mistresses Anonymous, a group to share secrets and help each other. My organization made me a national celebrity. Apparently there were more mistresses out there than I or anyone had imagined. So many women wanted to join up, I couldn't personally meet with them all. Hence, I wrote *The Mistress' Survival Manual* (Berkley Books, 1978), the official Mistresses Anonymous program that every mistress could consult for help alone or in a group. My *célébrité* made me the confidante of hundreds of thousands of women who related to the mistress dilemma. To enlighten society about the real mistress vs. the myth and to set the record straight, I then wrote *The Making of the American Mistress* (Berkley Books, 1981). This is a unique report on why and how any woman can wind up in a triangle.

In between writing, TV appearances, and research, I married my married man. In going from mistress to wife, I made what I call the Triangle Transition. For me it was the happiest of endings to a very unhappy triangle.

Becoming a married man's wife should not be regarded as an end for the mistress. It is a beginning. It is the beginning of a new life. If you go from mistress to wife, you are not becoming an ordinary wife. You are becoming his second wife. What does that mean? Here is how one mistress-to-wife summed her triangle transition up:

"Although my years of mistresshood led me on a journey of roller coaster highs and lows, towering plateaus of euphoria and deep depths of despair, I finally emerged my married man's second wife. Not before emptying my thousandth box of Kleenex, though. I remained emotionally and physically drained and war-wounded for months to follow.

"Our new life together now consists of three years and several months. I think I need another book, only this time perhaps you could write 'The Second Wife's Survival Manual.' If I were able to write, it could be based on my experiences. My tale runs the whole alphabetical gamut from:

                    A—Alimony, Child Support expenses
                    B—Belated beginning for us
                    C—Children—a real eye-opener for a non-
                        parent like me
        to: X—X-tra bills, X-tra headaches, X-tra house-
                        hold to support, X-tra phone calls from X-wife,
                        Xcetera
                    Y—Your sanity
                    Z—Zero level of tolerance.

"I feel that it is safe to say that the new wife does inherit a husband's problems from his other life to some degree and she must be equipped emotionally, maybe even financially, and ready to handle each new (old?) crisis. I love my husband and we share many happy times, don't get me wrong. It's just that I could use some HELP! I need another Manual right away!" *(Wisconsin)*

As a second wife myself, I knew what this woman was talking about. I began getting more and more letters from mistresses who became their married man's wife. They had questions and points to make. So with their help and inspiration, and my experience, here is the book about what it's like to go from mistress to wife.

In designing the book, I thought it could be most useful to gear it to the mistress—because every mistress is a candidate for second wife! Life is unpredictable. You are a mistress now, but you could wind up as I did, making the Triangle Transition.

I want you to think about that now. Could you go from mistress to wife? Would it be a happy ending for you? Don't answer yet. Wait until you reach the end of this book. It is dedicated to helping you find the right answer to that question. *The Mistress' Survival Manual* was devoted to helping you get or give up that married man. This book is devoted to helping you find out if you are cut out to become his second wife. The decision is yours as well as his.

Why all this fuss about the Triangle Transition? Is becoming a second wife really so different from becoming a wife? Yes, yes, a thousand times yes! As a mistress, you are not the ordinary fiancé contemplating an ordinary marriage. Your married man is no ordinary fiancé, either. You are not simply contemplating marrying a man, but a father, a debtor, an infidel, a "criminal," and possibly an indentured servant of sorts. Just as your affair is a taboo, a mistress marriage also takes place in taboo territory.

Society at large is not ready to accept the mistress marriage. The mistresses who do get sympathy are few and far between. The mistress who marries her man is jinxed with superstitious forebodings, not congratulatory wishes. It's almost as if a woman who goes from mistress to wife has committed some crime. Perhaps wife-a-cide?

While the scarlet A stigma attached to mistressing is well-known, the stigmas attached to second-wifehood are less clear. Yet they do exist. The Triangular Transition subjects you to pitfalls, trials, and challenges. It also sets you up for untold joys, happiness, and the fruition of a host of fantasies.

As in confronting any taboo, there are warnings implied in the challenge. As a second wife candidate, you should ask yourself: What kind of trials are waiting for me on the other side of that threshold? Am I cut out to weather the stormy transition from mistress to wife?

In the passage from mistress to wife, some education and some enlightenment can guide and help you. This book will reveal many common experiences of the mistress marriage and suggest strategies. The tales and the advice compiled here come from many second wives.

The first part of the book deals with rites of passage, rites you will travel through in going from mistress to wife. These are strategies for choosing, for deciding about him as well as other aspects of your relationship. Does your affair have the ingredients to make a good marriage? Does your married man possess appeal to keep you interested for a lifetime? Will he take another mistress, once you become his wife? How can that chronic question and chronic fear be answered? Will the past repeat on you, resurrect jealousy, rehash old traumas? Every mistress who opts for the Triangle Transition must pass history tests. So must the married man. Can you accept him, his total person, his past?

Decisions are your first responsibility. Decisions involve choosing. Part I will help you choose so that your team will be a happy marital partnership.

The second part of the book deals with some strategies for living. In some aboriginal tribes, the groom paid a bride-price for his spouse. In mistress marriages, the reverse is often true. If you go from mistress to wife, you will probably pay a "groom-price." Married men don't come cheap! The price is paid in emotion, in sacrifice, and in money. The legal system provides the gameboard. Playing judicial monopoly well can save your new life. Playing naively or irrationally can leave your married man childless, penniless, and hopeless—a cruel life sentence. A life sentence that you will share. Surviving judicial monopoly is possible once you learn the rules, the odds, and the advantages.

How can you prepare for your new life as his second wife? You must plan "lodge-istics" so that you don't wind up without a roof over your heads! Take stock of your assets and liabilities with this married man. There are money matters to consider, because money will indeed matter. Learning appropriate strategies for living can make or break your mistress marriage. How will families react to this triangular switch? How should you react to their reactions? This transition shakes up any family tree. Can you pick relatives the way you pick friends? Going from mistress to wife is like going from outlaw to in-law. The last chapter of Part II will help you deal with various aspects of your new life—the where's, the how's, and the who's.

Part III considers your new family roles and relationships. These are akin to initiation rituals. What will life be as a second wife? You, in all likelihood, will be marrying more than a man; you will be marrying a father. Developing strategies for parenting is, therefore, a must. For many mistresses, wedding the package deal (the man with children) means marrying crises. After his divorce, your married man will probably suffer a paternal crisis. His paternal bind is your bind. Are you qualified to help? Then there is stepmothering. What are your expectations about step-parenting? If you have children, do you have a strategy for your new blended family? If you are childless, will maternity be an issue that will plummet you into an unusual maternal crisis? Married men get you in the womb, in the heart, in the mind, and often wreak havoc everywhere. Parenthood in all its aspects is a huge commitment for the second wife. Are you ready? Can you get ready? Are you willing to become a family member as well as a partner?

The fourth part of the book is designed to assist you in coping with all the challenges of becoming a second wife. It will help you sort out good strategies for coping. It will train you in sustaining for a lifetime the romance and passion you now feel. Second marriages are especially blessed in some ways. In others, they are especially cursed with complex pitfalls. You can learn the valuable role of temperament, and you can temper your temperament if you need to. You can learn to keep the magic of romance alive. Romance is not a commodity that has to be forfeited on the other side of the threshold. Yet, so often that seems to be the fate of romance. Why? Can you get romance insurance? How can you keep a little of the mistress in your marriage? And can you keep communication as intense as it is now? Can soulmates remain so for years and years? Learn the difference between the language of marriage and the language of love, and you've got a good warranty.

Going from mistress to wife can be a dream come true. It was for me. It can be a nightmare, too, if you are not cut out for the special trials and tribulations. Could you go from mistress to wife and go happily? Will the benefits balance the sacrifices for you? Only you can make the assessments, the judgements, and the calculations, with the help of your man. I can give you tests to clarify issues and help you learn more about yourself. I can supply a wealth of testimony from second wives. I can give you advice, suggestions, thought-provoking data and hints. But in the end, only you and that married man can make the final commitment.

Sounds serious, doesn't it? It is. At this moment you may be only a mistress, but at the same time that makes you second-wife potential. Married men get you, and sometimes that means right to the altar. And I want you to be sure you don't wind up feeling like a sacrificial lamb on that altar!

"It sure is easy to say 'I won't get involved' when you're a mistress. But it happens before you even get the words out of your mouth!" *(St. Paul, Minnesota)*

Ten years ago if someone had predicted that I would fall in love with a married man, fall prey to a triangle, and become a mistress and then his wife, I would have thought they were nuts. Life is so uncanny. It takes us around in circles and sometimes that means through triangles.

Many times a mistress chooses a married man because she is in some period of transition. Possibly she has just divorced and a married man seems safe. Possibly she's questioning her marriage and a married man seems like an elixir. Possibly she is committed to a career and a married man seems convenient. Unexpectedly, though, a choice motivated by transition can propel an unprepared mistress into a transition she never dreamed . . . the Triangle Transition.

Nearly every mistress I have met has said to me, "I never thought this could happen to me," or "I never meant to fall in love with this married man." It seems each mistress is borne in surprise, passion, and disbelief.

If that applies to you, beware. Because every second wife also expresses disbelief at her new married status to that ex-married man. Show me a second wife who was formerly a mistress, and I'll show you a woman who never thought it could happen to her!

When you are in the grips of a triangle and in the arms of a married man, it is very important to try and get your footing. Your affair will be going somewhere, no matter how hard you try not to look at the future. Mistresses and married men relish the present but time still marches on and forward. Where you and he wind up should be given much thought.

I am more concerned with you, the mistress, because no one has given you enough concern. What will a triangle do to your future? You must try and find the answers yourself. If you don't, tell me then, who will?

Where do you want to go from here? Today you are a mistress. What do you want from tomorrow? From that married man? Many of the mistresses with which I deal are not sure of anything anymore. If you are desperately in love with that married man, get in touch with your desires for the future.

Some mistresses admit that he won't divorce and yet they don't believe it. Deep down inside, many a mistress wants marriage. What about you?

Do You Secretly Desire The Triangle Transition?

An affair with a married man oftentimes has clear-cut limits. Divorce and remarriage are usually out of bounds. How do you react to those limits? Are you being honest with yourself? Some mistresses accept and even express satisfaction with the limits of an affair, while others harbor clandestine rebellion.

Secretly do you desire the Triangle Transition from mistress to wife? As I look back at myself in the mistress period, I see now that I did want to be my married man's wife. I called upon all the rationalizations I could consciously, and yet my heart was leading me on a different course. And while I stifled, silenced, and starved those secret desires, they were leading me into the Triangle Transition.

Wishful thinking and positive thinking, even done secretly, can influence the course of your life. Many experts agree on that. Therefore it is useful for you to explore your own behavior and see if you are showing signs of secret desires to go from mistress to wife. Be careful and, more importantly, be knowledgeable about your wishes.

The following test is designed to help you see your secret desires. Answer honestly and, in exploring your behavior, fragments of the wishes you harbor will begin to surface. Could you make the Triangle Transition? The first clue is in your desire.

Directions: The test is a True or False test. Simply respond honestly, either True or False, and write in your answer in the space provided. Then proceed to the scoring and an evaluation of your score.

1. You have found yourself absentmindedly
   scribbling "Mrs. _____" on paper, the
   name you would have as his wife.

XX   THE SECOND WIFE'S SURVIVAL MANUAL

2. You have introduced him to people close to you, not as your lover, but in disguise, because you wanted him to meet them. _____

3. You have been introduced to his children, or he to yours; again incognito. _____

4. You have fantasized the kind of wedding ceremony that your marriage to him would entail, given the special problems. _____

5. You have imagined him in the social situations of your life, at parties, in family gatherings, social functions. _____

6. You yearn for the ordinary things, like going to movies on Main St., or doing shopping together at the Mall. _____

7. You have deliberately explored his attitudes and values on things like politics, child-rearing, religion. _____

8. Your attitude towards marriage has definitely changed (either pro or con) since this married man has come into your life. _____

9. When you and he are together, your conversation is laced with fantasies of how it would be as man and wife instead of mistress and married man. _____

10. You have begun to map out a plan of where you and he would live if you were together. _____

11. The romance and the isolation of your affair isn't as pleasurable as it was; now you yearn for more. _____

12. You have calculated at least once the financial possibilities and liabilities of you and he living as one. _____

Scoring:
Each True answer is worth 10 points. Each False answer is worth 0 points. Give yourself 10 points for every True answer and total your points. Then see below if you secretly desire the Triangle Transition?

Evaluation:
    0–30 points: The Daydreaming Mistress. If you scored in

a low range on this test, you have occasional daydreams about the Triangle Transition from mistress to wife, but they are fleeting and isolated. Affairs so often have such a make-believe aura about them, due to their intrigue and romantic flavor, that the fantasies are consistent. The key to understanding your secrets is in looking at your moderate inclination to daydreaming about being his wife. Your mind is surely occupied with other things, other goals, and other problems. Your future may or may not involve your married man, but certainly it does not depend on his becoming your husband. Keep a meter on your fantasy behavior, though; things might change. In the meantime your daydreams are not signaling a strong desire to go from mistress to wife.

40–80 points: The Closet Wife/Mistress. If you scored in a middle range on this test, your desires are secrets that still remain in your own private closet. You exhibit some of the fantasy behavior and some of the inclination towards the Triangle Transition, but you still vacillate. Perhaps you will go further toward wanting to be his wife; perhaps you are just indulging a romantic imagination. Go back and examine your True answers. Some are more pregnant than others. Are you value-testing your married man for compatability? Are you bringing him into your family and social circles to get opinions and reactions? Are you planning financial and living scenarios? Action is what you should look for, as opposed to doodlings or creative imaginings about a wedding ceremony. Identifying the degree of your secrets is important for you. You could go on to becoming the Bride-to-Be Mistress, preoccupied with going from mistress to wife.

90–120 points: The Bride-to-Be Mistress. If you scored in the high range on this test, your desires are probably not unknown to you at all. You know that the Triangle Transition is occupying much of your time, your thoughts, and your fantasies. You are in a bride-to-be state of mind. Much of your energy is focused on going from mistress to wife. Your conversation with your married man is full of not only "if only" but "whens." Chances are you've calculated the risks, the assets, and the odds about becoming his wife. You have a nuptial game plan all prepared. You've value-tested him hopefully and tested him out on relatives, friends, and in social scenes. What you should do now is find out if your bride-to-be state of mind has a future. Does your married man know of the intensity of your secret desires? Have you really looked at all the pragmatic questions of compatibility and drawbacks? Or are you locked in the romantic angles of animating your doodlings? Learn to be honest, straightforward, and vocal about your secret desire to become his wife, or you may wind up waiting a lifetime for him at the altar . . . alone.

In Conclusion:
Whether your desires to go from mistress to wife are mere daydreams, recurring fantasies, or incessant preoccupations, acknowledging them is the first step. This entire book is dedicated to taking you on a journey to see if you could go from mistress to wife in reality, not fantasy. And more importantly, if that Triangle Transition from mistress to wife would make you happy. For you, would it be better or worse?

Think about those marriage vows. Think about your married man married to you. And above all think about what it will be like if you go from mistress to wife.

"I always hated the stigma attached to being 'the other woman.' I was viewed by others and even my own mother as an evil woman because I was a mistress. Just because I was courageous (and foolish?) enough to express my taboo—but genuine—love." *(East Lansing, Michigan)*

It is quite common for any mistress to feel imprisoned in a world of taboos. Is there any way out of these aboriginal limits? Is a mistress destined to feel like an anthropological oddity forever, even after she crosses the threshold?

For some that answer is yes. Mistresses are different, outside social norms. Second wives remain different, too. There are always elements of life that are extraordinary in a mistress marriage. However, that doesn't always mean that different is bad.

In some primitive societies after the marriage ceremony, the bride's father and relatives would grab clubs and start chasing the newlyweds. The new bride and groom would run for their lives. That anthropological cameo reminds me of the mistress marriage, because the second wife and her new husband will have to run, from harassment, from prejudice, from fiscal discrimination and from spiteful ex-spouses. Yet there are two ways of looking at this great escape. You may be running away from ill-willing enemies; you may be running toward unprecedented romance and bliss. The way you define that escape can be a prediction of how you feel about a mistress marriage.

Marriage is a serious step. As you watch your married man dismantle his marriage or as you dismantle your own, that lesson hits home. Before you marry that married man, weigh the pros and the cons and be sure the odds are in your favor.

Any mistress can go from mistress to wife. It could be you. Your responsibility is to find out if that fate would add to your life. I hope this book helps you.

Every person has a future, even a mistress. Plan out your future so that it includes all the best things in life, love, and marriage. All the things that you deserve!

PART I

Strategies for Choosing

CHAPTER 1

From Soulmates to Roommates

Sometimes I feel like I am writing the memoirs of a fairy-tale princess. I am like the star in a fairy tale. His kiss changed me from a tearful mistress to a blissful wife. The tale is too long to retell here. But it was full of grim episodes, dragonesque obstacles, and romantic flights. Here, I will tell you a bit about the happy ending.

It was not hard leaving the mistress era behind, as you can well imagine. When I look back at my mistress past, one picture I still see is me holding and smelling a flannel shirt *he* once left behind. I'll never forget that brown and gold flannel shirt. I still have it. When *he* wasn't around, which was ninety-nine percent of the time, I would wear that shirt or just sit and smell it because it smelled just like *him*. Sounds pitiful, doesn't it? Well, being a mistress is, in some ways. You have to live without the most important thing in your life . . . *him*. So instead you live with memories of him, longings for him, and maybe some momento that conjures up his fragrance or his presence.

One day he came to me with the rest of his clothes. The mistress era was ended. I don't think I can adequately portray the joy, the relief, and the pleasure that followed. We lived in a tiny two-room dwelling stuffed with all our belongings. We had little money. His was all tied up in his past. He had enormous legal pressures. He worried endlessly about holding on to his relationship with his two small children. We had nothing. And yet we had everything. We had each other. We were hopeful and happy. We had a future. We had been soulmates. Now the perfect coupling of souls were roommates. The married man and the mistress became husband and wife.

What is it really like living at last with your dream man? For one thing no matter what your floors are made of, you could swear they were all carpeted with clouds. When you awaken in the morning, he's not only on your mind, he's right there. Before and after you rub your eyes. Then there's waking up at night somewhere in between your dreams and feeling him next to you. For the mistress who goes on to wife, each and every ordinary part of being married is a special blessing. All the simple things that married people take for granted, the mistress/wife never does.

Remember the rush you felt as a mistress approaching that rendezvous moment? The culmination of passion and longing? These feelings are now with you twenty-four hours a day. There are no tortures like there once were. He is no longer unavailable; he lives with you. He is not someone else's husband; he is your husband. All his wonderful traits will be dedicated toward building a life around you and for you. His paternal qualities will now be expanded to include a child of your mutual conception. The romance that surrounded you both now surrounds daily life.

If I could compose music, I would have written a piece called "The Candlelight Sonata." Because going from his mistress to his wife was like entering a world of violins and candlelight, of arpeggios and whispers. A world where hot passions no longer had to cool for any reason. There were no longer endings everywhere. Instead all was beginnings.

I was positive that I was the luckiest woman on earth. I had to have that superlative honor because only I was married to *him*. However, there were other women out there who challenged me. They, too, had gone from mistress to wife. They, too, had gone from soulmates to roommates.

"At first, the thought of his being married never crossed my mind. We went out for a whole year before it hit home. I was too in love then to give him up. Whenever I thought of not seeing him again, I couldn't breathe. So I hung on and became a mistress. I went straight down into a world of hell. I could not break up with him, nor he with me. Then he divorced and married me. I went straight up to heaven and I'm still there after seven years." *(Cleveland, Ohio)*

"I love him so. Makes an intelligent person into a damn fool. Luckily for me, by some miracle he married this fool.

Sometimes I still feel I don't deserve all the happiness I've found." *(Okemis, Missouri)*

It doesn't matter how each mistress expresses her joy at becoming her man's wife. The feelings are universal. The language of love is understood without any need for translation. The initial transition naturally is wonderful. It is the culmination of a fantasy.

If you go from mistress to wife, you can expect that aura of bliss as a wedding present. However, after the newlywed stage is over, then what? As a mistress you lived *for* that married man. As a wife you will be living *with* that married man. Will he still be that dream man after his married man appeal fades? Will he be as wonderful a roommate as he was a soulmate? Or will you utter desperately one day, "You're not the man I married!"

The purpose of this chapter is to explore the married man thoroughly on this side of the threshold. Right now, your married man is the man of your choice, the man you want. If you go from mistress to wife you will have him. When you do, will he turn out to be the man who can make you happy for a lifetime?

The purpose of this chapter is to verify your choice. Can picking a man be romantically right and scientifically sound? Is your love for this man based on reality or is it blind? Are there any special pitfalls that you should be alerted to because of your triangle status? Are your romantic assertions valid? Is there a method that can tame the madness of love and validate your choice?

In this section we are going to look at several mistresses as they choose and marry their men. We will analyze their methods of choosing. We will dissect fantasy. We will study motive. As we see these women in transition from mistress to wife, we will see the impact of that change on their relationships. Their learning processes will become yours.

Some say that familiarity breeds contempt. Although that is a depressing assessment of long-standing relationships, some truth lies between the lines. And yet, familiarity can also breed contentment. If you go from mistress to wife, which will it breed for you? Will familiarity breed contempt or contentment? Your answer will depend upon your married man, the man you pick.

A soulmate is one thing, very beautiful and unique. A roommate is quite another. A man may be good at one of these roles, and turn out to be horrid at the other. Married men often are instant soulmates. But mix that same man with marriage, and the brew can be bitter. That is something that Megan learned too late.

Madness and Sanity

"I can't stop writing. I've never laid it out this way, only in my head again and again. And in my diary. But I stopped making entries there, too. I'm afraid of my diary."

Why is Megan afraid of her diary?

"When he calls and asks me what I'm doing, I used to say, 'Nothing,' or 'Knitting,' 'Cleaning.' Now I have a new one . . . 'Feeding the baby, our baby.'
"The baby was a month early. My whole body was so tense and anxious all the time, that baby just wanted OUT. I know the feeling. I used to feel my mistress years were full of nightmares. Now nightmare is a gross understatement!"

Megan's fears are striking, even if her explanations aren't clear. Let me start at the beginning of her tale and briefly fill in some details. Megan met Mat at an Alcoholics Anonymous meeting. They were both recovered alcoholics. Mat was married, for fifteen years, but the marriage was childless. It was a confusing time in both of their lives. The confusion was compounded when they had a brief affair and Megan found she was pregnant!

"I considered abortion, even went down to a clinic and talked it over. But I'm thirty-five. I chose to approach this baby as a gift from God and of that decision I have no regrets. The regrets are for all the other decisions I've made."

Mat was overwhelmed at the prospect of fatherhood. It had been something he always wanted. Impulsively he left his wife and filed for divorce. Megan was all wrapped up in the miracle of her pregnancy, too. She accepted his marriage proposal. It all seemed too easy. That premonition was apt.
Mat divorced his wife and married Megan, but he never

really left his wife. He was juggling two lives, two wives, and everyone was miserable. And Mat started drinking again.

"I thought I knew Mat. I thought I loved him and that our marriage seemed perfect. Now slowly I am realizing it was a mistake. I didn't really know him at all.

"I go through little playlets in my mind all the time. Imagining this and that. The three of us, Mat, myself and his ex-wife have all entered counseling. I want to survive this for my son. I want to be the best parent I can be. And now all I can do is rock my colicky baby around the house and cry.

"The therapist sat me down last evening and asked why in the world I couldn't let this man go. He made some brief comparisons of 'me' and 'her,' and 'me' and 'him.' He said my growth potential so far exceeded this man's that I would bore of him quickly if I hadn't already. I had and I knew it. He said that my man's instability, his sense of utter failure to cope, was a crutch I hardly needed. He ventured our marriage was a mismatch hastily sealed in some feverish circumstances. I had to agree. I cried and protested and said, 'But I love him.' But I knew the real truth. I realized it wasn't the man, it was the married man I loved. Mat, the husband I lived with, I didn't like him with his weaknesses and his excuses and his indecisiveness. I didn't think about him as a person during our affair, just as the main 'thing' in my life. Then came the baby. Having him for husband and father became an obsession for us both. It could have been a drug I was addicted to. I was possessed and now that I am seeing things more objectively, it has all been a terrible mistake."

Megan and Mat were casualties of romantic madness. Megan's judgement of Mat was blinded by passion. Megan's expectations were inaccurate of Mat and impossible for Mat. Triangle trickery confused them and was compounded by the primal promise of reproduction. These forces created havoc in their lives. Hence a time of insanity.

"When I was a child," Megan recalled, "I had a horse named Sanity. I would literally gallop for miles over the Montana hills, and leave behind any feelings of weakness. I was free and in control whenever I rode Sanity. I wish I had that beloved animal now!"

Megan's passage from mistress to marriage was a disaster. Her story is melodramatic, thus providing an excellent lesson.

Megan chose a man steeped in married man appeal, and not the real man underneath.

Sometimes a mistress falls in love with the phenomenon of the married man. Married men come packaged in romance and intimacy. They seem equipped with strength, because they have the power in the relationship. They come across perfect and loving, because that is the only side a mistress sees given the limits of her affair. Married men seem deep and profound as they communicate their souls and their needs.

When a mistress falls in love with this aura, sometimes it clouds the real person. She may be falling in love with a persona of perfection, of sensuality, and of intrigue. A married man who goes on to become a husband loses some sensuality with familiarity, loses his intrigue with respectability, and loses his perfection with ordinary living. If you marry a romantic persona and not a real live person, you are bound to be disappointed. Some married men are illusions. They are all in your mind. And on your mind obsessively. If you are married, your own husband pales in comparison to this married man. Be wary of illusive judgements. Illusions make poor marriage material. Illusions never materialize. If you divorce and remarry an illusion, you will be doubly disappointed.

Psychologists have warned us about love's romantic madness. People in love have a tendency to magnify the attributes of their loved one. The tendency is called crystallization. Do you fail to see any bad in your married man? Do you only see superlatives? You are crystallization in action. Or worse you could even be idolizing him! That is psychologically defined as ideation. Is your married man perfect in every way? If you are answering yes, beware. You may be manufacturing the persona of your married man to your ideal specifications. Is your ideal the same as the real man who lies under your romantic images? Romantic perceptions are very tricky. Both crystallization and ideations are common, dangerous, and misleading. They are pitfalls that can have severe consequences upon your life and life decisions.

Add the complications of a triangle, and these pitfalls take on new dimensions. Triangles escalate passions. They further confound rational thinking. Life takes on a melodramatic cast. Having that married man or not seems the only important thing, worth any price. A mistress is warped temporarily in a triangle, both romantically and rationally. She is prone to even more blindness than ordinary love tends to inflict!

It's scary to acknowledge that you may not be able to trust your instincts when it comes to judging your married man. How can you assess him as a partner, if your instincts are hazy?

You must be careful. The next profile will help you see where the emphasis should really lie.

Puzzle Pieces

Natalie became very introspective after her divorce. She spent several years looking at the broken pieces of her marriage. She was just twenty-five, but she felt much older. Introspection came easy. Natalie always preferred the intellectual side of life to the physical side. That is until she met Spencer.

"I'm not passionate by nature. I began to feel that was the downfall of my marriage. That brought on grave doubts about my sensuality and my self-esteem. I had lost faith in everything including myself until I became friendly with Spence."

She met Spence at work. In the middle of her quandary about life and love, Spence began to help her find answers. It almost was as if he was the missing piece in the puzzle that her life seemed to be.

"Spence and I spent long hours talking at work, at lunch and soon after work. We became good friends. He was kind and he listened. He is sensitive, and appreciated me as a friend, a person, and then as a lover. I was so fearful of having sex and finding that it would be as bad as it was with my husband. But with Spence, it was beautiful and such a relief to find that I was certainly more than adequate! I began to realize that this sweet caring man was what I really wanted."

Natalie couldn't have Spencer because he was married.

"I hid my feelings for him for nearly four years. But all that time I watched him. I watched the way he handled people at work. I evaluated him as a father each time that he told me a story about his family life. I even made a list of qualities and rated him. I graded him on disposition, ambition, and purpose in life. I think I was looking for things wrong with him. But the more I looked, the better I liked him. With each passing year, I became sure this was the man I wanted."

Spence decided to divorce. He said that the decision was inevitable. He had never been in love the way he was with Natalie. His marriage had been stagnant for years. When he tried to think of reasons why it should be saved, he came up empty.

"We have a positive impact on each other. We like the same things. In fact, sometimes he says things that I have been thinking, but was afraid to say out loud. He's uncanny!"

Natalie and Spence lived together till his divorce was final. Then they got married. She realized that all the things that a man should have, her new husband had. Her last husband lacked many of them. Suddenly her first marriage failure made sense. Her past wasn't so confusing anymore.

"Spence was like the last piece to a puzzle. Now I feel complete. I was much smarter and surer the second time around. I wanted Spence because of the wonderful man he is. And I look forward to growing old with him near me."

Natalie's story is really the tale of a friendship that blossomed. First the friends became confidantes. Then the confidantes became lovers. Natalie knew that communication was important. Yet she knew that intimacy wasn't enough, verbal or sexual. You had to like the person as well as his capacity for intimacy. Marriage can dampen intimacy. That, her first marriage had taught her. Intimacy can be renewed only when genuine love for the other person sparks it. And to love him you must know him. Knowing him by heart is almost more important than knowing his heart.

Natalie's process of rational, careful selection is wise. Affairs are passionate peaks. Marriage is more level. Level can be better if the person you share it with suits you. You must know him, good points and bad.

Being soulmates can be a deceptive basis for judging. After the souls are bared, profundity cannot be recaptured on a daily basis. Being roommates is still sharing souls, but it is sharing more. It is sharing towels and toothpaste, sharing troubles and tedium. A husband loses some of the magic that he had as a married man. He is there in the shadowy romantic hours, and in the grumpy daylight too. Will you love him in his least attractive moments as well as his most appealing? You must know all the perimeters of his behavior and personality before you can answer with clarity. Or else familiarity may lead to contempt and discontent.

I've heard people say that you don't really know a person until you live with them. If your man is married, you cannot live with him until you have already committed yourself. So beware of your situation and compensate for it. Go to all lengths to get to know him in his entirety. Be objective. List his bad points. Be inventive and creative in your investigation. Don't settle for a naive estimation of him!

At this chapter's end is a test to help you sort out the man who lies beneath the married man appeal.

Falling in love with a married man is so easy. No man loves you like a married man. They are instant soulmates. They wear their souls on their sleeves. Their hearts, though, are a different matter. Their hearts and yours rarely emerge from a triangle intact. A married man needs you so much. No man will ever need you the way a married man does. Yet his love, his need, his intimacy are all incomplete so long as you have only half of that man.

Even half of a married man is overwhelming. But if you marry without knowing the full picture, your emotions will be make-believe like your lover.

"He seemed so perfect in the beginning. He brought me roses. He told me secrets he said he couldn't tell anyone, not even his wife. I couldn't live without this man. That is how I felt. I even divorced my husband. Now I live with my married man, but I'm not living with that man behind the bouquet of roses. And the secret thoughts I have now, cannot be shared with him. I can hardly face them myself." *(Tulsa, Oklahoma)*

Mistresses certainly have no monopoly on falling in love with love. How many women marry someone they perceive as wonderful on the basis of courtship experience and wind up with a husband who is different? Choosing a mate for the wrong reasons can happen to anyone. What I'm trying to do here is narrow "anyone" down to you, the mistress.

Sometimes your choice of a man can be based on a fantasy. Ideally your choice is based on his reality. And yet at other times your motivation has nothing to do with the man himself, the real version or the imagined. Some mistresses choose to play out a drive and the married man figures in the cast but he is not the star.

Rescue Me!

"It seems that before all this started my life was running so smoothly. I had friends to socialize with and inner peace which I gained studying yoga and meditation. I was enthused about my career and how successful I was becoming. That was before I married Ted. Now I'm wondering if it will ever be smooth sailing again?"

Rita said that everything seemed so right in the beginning. Ted was in his second marriage, but he was being used. His second wife treated him badly even though he worked hard, supported her and her two kids, and gave them all stability.

"Ted was so full of negative feelings about his wife. He even told me his wife didn't love him. He was a convenience. He said he married her because he wanted to be the eternal rescuer. He was aware of his weakness for Cinderellas because his first wife had been one too.

"I guess I became the rescuer. I made him feel good, appreciated. I made him feel loved for the first time in his life, I think! It was only logical that he would want me for a wife."

In the first few months Ted became insistent that he was going to marry Rita. Rita said she kept pulling back because she'd seen too many bad marriages.

"I kept saying that I couldn't get permanently committed. Eventually though, I found I was relinquishing my stand. He separated, divorced. And then I married him. He loved me. I loved him. But. There was a big 'but' that neither of us could figure out. I took a second job that involved travel. He didn't like that, so he took on extra work too. That cut our time together to a bare minimum."

Too much work and too much stress got to Rita and she became ill. Her doctor prescribed plenty of rest. The rest enabled her to spend a great deal of time thinking about why she and Ted were literally avoiding each other.

"With all this behavior in front of me, there had to be a reason. I'm certain that I have always made poor choices in men, feeling I should be the helpmate with the heavier load.

As I looked at Ted and the men before him, I saw that I never created a balanced situation. I was as much guilty of the Cinderella complex as Ted, only the reverse. Show me an underdog and I jump to the rescue."

Now that Rita began to understand her need, why she chose Ted, and why she resented the imbalance in their marriage, she knew why she had been running away.

"I had to decide, should I keep running? Was Ted worth it? He is. I am feeling an inner peace growing within me. I am going to start taking positive steps to mend my marriage. I always liked rescuing, perhaps it's about time I rescued me!"

Rita and Ted may not be the love story of the century, but just another story of love and commitment. Marriage isn't always an easy love story; many have to work at it to enjoy the fruits of their labor.

The "rescue me tendency" can have a number of applications. Some married mistresses find a married man to rescue them from a bad marriage. While he can be their savior in helping them acquire the strength to divorce, he may not be the incarnation of the perfect husband.

"My marriage was the worst. I don't know why I stayed in it so long. Scared, I guess. Falling in love with my married man gave me strength. He taught me that I deserved better. He showed me what true caring can mean. Once I divorced, though, his mission was complete. I no longer wanted him nor my ex. I said, 'Thank you very much,' and moved on." (Sarasota, Florida)

Some of us want to save ourselves or save a misunderstood married man; either way we are driven by missionary-type motives. Beware if your married man is synonymous with a deliverance drive. As husband and wife you and he may find deliverance, but deliverance to where?

The last word of warning is about fantasy once again. Only this time watch his fantasies. Make sure your married man does not see you as a pure fantasy. Some men tend to see their mistresses as 100 percent fantasy. And we all, as mistresses, at one time or another have tried to fulfill our married man's fantasies. We have all held back some of our innermost selves, perhaps because of fear of rejection or perhaps just because there wasn't time enough to unravel. All that I have already said about falling in love with romantic personas should be a lesson you give him. Make sure he sees the total woman and not some girlish geisha.

"I've known two married men in my life. Both of them were too busy tailoring me to their dream woman to meet me half way in the real world. When I asserted myself, they said I was acting like their wives. They were both bad bets as lovers and husbands: Amen to the fantasy and hypocrisy of these married men!" *(El Paso, Texas)*

Her judgements and generalizations are harsh. However, the fantasy trap can be alluring for your married man. You must unveil your whole personality and not only your soul.

The reasons for choosing a mate are as diversified and as individual as the selectors themselves. However, as we have discussed, there are similarities. There are generalizations. There are methods to some of our madness, and methods to save us from madness. Learn to question your motives and your married man's motives. When it comes to choosing your husband, be certain that the man is the motive. Be equally certain that the motive is not totally removed from the man himself.

Much of this advice could be applied to any woman. But I want you, the mistress, to especially take heed. Why? If you have lived in a triangle you have had enough unhappiness. If you go from mistress to wife, go to a marriage that has the best things in store. Go to a man who is the best mate, teeming with surprises that are only good ones. Then your marriage will be the fruition of fantasies. And the honeymoon need never be completely over.

If your married man is your soulmate that is a solid foundation. If he is truly your best friend add a few more layers of plusses. But remember, you must know more than his soul. You must know his mind, his manners, his lifestyle, his goals, his head, and his limitations as well as you know the color of his eyes.

Familiarity will chip away his romantic aura. After you are married awhile, your heart may not skip a beat each time he looks into your eyes. He won't make earth-shattering revelations each and every time you get into a conversation. His smell and touch will not be so rare as to be savored and remembered with longing. As often as he'll leave you sensually in rapture, he'll leave you with dirty laundry and dirty dishes.

Yet, if you are getting the man who is right for you, your transition will not feel like loss. Oh, your communication may not seem so profound, your emotions may not seem so roller coaster wild, but you will have a new high being his wife. You can look forward to planning the future with its new joys around every corner. Looking forward is one of the nicest things about being married. Looking forward together as soulmates and roommates.

I must confess that I don't caress that brown and gold plaid flannel shirt anymore. And for two reasons. One, now I wash and iron it in my busy frenzy of chores. But two, because now it doesn't smell like him. Now we both smell the same because now we are one.

I'm not the fairy princess, though I still feel that way sometimes. He's not the prince. No longer, though, am I the mistress or he the married man, in that old unavailable sense. I am a wife and he is my husband. He was a good choice because living *with* him is far better than living *for* him!

If you go from mistress to wife, be able to say the same for your choice! Soulmates are captivating, but souls are intangible. Life is not, so concentrate on the roommate.

Is Your Married Man a Pedestal Person?

Do you put your married man on a pedestal? Surely you have heard that expression. Putting someone on a pedestal means that you tend to idolize that person. In other words you see that person only in special superlative terms. How do you see your married man? Do you have the pedestal prejudice? Is your married man a Pedestal Person?

One of the best ways to find out whether or not you have the pedestal prejudice is to explore what you know about your man. Of course we know he is warm, communicative, and wonderful. In fact you are probably well-versed in his romantic persona, but what do you know of his mundane side?

The following test is designed to explore how much you really know about your married man. After reporting your knowledge and checking it with his, you will get an idea of who he is. Then and only then will you know if you have the pedestal prejudice and if your man is a Pedestal Person.

Why should you know all this? Because if you are plagued by the pedestal prejudice, you are vulnerable to its pitfalls.

Directions: Answer all the questions below. Keep your answers as brief as possible. Then give the married man the same test. Compare your answers with his. For every time your answers match his, you will get points as the scoring section will explain. Good luck!

	Your answer	His
1. What newspaper does your married man read?		
2. How many hours of television does he watch on the average night?		
3. Name the household chores he does on a regular basis.		
4. Did he attend a cultural event (ballet, concert, museum, art exhibit) in the past year?		
5. Does he ever do the grocery shopping?		
6. Is your married man a sports zombie?		
7. Does he go drinking with the boys at least once a week?		
8. Is gambling (card games, horse racing, numbers, etc.) one of his pastimes?		
9. Did he vote for the Equal Rights Amendment?		
10. Is he a workaholic?		
11. Does he want more children?		
12. How many hours a week is he in full charge of the children?		
13. Does he call that "babysitting"?		
14. Does he believe in fidelity?		
15. Does he think that monogamy is realistic?		

	Your answer	His

16. How many times a month does he have dinner with his in-laws?

17. How often does he see his parents?

18. What radio station does he listen to regularly? (or what kind—news, country, rock, jazz)?

19. What is his favorite television program?

20. What book, if any, has he read in the last year?

21. What outfit of clothing is he most comfortable wearing (work clothes, suit, athletic garb)?

22. Does he write out all the bills each month in the household?

23. Does he subscribe to a monthly magazine?

24. How often does he go shopping for anything?

25. Does he go to parents' night at his children's school?

To Score:
For each answer that is the same as his answer give yourself 10 points. For answers that don't match give yourself no points at all. Now total up your points.

Total_____

Evaluation:
   0–50 Points: The Pedestal Problem. If you scored low on this test you definitely have the pedestal prejudice. And it is a problem. Why? When you think of your married man you see him uttering words of love, or holding you in his arms. You tend to see him in a working situation or in a situation

that is familiar to you. The man he is when he is out of your sight is still a mystery. You keep him on a pedestal where he is forever wonderful. Yet how little of his habits you know! How he spends his time, his money, what part he plays in child-rearing, what he reads or does for leisure activity, of these you know very little. If you go from mistress to wife, it is the real man that you will be living with, not the pedestal version. Learn all you can about the little things in his life. Otherwise when the pedestal falls, you will be hit the hardest. The man you have may be a stranger!

60–120 Points: The Pedestal Propensity. This score indicates you have quite a bit of the pedestal prejudice. It is for you very much a pitfall. The less you know about your married man, the more surprises you are in line for. And surprises aren't always pleasant. For instance, if you love to go to the theatre, the ballet, and he loves to sit in front of the TV set with a beer, will that alter your happiness after the altar? Is the man you think he is, really the man he is off that pedestal? You should go back and review all the answers that disagreed with his. Are they things that are significant? Are they meaningful to you? These 25 questions will give you more details and you must see if you like the clearer picture. Your propensity to idolize him could cloud his personality. Watch for the pitfalls or the bottom may fall out of your second marriage!

130–180 Points: The Pedestal Penchant. If this is your score, you still have a mild penchant for the pedestal tendency. However, you are in no serious danger. Apparently you have been quite inquisitive about the man without the pedestal. You know many of his habits, his plans, his play-time activities, and his values. There are still some empty holes in the total picture though. Chances are that the misses for you involve the domestic side of his other life. He may be reluctant to reveal his part in the marriage: chores, budgets, babysitting. And yet these very things are sometimes quite telling. For example, does he regard his time with the children as "babysitting"? What does that say about his parenting role? Look at all his answers and get the total picture. In all likelihood he doesn't have far to fall from the pedestal, but be sure that it's not your images and hopes that come tumbling down!

190–250 Points: Pedestal Proof. If you score high on this test, good for you! You are pedestal proof, which means that you don't have that man up on an unrealistic pedestal. You know what newspaper he reads, how much TV he watches, and what clothes suit him best. These are not menial things but rather indicators of his philosophy, his goals, and his routines. The more you know about your married man, the better equipped you are to decide whether he really is the man who can make you happy if you go from mistress to wife. After all, time and familiarity will chip away that romantic pedestal and you will be left with the sum total of all these questions. What you see is definitely what you will get from your married man and thank heaven your vision is not clouded! Pedestal proofing is a good exercise for any couple to ensure living happily ever after.

In Conclusion:
A pedestal may be a lovely place to be in fantasy, but in reality putting your married man on a pedestal is a mistake. We are all inclined to do this in the initial stages of romance. If you had that penchant, after this test you are already on your way to overcoming the pedestal prejudice.

Now your married man is no longer going to be that Pedestal Person and that will help you from making any mistakes in an important area of your life!

CHAPTER 2

Is Your Affair Marriage Material?

Does your affair possess the potential to make a "good" marriage? That is a tough question. It probably raises more questions in your mind, too. For instance, questions like "What is a good marriage?" Or questions like "How can anyone predict the good marriages from the bad?" In the next pages we are going to attempt to explore the issue of marriage potential.

If you go from mistress to wife, you are going to make the move of a lifetime. What sort of move will it be? Will your mistress marriage bring you a thousand new joys or a thousand disappointments? You and he as married man and mistress may add up to a wonderful affair, but as wife and husband what will be the end result? What kind of a team will you two make?

Team is the word I want you to keep in mind throughout this chapter. We are going to meet several second wives who were formerly mistresses. With each meeting we will be looking at some relevant lesson about marriage potentials. What makes some marriages successful and others not so? Are the relationships that follow founded on love or logic? Which is better? Does a good marriage take one or both or either? At the chapter's end you will have to apply these lessons to your own affair. A test is provided to help you. Because in the end, you and only you can decide whether or not your affair is marriage material. As a mistress you are probably absorbed in the present. However, now is the time to assess the future of your team.

Long ago when I was a mistress gripped in uncertainty, a dear friend of mine and her mother used to tell me, "If a man loves you he will move mountains for you." So often I have thought of them and their words. My only editing would be that sometimes a woman too must move the mountains. The next story of a mistress/married man marriage brought those words to mind again.

Mountains and Moving

"I loved Bob so much that I would have moved heaven and earth for him. He felt the same way about me even though we were both married to other people at the time. I honestly believe there comes a time in a person's life when they have to choose what's best for themselves. Then they have to make their move no matter what it takes."

Darcy wasn't simply a woman of words. She was a woman of action. She didn't have to move heaven and earth for Bob, but in her own way she sure did have to move mountains. So did he.

"I was married for eighteen years. My children are old enough to understand that I was unhappy and that I wanted a divorce. My husband threatened to kill me every time I broached the subject. I knew a divorce would mean a long bitter dragged out feud. I got to the point where I couldn't go home anymore. I knew the only way for me was to go as far away as I could so my husband couldn't find me. Only then would he realize that divorce was inevitable."

Darcy left and moved west, over the Rockies and to California. She left behind her children, her house, all her possessions and assets. It was a choice she felt she had to make. The one thing she didn't leave behind was Bob.

"Bob said that he would leave too because he couldn't live without me. I felt badly for his wife at the time but mostly for his kids. But his wife was being stubborn too and wouldn't consent to a civilized divorce. Truthfully, I couldn't make my life miserable staying married to a man who wanted to be set free. Wives that do this are beyond my understanding."

In California Bob filed for residency and for divorce. Darcy's husband filed for divorce too. In time the divorces became final and Bob and Darcy were finally married.

"I feel so lucky because Bob and I are so happy. We give each other all the love and understanding that a real marriage takes. Life holds new hope for us now. In time we hope to straighten out all the loose ends we left behind. Not that it's been easy. It has been heart-breaking for us both because of our children. We are planning to go back east soon to visit and hopefully we can move back there. We both gave up good jobs and had to find new ones out here, but when you really want something badly enough, you go out and do whatever it takes."

Darcy told me that they had to sacrifice a lot at first, but that they had their love to keep them going forward. And that it was worth the price they had to pay. They knew it would be. That is why no mountain was too high for them to tackle. They moved and in so doing moved mountains and reached new heights.

The point of introducing you to Darcy and Bob is to emphasize that planning a marriage means making choices. These two who were very much in love were also very much aware of their options and losses. They calculated that their affair would make a good marriage if they survived the tumultuous transition of divorce and missing time with their respective sets of children.

Going from affair participants to marriage partners means changing your lives totally. The pragmatic details have to be planned in advance. There has to be a logic beneath all the love. That logic has to alert you to any sacrifices, any losses, or any demands the new team will necessitate. You and he as a team must jointly make those choices and decisions or else you find yourselves victimized and unawares. Choices can range from jobs to children or to any lesser stresses.

Sometimes the "lesser stresses" can be a tall order to master. The emotional obstacles that Ellen met almost ruined her transition from mistress to wife. There was almost nothing left to the team.

Faculties

"Every woman in our position, [the mistress] needs to be brutally honest with herself. My story ended very happily. Rick and I were married two years ago after three years of hell, punctuated of course by the inevitable periods of heaven that keep every affair going. And although I have been married for two years now I still think back sometimes and marvel at our final outcome."

Ellen's transition from mistress to married was a real horror show. And yet her ordeal is typical of what many mistresses must go through with her married man before arriving at the threshold of a new life. So let's go back two years and review her passage.

"Our affair began two weeks before my thirty-first birthday. I was a graduate student and my married man was a professor on the faculty. He was married of course, ten years my senior, and with a new baby. If one can be platonically in love, I had been in love with him for a year or more. I knew if he ever made overtures I would accept. I knew he would be interested in an affair for fun, not love. Then three weeks into the affair, complete with sexual overtures, Rick told me he loved me. I, cautious soul, waited a week after that before making my confession."

The acts of love were followed by other acts. Acts of guilt, acts of separations, acts of reconciliation, acts that brought enormous pain and passion to them both. He proposed marriage one week, left his wife the next and then went back home. After a long thirteen months of this Ellen packed up and left the state.

"I moved. I went to movies. I threw myself into looking for work. I loaded my bulletin board with all the poems I could find about recovering from a broken heart but also about the power of love to overcome all obstacles. Then I moved back and began working again on the faculty with a firm resolve not to see Rick again, romantically. But of course we did go back together, and inevitably there was another hellish period."

Ellen needed a solution. She applied to new graduate schools and was accepted. She said, "I couldn't continue to go on living not knowing where my personal life or my career were going. I couldn't go on living with his waffling and indecisiveness even though I knew he loved me."

Ellen finally issued an ultimatum. She was dead serious this time and Rick knew it. There really is no right time to divorce, but any time is the right time for an ultimatum. It worked. Rick moved out once and for all. Now they are married.

"Are we happy? Yes, deliriously. Are there problems? Yes, but the problems now pale in comparison to what we already survived. But life is settled now and we're making it together in spite of financial strains, family ties, and the rest."

Ellen is now an associate professor on the faculty. So is Rick. But it was their collective faculties for love and strength and endurance that made a success of their marriage.

An affair must be founded on friendship and logic. An affair must also be founded on a firm base of love. Otherwise it will never survive the Triangle Transition to marriage. The ups and downs of divorce, separations, and reconciliations take a tremendous toll on the quality of love. For many mistresses riding that married man to the courts and to the altar is like riding a bucking bronco. If you can hold on tight enough and close your eyes, maybe your love will triumph. But it's a tough, dangerous period.

Some mistresses find that those final months of the affair are the final turnoff. It's as if their threshold for stress has just peaked. When the married man arrives at the doorstep free at last, it's the mistress now who wants to be free of him.

"I just ran out of everything at once . . . love and patience, strength, too. He had lied to me and run back to her and back to me again one too many times. When he came for real, I cried wolf at him. I told him I was drained, all loved out I guess. And I meant it. I didn't want to be his mistress anymore or his wife either." *(New Paltz, New York)*

If your affair is to be marriage material it must be stronger than most relationships. The bondage to each other must withstand enormous stresses. The friendship that you share must have forgiveness and understanding ingrained firmly. It takes more than romance and passion to turn an affair into a marriage. It takes a commitment to the future of the team so that the present can be put into perspective.

"I was there. I was his mistress for a short time. I wouldn't let that last any length of time as I knew I couldn't handle it.

And besides there are too few years in a lifetime and who wants to see them wasted. We knew we were right for each other. We knew it in our hearts and we knew it in our minds. Luckily for us everything worked out fine. We each divorced our spouses as we had been very unhappily married, and married each other. It will be nine years married for us, not without problems, but what marriage has none? All in all we were right. We have been happier than either of us could have imagined." *(Akron, Ohio)*

Underline one sentence from that quotation, "We knew it in our hearts... and our minds." Your affair must be able to surmount the pragmatic obstacles and the emotional turmoils. It must be based on love, but it must also be based on the logic of the mind.

Sometimes the difference between the successful and the unsuccessful marriage is easy to assess. It is often a matter of logic. If the mistress/married-man match is an illogical team then the chances of success are less.

Logic sounds so easy to grasp, doesn't it? However when you are gripped in the swirling passions of a triangle, logic can elude you. If you are a mistress and immobilized in the present tense, sometimes the picture of the future is hard to foresee. You and he are in love and right for each other now and so it is often natural to assume that means forever. Beware of romantic predictions.

Your affair must be founded upon logic, if it is to be "forever" material. As the passions and romance flow and ebb as they do in marriage, your affair must have a firm base to see you two through. Only a rational framework will make a team stable. A rational framework usually means compatibility. Your union, in addition to being passionate and romantic, must be stable.

How does one assess the stability factor in a potential marriage team? By focusing again upon pragmatic considerations. In the beginning of this chapter we looked at obstacles your team would have to face in moving from an affair to marriage. Obstacles on the outside like careers and children. Now we are going to look at obstacles from another perspective. What do you and he add up to as a team? If you are compatible your union will have few obstacles. If you are not compatible, watch out. The less compatible you are, the more obstacles you will pose to each other.

There is only one thing scarier than discovering that you and your married man are incompatible. That is learning that you and your new husband are incompatible.

The Politics of Incompatibility

"Shortly after my marriage to Glen, I entered an assertiveness training program. I was so confused. I was super-high over the marriage, I had confidence I never had before. Yet I was also devastated in a vague way, panicky, and slightly suicidal in my fantasies. This didn't jive with what a newlywed was supposed to be. So I decided I would try getting help."

Lorraine was twenty-five. She told me she had been looking forward to being a wife and a mother all her life. Glen, her former married man, was fifty-four. He was a doctor; she a film crew worker. Sounds like a strange pairing, doesn't it? It was. They met in his office once when Lorraine was sick.

"My depression started over our married sex life. Our affair had been super sexually. After marriage, though, he changed. He was always too tired. A few times he came up impotent. I wanted to get pregnant so much I became very frustrated and upset. He had grandchildren. I was a step-grandparent and yet I had no child of my own. I love Glen very much, but I am scared now."

Lorraine worked for the church and started to become more religious as time went on. She began talking more to God and less to Glen.

"How could I confide in Glen. Could I tell him I feared we had made a terrible mistake in marrying? Could I tell him I was afraid that he was too old to give me a child? As time went on I felt we were mismatched more and more. He played golf with all his golf cronies, who began looking to me like old men. He didn't even know what a film crew did and he cared less. The love that had drawn us together so fiercely seemed to be laughing at me. Was it because I did something wrong? Was I being punished for loving a married man?"

Lorraine was being punished in a way, but not for breaking

some commandment that she so feared. She was being victimized by bad logic. She hadn't thought that Glen and she would make a strange pair before the marriage. She had only thought of long white veils and rice. The age difference, his sexual pace, his desire to begin a family: these are significant considerations. The different worlds from which they came, their combination should have been thoughtfully discussed and assessed. Now it was too late for everything but hindsight. Lorraine was getting a fast lesson in the politics of incompatibility.

The single, most common reason why mistress/married-man marriages fail is incompatibility. That feeling of being mismatched may manifest itself in several areas. You can discover you can't handle his children or he yours. Or that you share little in common where values are concerned. You find that your life goals are opposite. Or that you don't approve of his lifestyle or he of yours. When there is a mismatch in the team the potential problem areas are many. This rule holds true for all marriages. However, mistresses and married men are more prone to the politics of incompatibility because they are usually deciding things under the duress of a triangle.

Affairs are not like ordinary courtships. Triangles have their own trickery. They have swirling passions and larger than life destinies. When a mistress and married man share a rendezvous, all is sublime. The affair doesn't take place in an ordinary day by day world. It takes place in a fantasyland. Unfortunately, triangle trickery eludes many couples. They think because they are perfect lovers and perfect friends they will make a perfect marriage team. Such is not always the case. The next story explains this trickery in a most interesting way.

Verbal Seduction

Gloria was a counselor, which gave her an extremely articulate grasp on her dilemma. Unfortunately she didn't grasp all in time to avoid the mistake of a lifetime.

"I think it is particularly important to stress the verbal seduction that takes place between a mistress and her married man. A mutual verbal seduction took place in my case for over four years. In the beginning I was married to my first husband. However, at work I met Zach and found my intellectual soulmate. It got to the point where verbal and nonverbal communication existed. It was a kind of total communication I had never had with another human being. My husband couldn't measure up to this newfound oneness. Not verbally and then later not sexually."

Gloria's husband got a job transfer and she found she had to make a choice. Their marriage had not been unhappy, it simply paled in comparison to this passionate ethereal union she had with Zach.

"I was totally emotionally, physically, intellectually addicted to Zach. I could not go with my husband. I let my fifteen-year marriage and my son move out of my life. I gave up all financial support from my husband and did a downward financial spiral and had to go through the most difficult year of my life in terms of personal loss, guilt, feelings of worthlessness, and incredible unforgettable nights of suicidal ideations over my marriage. Zach's leaving his wife in the middle of all this didn't help. I realized that he was an illusion. Once having left I couldn't retrace my steps and go back. So instead I married Zach."

For Gloria it was the old "two wrongs don't make a right."

"There are times when I can say that the new marriage I have with Zach is worth all I have given up, but that's only one percent of the time. I look back and try to understand what happened to me. I felt that I had something so precious and so unique, that it justified giving up everything else in my life. Zach was that 'once in a lifetime' trip and I took a tremendous gamble in leaving my stable but relatively mediocre marriage. Now I cannot go back in time, nor can I go forward without this regret if I look honestly at the situation. I am sitting in the middle of a timebomb and when it blows, I don't know where I'll land."

Gloria was verbally seduced by Zach and by her own protestations of passion. However, she was also seduced by the tricks of the triangle. Her own mundane marriage and family life didn't measure up to the fantastic illusions of what marriage to Zach would be. She based her decision to divorce and marry Zach on an ideal concept of love, not on the reality. Her dream of a future with Zach was inconsistent with the past that she too readily deserted. Gloria the mistress was incompatible with Gloria the total person. However, I have faith in Gloria. Someone so articulate about the triangle trickery can resolve it in time.

All the old references to love being blind are so very true. Triangles heighten all our expectations about the marriage that will triumph in the end. Mistresses and married men envision their life together often as one long lifetime of rendezvous. It is hard for any marriage to live up to that expectation. When the fantasies fade in the real light of day after day, there has to be more than illusions within the union. The team must have more going for it.

If the team doesn't have more than passion, realize it before tying the nuptial knot. That may be sad, but certainly not more tragic than discovering triangle trickery got the better of you after your marriage.

"What happened to Jack and me is sad. When he got his divorce and married me, I thought I had it made. So did my mistress friends. I don't know what happened to us exactly. All I know is that our desire to be near each other and talk all the time has seemed to vanish into thin air. I love Jack but I don't like him. He's too opinionated, too selfish, too old-fashioned, too unlike what I thought he was. We have nothing in common except we were once bewitched by some triangle black magic." *(Lindsey, Ohio)*

"I was a sociology major in college. Of all people I should have known that class differences can ruin a relationship. I was counseling in a hospital when I fell in love with Al. He was on the maintenance staff. I found his life fascinating because it was a different world from mine. The first year of our marriage the fascination ended abruptly. Instead of intrigue, I saw vulgarity, ignorance, and more, when I looked at him. Needless to say we are in the process of getting a divorce." *(Bronx, New York)*

"I am still a mistress and very attached to my married man. I really don't think that I love him anymore though. I guess I did at one time and will miss him a great deal as a friend if I end it. But I have been nagged by the differences between us. I can't see us as a team. He's got too little money and too many children. I've got too much education and I have always wanted a large family. I really can't imagine us in the future ever finding real happiness. I don't want a mistake to haunt me for the rest of my life." *(Boston, Massachusetts)*

Going from mistress to wife for some women can be going from the frying pan into the fire, if you'll pardon the cliché. Surely that is a fate that we all would like to avoid.

I receive so much mail from mistresses who are all potential second wives to their married men. They seem to be looking to me for judgements. How much time should they invest in the waiting game? How much should they give up in terms of time or in terms of goals? How can they tell if he really will get that divorce? Many of the agonizing writers are stressing the man too much. They seem to be fixated on *will he or won't he get that divorce*. They seem to assume that and only that is the obstacle to happiness. The stress has to be not on the man's fate alone, but on the fate of the team. Will he and you make a happy match?

I cannot make that judgement. No one can except you. You must look at your married man and you and make an individual assessment of the match. You must look at your collective goals for a life together, your mutual values, and your compatibility factor. The choice is yours alone. No one else is qualified to make that selection. No one else will live with the consequences of that decision.

In a sense this book will keep returning to ways of helping you look at different aspects of compatibility from parenting to finance, from the emotional aspects to the practical ones. Making a good match will certainly enhance your chances toward making that "good" marriage. Going from mistress to wife can be the best move or the worst. It is all up to your personal discretion.

"I have never been as happy in my whole life. When I was a mistress I knew ecstasy, but I knew agony too. Now the ecstasy isn't so overwhelming anymore. But there isn't any agony. And when I lie in bed watching my husband sleep, I still think all this may be a dream. But it isn't. It is a dream come true." *(Lisle, Illinois)*

There are many, many mistresses who do find their happy ending. I was one of them. In my case and others, it is due to the strength, the love, and the logic of the team. In each case that judgement must be made by the mistress and her married man. I am not going to leave you with the weight of the future on your shoulders without a test to help you in judging your own team.

Take the next test and assess your team. Find out right here and now if your affair is really marriage material.

A Very Private Screening

You are invited to a private screening. Usually, I'm inclined to encourage the mistress to dispel her fantasies. But not this time. This exercise is going to depend on your imaginings.

What will it be like after you and he untangle your triangle and finally tie the nuptial knot? You and he, no longer mistress and married man, but husband and wife. What kind of couple will you make? How will your coupling determine your marriage? Can you visualize the team you and he will make? How alike are you and he and how unalike? Which do you think is more important between couples: common ground or the attraction of opposites?

The test that follows will help you design a picture of the future for your very own private screening.

Directions: This exercise is basically a word association test. You are to read each word and then select from the two choices the one that fits you best.

For example: gender   man or woman

You as the mistress would choose "woman."

After you complete the test give it to your married man. Then you will compare your answers and see what it says about your particular coupling.

			You	Him
1.	sports	spectator or participant	_____	_____
2.	socially	extrovert or introvert	_____	_____
3.	financially	saver or spender	_____	_____
4.	food	nutrition or gourmet	_____	_____
5.	sex roles	feminist or chauvinist	_____	_____

		You	*Him*
6. religion	relevant or irrelevant	_____	_____
7. persuasion	liberal or conservative	_____	_____
8. energy	consumer or conserver	_____	_____
9. communication	open or intimate	_____	_____
10. preference	leisure or career	_____	_____
11. schedule	day or night	_____	_____
12. politically	activist or non-involved	_____	_____
13. family	children or relatives	_____	_____
14. education	important or unimportant	_____	_____
15. job	work or career	_____	_____

To Score:

For every time you and he select the same answer you get 10 points for the match. Your score, therefore, can range from 0 with no matches to 150 with all fifteen answers matching. Now look below to the category that best applies to your score.

0–40 Points: The Night and Day Match. You and he are as different as night and day. Very few of your responses were the same. In order to see just how different you and he are, just go back and discuss the differences in how you and he answered. Chances are he's the saver and you're the spender or it may be vice versa. Or you're the liberal and he's the conservative. Difference in itself is no cause for immediate alarm. It is how you feel about the differences that matters. Some of us like opposites. We like diversity, conflicts, etc. in our lives to keep it changing. Others of us find diversity a threat and a cause of anxiety. You must take a good look at the differences between you and him. Will his different ways and opposite persuasions add to your marriage or will they only add problems? You and only you know. And remember, you can't change him!!! People don't change. This test delves into life goals, lifestyles, and life values. You and he are like night and day. Will that make for beautiful sunsets and sunrises as you trade and teach each other, or will it make for mismatch misery!

50–100 Points: The Hodgepodge Match. Your score is the most difficult to discuss. In some ways you and he think alike and in other ways you and he think quite differently. Therefore it is hard to make any generalizations about what kind of a match you and he will make. Your coupling is really a hodge-podge of mixed values, varied preferences, and diversified goals. The best thing for you and he to do is to go back and look at your collective differences. And then see just how you feel about those differences. Some can be inconsequential. For instance, if you are a nutrition nut, you can still enjoy food. However, if you are politically and feministically active, you could become intolerant and hostile about his noninvolvement or his chauvinism. In the courting days, these things may seem "cute," but after marriage, the differences could lead to walls. A hodgepodge match could be fun and lively or it could be incongruous and painful. And then again your hodgepodge score may only point up silly little differences. In the final analysis you are the judge, since you will be writing the script for your future.

110–150 Points: The Pea Pod Match. You and he are like two peas in a pod. Many of your answers matched. That means that basically your lifestyles are similar, you want the same things in life, and you tend to think the same things are of value. Probably your political philosophies are similar, your feelings about your work or education are the same. Your coupling will be harmonious. Decision-making will rarely mean a struggle or a compromise. Plans or sacrifices will be mutual. For many this match is perfect, but not for everyone. Some would find a pea-pod match boring, stagnant, and too predictable. If you value common ground in a relationship then congratulate yourself. If not, take a second look! Marriage is a blend and the contents must be to your liking.

In Conclusion:
What do you think of your private screening? Can you see the future a bit better after probing each other? Do you like what you see in the future? Do your future imaginings sketch lovely compromises, mutual agreements, or the best of two worlds? Is the script lively, boring, or full of shouting?

Visualize the team you and he will make. Your vision will be a prediction if it is truthful. If you are going from mistress to wife, make sure you are going somewhere not nowhere!

CHAPTER 3

The Chronic Question

When the word was announced that I had married my married man, I wish I could say that we were deluged with congratulations. I wish I could say that best wishes echoed. Of course, there were words of happiness and hopefulness from friends and some close relations. Yet from coast to coast as Michael and I traveled and spoke, one question reverberated throughout every audience. The most frequently asked question was "What will you do when your new husband cheats?"

I call that question the chronic question. The common assumption was that my husband would soon take a mistress, and then it wouldn't be I who had the last laugh! It's odd, but no one assumed I would repeat my past and become a mistress. It was always the perception that my husband would repeat his past and enlist a new mistress.

Many people resented my mistress marriage. There are widespread misogynistic attitudes toward mistresses. Sometimes I could feel the sentiments of bad luck directed toward us. Audiences tried to make us feel at times that our marriage was doomed. Jinxed because of our pasts. Not blessed because of our love, our struggles, and our success.

Michael and I are in a prominent public position. We are subjected to public prejudice and judgement because of that. We faced the chronic question innumerable times. In all my dealings with mistresses I found nearly all of them also face the chronic question. Either it is posed to them, or they pose it to themselves. If the married man cheated on his wife, will he cheat on me if I go from mistress to wife???

I have never been one to hedge a question, so in this chapter we are going to face the chronic question head on. Are there any insights into this chronic fear? Are second marriages jinxed somehow because they were conceived in triangular circumstances? Or are second marriages blessed because they survived frightful odds? Has your mistress experience helped or hindered you with regard to your future as a second wife? Is there a way to insure your marriage against triangular temptation? What are your chances for happiness, if you go from mistress to wife? Can your marriage last a lifetime?

I cannot guarantee that your new marriage to that married man will last a lifetime. I cannot even guarantee that my marriage will, although my husband and I are committed to that time period. Neither life nor love holds 100 percent guarantees. However, as for the chronic question, I can guarantee that I will never become a mistress again. I can guarantee that my husband will never be another woman's married man. How can I be so sure of our mutual fidelity? How dare I pompously declare that my man will not stray in view of his "imperfect" past?

Tell me, who is more qualified to predict the fidelity factor in my marriage? Who has control? Who do I believe has the answers? Fate? Does fate have the key to my future? Should I give allegiance to human failings and assume he or I will succumb? Fidelity is in our control. I believe it is up to us. We believe in our mutual commitment and ourselves. Each set of spouses sets the standards for their marriage. Each husband and wife, in other words, determines which behaviors will be allowed and which will not. It's not what our mothers told us "men are like." It's what we as spouses strive toward and permit. We all make the standards that prevail in our marriages. For Michael and me infidelity is unacceptable. Faithfulness is the standard by which we run our marriage. I have no doubt that we will live up to that commitment. If either of us finds it impossible, we will dissolve the marriage.

Why is that so hard to believe? People assume that he'll stray and I'll back down and silently accept double-dealing rather than divorce. Too many people in this society expect less than perfect marriages in the area of fidelity. That is exactly why such marriages proliferate. Husbands and wives tolerate and create their own triangles.

My husband and I have already ridden the torrent and the torment of a triangle. We know that an affair is not the simple elixir to marital discontent so many feel it is. We know that an affair brings compromises and complications. We know it is not easier to take a lover than to take problems head on. We know having an affair will not save a marriage. An affair is tumultuous. Far more tumultuous than anyone realizes, unless they have experienced it. Once was enough for him and me! Nothing, not even a divorce, could put us through pains we have survived while victimized by the triangle. In our hearts and in our minds we know this. We know the truth about affairs, about each other, and agree that there is a better way to go through life than within a triangle.

If you go from mistress to wife, you should be as sure about your man's capacity and commitment to fidelity as I. Many a mistress gets bogged down in the cliché, unable to resolve that chronic fear that he'll do "it" again.

"I can't shake this feeling about my married man. He makes love to me, makes promises, and I wonder does he do the same with her? Once we're married, will he do, with a new woman, this mistress routine? I can't help but fear him as my husband. Can he ever be trusted?" *(New Orleans, Louisiana)*

If you have no trust, then you shouldn't go from mistress to wife. No one except you can assess your married man's capacity for honesty and fidelity. However, do not get side-tracked by the sexist theories about men, all men do not have to cheat. Do not get sidetracked by the jinxing sentiments of others, all ex-married men are not doomed to repeat this adultery. Have faith in yourself and in him. Trust begins in your marriage and cannot be assessed by others.

Chances are your second marriage will have problems, but his infidelity isn't inevitable. If you are a mistress going to wife, it is natural that you feel jinxed as well as blessed. In some ways you are jinxed because mistress marriages do bring special difficulties. You will have to do your share of trouble-shooting, but your target is not going to be another mistress!

Are second marriages better? Is love lovelier the second time or easier to preserve? Divorce statistics are very close whether we are talking second or first marriages. Yet there is still a difference. Second marriages usually involve a stronger commitment. There is usually a firm resolve on the part of the spouses not to "fail" at marriage again. Second marriage partners are usually wiser and more prepared for the strains of marriage. Does that make them better?

"I was a mistress. It was a painful way of life except for the sweet moments of togetherness with the one you love. I would not recommend it to anyone. It takes an extremely strong relationship to withstand the pressures and pain. Eventually my married man did get his freedom (after being stripped financially). We have been married for nine years now. Neither of us worries about fidelity because we know what the other needs to keep him/her happy. This is a second marriage for both of us. Second marriage I would recommend highly. Neither of us looked for an affair, but something was lacking in our first marriages. Our second marriage helped us find what was lacking, plus we both try harder." *(Cincinnati, Ohio)*

"To make my long story short, I lived with my married man after my divorce was final. He was getting his. Now I have been married to him for three years. It's a beautiful relationship. We're open and honest with each other. We both brought lessons from living to our marriage. I feel I am a better wife, to say the least of being a better person, too. I think second marriages are better, at least that was true for us." *(Swift Current, Canada)*

Second marriages may not be absolutely better right across the board. That will always be a debatable generalization. However, people in second marriages do try harder. They have less romantic baggage. Chances are your married man does not ever want to go through the divorce process again, either financially or emotionally. If you, too, are a divorcée you probably share his feelings. So even when things get rough and the problems get complicated, second marriage partners don't throw in the proverbial towel so easily.

If you go from mistress to wife you are going into a special category of second marriage. Your triangle history gives you a few disadvantages. Yet your triangular past gives you an added bonus. You have acquired a skill that no other bride brings into the marriage. You'll see potential disadvantages in the later pages of this book. Now we are going to look at your bonus, your unique skill that I have dubbed "hindsight/foresight." The next story animates the skill in a most unusual light.

Slide Projections

Tuesday was creative, she was compulsive, and she was an

avid collector. To that list, add mistress. Then cross out mistress and pencil in wife. Tuesday married the man who once was her married man.

Tuesday's affair had lasted about three years, as so many mistress affairs do. During those triangle years, Tuesday threw herself into her creativity. She painted, and she cartooned even when there wasn't much to laugh about. She seized upon photography and soon became quite expert.

"I was compulsive about my new camera because I was trying to block out my loneliness. My camera solved the problem. James was my favorite subject, naturally. I snapped pictures of him whenever we were together. Then when he was gone, I could develop them, study them, enlarge them. It was my way of having him around in my empty days and nights."

Tuesday even took her favorite photographs and converted them into slides for her home projector. The settings were limited because they lived in Boulder, a rather small world. So most of her favorites were of him or them in her apartment or up in the mountains. But her all-time favorite photograph was their wedding picture!

It was Tuesday's first marriage and it was her fantasy. It was James's second marriage. For him it was a little less fantasy-oriented, but the reality pleased him even more. There were problems, financial ones, so Tuesday kept on working. There was a big emotional obstacle because James's ex-wife was threatening to move East with their children. But Tuesday and James lived through the bad moments and the good. They lived through six years that seemed to simply fly by.

During the seventh year of marriage, Tuesday was feeling odd. The high romance of the past seemed so far away. The tedium of marriage with its problems seemed to be getting to them both. They weren't having as much fun as they used to. Tuesday got out the old slides of the triangle years.

"I cooked an elegant finger-food dinner in front of the slide projector. We previewed our affair years for the first time in seven years. We reminisced about hard times back then and realized how lucky we were to have marriage—monotony, aggravation, and all. Now whenever we tend to slip into a rut I get out the slides and project the past. It always works and gives us a new lease on our love."

Sliding back into the past and acquiring a sense of how far you've come is a good practice for any couple in a mistress marriage. It helps to rekindle the warmth and the closeness that brought you through your triangle and into marriage. It recreates the passions you've known and reminds you of all the reasons that you fell in love. It reviews the problems in his past marriage and in your past life, problems that you can now watch out for and avoid. If you go from mistress to wife it will always be a good idea to *keep a little of the mistress in your marriage!*

When I suggest that you keep some of the mistress in your marriage, I am saying that you should never lose sight of your mistress roots. Those mistress years exposed you to invaluable lessons. As a mistress you were privy to your married man's soul and the struggles that plagued it. You had a ringside view of why his marriage failed, and how he and his wife contributed to its demise. Inherent in your ringside view were a few lessons about marriage, familiarity, and relationships. Mistressing may have scarred you indeed. More importantly, it equipped you with "hindsight/foresight."

You've already seen your married man's patterns, his hopes, and his needs. You know firsthand what makes him happy and what doesn't. You have hindsight, only you can now apply it to your own mistress marriage when you become his wife. You have hindsight upfront, which makes you especially enlightened! Your hindsight can give you an insight into your future with your new husband. Your "hindsight/foresight" can trigger an alarm when potential problems begin to chip away at your friendship and communication. Because you were once a mistress, you know what your relationship can be. If you go from mistress to wife, you have a bonus skill, an inner warning system, and a sense of the past to help you maintain your close relationship.

Most people only have hindsight as they look back and regret. Their hindsight serves only a negative purpose, bringing guilt and remorse for not having done it another way. You know, the if-only-I-knew-then-what-I-know-now saga. You know what makes a good relationship from experience and you can apply that experience to your marriage! It is like you have a tailor-made insurance policy against marital mistakes and misconceptions.

No other bride was once his mistress. No other bride knows the keys that unlock his past. Your "hindsight/foresight" is a blessing, a tool, and a power unique only to mistresses. It is one mistress memento that you should rightfully cherish. It will help you keep the mistress perspective relevant in your relationship. It will sustain the romance in your marriage. It will signal you when to begin attending to trouble spots.

I want to add a note here with a point for your ex-married man. He, too, has "hindsight/foresight." He should never lose sight of the affair and why it blossomed into marriage. He must never totally divest himself of that old married man magic, its emphasis on intimacy and romance, verbal and otherwise. If he keeps his married man appeal as a part of his persona, he will always be appealing to you as a confidante, a lover, and a friend.

For you and that married man, retaining your sense of the past gives you an edge on succeeding in your marriage. Your experience equips you with a special triangular sense that will enhance your years together, if you summon its power. It is a good idea to keep some special souvenir from the affair era to remind you of this unique bonus.

Up to this point, we have looked at the positive prospects of a mistress marriage versus the prejudices that permeate it. For most of you, the chronic question is a fear that threatens your peace of mind more often than your marriage. However, I cannot end this chapter without confronting the ultimate possibility. Suppose chronic "cheating" or infidelity does happen? What if your husband harbors the belief that extramarital affairs are growing, necessary experiences? (A belief that you should already know before marriage.) Suppose you go from mistress to wife and the unthinkable happens? Suppose his ex-wife becomes the mistress. And your marriage becomes a triangle?

While most married men who marry their mistresses will not, I repeat, will not take another mistress down the road, a few will. Some men will find fidelity impossible. Some people think monogamy is unhealthy and inhibiting. You should know each other's values about such things before you exchange vows.

But if you think you know him, and suddenly you realize you were wrong, then what? If you learn that your new husband has a mistress, what should you do?

The next story tells of a triangle that can happen in the world of musical mates.

Change Partners and Cheat

Don't mistake the title as implying levity in this situation. The letter that I received from Sue was not a laughing matter—for Sue to write or for me to read.

"Our situations are very similar in that we both married the men to whom we were mistresses. I have never written any letters seeking advice of any kind; in fact, I rarely write letters to anyone. However my mind would not rest until I took pen in hand. Here's my riddle. What do you do when the mistress becomes the wife, but the ex-wife becomes the mistress? That is what is happening to me."

Sue had met Lee on and off for several years in various social meetings. Then at one party they really got to talking and liked one another.

"I can't explain it, but I had a feeling that he was married, though I never saw him with a wife or anything. He told me he wasn't. I still suspected so I took the initiative to find out for myself by looking up his marriage license. We were now five months into our affair. I got the certified copy and confronted him. We went through a whirlwind for the next three months."

Sue was not going to become a mistress and that was all there was to it. She cut Lee off and refused to see him or talk to him.

"Then at the end of January, he called and said that his wife was serving him with divorce papers and he was free. Where should he go? To his Mom's or did I want him to come to me? Naturally I was still in love with him so I welcomed him bag and baggage."

Sue confided that she couldn't believe all this was happening. She gave up the man she loved because she feared spending years in a situation waiting and hoping. Now her dream was hers! Was it too good to be true? It wasn't, but he was.

"We married and it was like a dream. We moved into a new

house. Everything was wonderful and still is, despite the episode when I found out he was seeing his ex-wife. We had always had a very deep, spiritual, and mature feeling for one another. We prided ourselves on knowing each other's wants, needs, and even thoughts. I couldn't believe all this!

"His ex-wife had called me and said it would be to our mutual benefit to meet and not tell Lee. When I arrived she asked me if I had been served with divorce papers. Me? She recounted times when Lee had been with her, times which did correlate with his absences. She told me Lee was promising to divorce me and remarry her."

After the shock subsided, Sue did some thinking. She realized that things couldn't be going so smoothly for the ex-wife or else she wouldn't be seeking Sue out to see where things stood. She knew that her relationship with Lee was happy. She controlled the money and so he wasn't forking anything over to the ex. There was no trouble in their sex life. In fact, how had he strength for anyone else?

"I have a background in psychology and I am trying to employ it now at this time in my life. I love Lee and I want to see us make it. I know his ex is a desperate sort. And yet, how does one handle this? Should I confront Lee with his infidelity, throw him out? Suppose I force him to go to her with that ultimatum? I need some help."

Going from mistress to wife can be wonderful, but never when you find that the ex-wife or any other woman has taken over where you left off. No doubt about that! If your biggest mistress fear becomes your reality as his wife, what then? If all your insecurities about his love for this other woman are founded in discovering they had renewed their relationship, where do you go from that hellish revelation?

That is a trouble I would not wish on any new wife. However, if it happens don't stick your head in the sand. First of all, Sue shouldn't meet with the ex-wife. No wife should ever conspire with a former wife to share secrets or suspicions. If you have doubts, go to your husband. Ask him, "Why is your former wife calling me?" In Sue's case, once she heard the worst, she chose to keep it to herself. That, too, is a grave mistake. Now her silence is making her a co-conspirator in a triangle. Fear of losing him, fear of the unknown, neither of these is a good rationale for silence.

Any wife who suspects a triangle lurks in her marriage should voice her suspicions. She should confront her husband quietly or compassionately, angrily or noisily. Any way so long as the suspicions get out into the open. Triangles cannot continue if one side of the triangle says "No."

Perhaps Sue will lose Lee, but if she remains silent she will only have half a man at best. Perhaps the whole story is a lie! How will she ever know if she keeps the ex's tale to herself? If the tale is true and she does nothing, she will be the loser. She will be trading a blissful marriage for a sham. She will be living with a man whom she no longer trusts and respects. She will forfeit some self-respect. No man is worth paying those prices. There are worse things than living alone. Living in a triangle is one of them. Sue didn't really have enough experience in a triangle to know its pains, but she's learning fast.

At the start of her story, Sue refused to accept years in a triangle as a mistress. As a wife she should expect no less. Cheating is a terrible reality to live with regardless of which side of the triangle you are on. If he changed partners and still is doing the same unfaithful steps, Sue should get off the floor. That move will determine who Lee wants. That ultimatum will prove to Sue that she has the power to run her own life, her way.

It takes three willing partners to keep a triangle whirling. Sue can unmake her triangle simply by opting not to participate. Every wife has the power to make or break her triangle, just as every mistress has that power. The rub is to muster up the strength to summon up that power. If you say "no," you may forfeit the man, but you will also forfeit the anxiety and pain that accompany triangle living. If you choose silence in the face of infidelity, you are choosing double-dealing as a way of life. It's your choice, no one else's. It's your choice, triangle or no triangle.

The only way to create and maintain a good marriage is to fight for what you deserve. If you go from mistress to wife, you deserve faithfulness, loyalty, love, trust, romance, and consideration. If you expect these things and stand for no less, your marriage will have these things. It is vitally important that you and your husband agree on these things. Don't forget the old golden rule, and if you set an example with these qualities you will inspire your spouse to behave likewise. This is the only way a marriage can last a lifetime, happily.

When the mistress marries her married man it is a unique kind of second marriage. The new marriage partners have unique insights into each other. They have a shared triangular past, which should solidify a commitment to faithfulness and trust. Experiencing a triangle can be like getting a vaccination. You should be immune to repeating adultery. This goes for the man and the woman. Neither the married man nor the mistress is destined in any Freudian way to wind up in a triangle again. Just the opposite is more applicable. You have a good chance at having a marriage that will be affair-proof. But if you do encounter fears or problems, face them immediately.

The chronic question is one which you will have to answer. However, don't buy the chronic cliché, with which "well-wishers" may taunt you. Men are not all back-stabbers, dishonest, and unfaithful by nature. Nor does one affair portend an inability to sustain a faithful second marriage. You and your married man can give each other any answers you need. During the mistress era, you discovered the real man, not the stereotype. Keep your sights on each other. Keep the mistress roots in that scope too. Ignore the gossip of chronic pessimists. No matter what the rest of the world may say, if you go from mistress to wife your marriage will not be inevitably jinxed. It will be especially blessed!

CHAPTER 4

History—Your Attitude and Aptitude

You can take your relationship out of the triangle, but you may never be able to take the triangle out of your relationship. If I am confusing you, let me put it another way. A mistress is labeled as a woman with a past. As you go from mistress to wife, suddenly you have the future. However, ridding yourself of that past label and its legacy is another matter.

In your future with your married man, the past will always linger. Even after a divorce, he will be fettered with souvenirs. His children, for instance, are souvenirs personified. His ex-wife is a part of his past that never really disappears. There are financial obligations with regard to his past. Do you see what I mean?

Since he was married when you met, he has a past. If you are now a married mistress, you will be bringing your past into your future marriage too. The past sounds like some abstract concept. However, it will be far from abstract as you proceed into the future.

Suddenly you are going to find yourself looking at a history test. Can you pass the history test? What is your aptitude for history? What about your attitude toward history? Will it be an asset or liability? What about your married man; how will he fare in the history tests?

In this chapter, I'm going to try and make an historian out of you. Since you cannot eliminate the past, you must learn to deal with it. The purpose of this lesson is to make a study of the past. Where will the past challenge your future happiness? How? Will the impact be all negative? Or is there a way to handle history constructively? How you handle the history test will be crucial to your future happiness. If you want to make the triangle transition, mastering history is a must.

Maybe history was never one of your favorite subjects. In the context of the triangle, when we say "history" we mean your man's first marriage and his first wife. Obviously that may not be a favorite subject either. However, as with any required subject, isn't there a reason for it being on the curriculum? Isn't something to be gained?

You will find in studying history that you have a choice. History can teach you gratitude or grief. The fact that you and he began your relationship in a triangle gives you a unique mistress past. That past can enhance your marriage. Your mistress history can also have remnants of tragedy. His former life can irk you and destroy your peace of mind, if you allow that alternative. It is really a choice. Either you concentrate on the good effects or the bad. Having a triangular past is like a double-edged sword. Relying on the right blade can give you an edge. The wrong blade can wound you severely. It is all in your attitude.

To further illustrate this point, here is Bliss's story. Her lesson in history taught her "the Cinderella quality."

Cinderella in Overalls

Bliss lived on a small farm in Indiana. Her husband left her for another woman when Bliss was thirty-nine years old. He left her with their three children and no more illusions about love or marriage. Bliss met her married man at a Hog Roast.

"Bart was in his third marriage (now don't come to any conclusions yet). His first wife died. His second had left him. His third had tricked him into marriage claiming that she was pregnant. In the year they'd been married, they'd been apart more than they'd been together."

After Bliss gave this background, she explained that Bart divorced again. After all, his luck with women couldn't be bad forever. He felt that his odds on Bliss had to be good. And so they were married.

"It sounds like it all happened very easy, but don't get me

wrong. His last wife moved to Florida alright. When she heard he was living with me, she came north all lovey-dovey again. He bought it for awhile and I lived through hell again. Only after my husband up and left, hell was no stranger. But then things just started working out right. He came to his senses and now things are perfect."

Bliss had been battered and bruised by life. She had scars from being a wife and scars from being a mistress. But she turned all that inside out.

"The day he put that ring on my finger I felt like I was really living out my fantasy. I love this man more than anyone in my whole life. I remember all the hard times and it only makes me see how lucky I am. He's so happy with me, it's like all those other women only make him appreciate me more. All the things we couldn't do before because of his being married, now we do 'em and I love 'em one by one. Going into town, the annual hog roasts, Sunday meetings, it's one dream come true after another."

Bliss realized that she was lucky. After her past and his past, she appreciated the present. It was as if all her fantasies were coming true one by one and day by day. She made the most of it. History actually enhanced her second marriage, with a Cinderella quality.

It is all in the way you apply the past, you see. The past can be used as a backdrop. It can be a source of reference. Take the present and compare it to the past. With that perspective, the past as a concept can serve you with something to be grateful for daily. Every woman who goes from mistress to wife is living her fantasy of togetherness with that married man. Just think about how many times you wish for a night together uninterrupted, a carefree day, the simple opportunity to do chores together. As the second wife, all your wishes come true. He is now your husband. Sure he has drawbacks because of his prior marriage, but things have changed. History can be learned as a lesson of luck and gratitude.

Not that it is always going to be easy. Jenny had not given history much thought. Slowly, she began to see it popping into her new life. She couldn't close the history book, but she did have a choice.

Jenny's Second Thoughts

"Are you crazy? Don't do that! You'll give yourself a hernia!"

Jenny's outbursts came because Bill was trying to pick her up. Oh, she had wanted him to pick her up and carry her over the threshold like any new bride, but she had second thoughts. Jenny was eight months pregnant.

"It took two years to save enough money for a down payment for a house of our own. I'm no spring chicken and no featherweight to start with. Being pregnant I weighed a ton. I didn't want Bill to rupture himself. More than that I was a tiny bit angry. This wasn't his first threshold."

In the beginning, Jenny didn't have any second thoughts. She was just so relieved and happy that Bill was finally hers. She had pinched herself all through the wedding ceremony. But at that moment, the second thoughts had begun if only in the faintest degree. It wasn't until she became pregnant that the second thoughts became a problem.

"When I found out I was pregnant I was so delighted. I couldn't wait to call Bill; no, I wanted to tell him in person. While all this was rushing through my mind, all of a sudden the joy exploded. I felt a sensation of pain. How had it been for him the first time? When his first wife announced her first pregnancy?"

In an instant and in a nutshell, Jenny had her first lesson in history. Yes, she was going to have to come to terms with Bill's past. All his *firsts* had already been used up. His first engagement. His first wedding. His first child. His first home. Jenny realized that it was going to be a rather long list.

"I knew Bill had a past. I was accepting the kids alright. The ex-wife, well, I put her out of my mind. I hadn't figured on all these second thoughts filling my head at the special times of my life, that's all. It made me angry and sad."

Jenny underestimated herself. She was doing a fine job

assimilating Bill's past. She had included his children in her wedding plans. They had been there to help pick out the house. It's just that Jenny had underestimated where the past would pop up. And when. It wasn't a pleasant surprise.

Jenny decided that she would have natural childbirth. Bill had never participated in that miracle. They had both been going to classes together.

"I started to tell myself, this is OUR first child. Our first marriage and our first life together. Bill and I are so close now as we wait for the baby to arrive. I can't forget entirely about his past, but I can make the present ours. It is special. It is different. I can't let his past spoil our marriage. I won't. It was a hurdle for me, coming to that wise conclusion. Finally one day I asked myself, wasn't Bill worth it?"

Past or no past, Jenny was certain that Bill was worth it. About that she had no second thoughts!

Jenny passed the history test with flying colors. She had met the past, seen the ultimate choice, and made the right decision. In the end, she had come to terms with the past. She was determined and able to put it in its proper place. The other alternative was letting his past ruin all the best moments of her life.

It wasn't always easy for Jenny. How will it be for you? It is a fact of life for all second wives that second thoughts intrude at times. You will have to confront the past and get it into perspective sooner or later. How you adjust is your particular choice. And let me repeat it again . . . it is a choice. It is a matter of attitude. It is something upon which you must work. How hard depends on you.

Your triangular history sets you up for second thoughts. That is one test. It also sets you up for a barrage of conflicting emotions, not all of them pleasant. Dealing with the vague concept of the past is one thing. Dealing with the specific concept of jealousy is quite another. Going from his mistress to his second wife subjects you to a challenge with the green monster—a somewhat unique challenge.

A Thorn in Her Side

"I was eighteen that summer of '78 when this gorgeous guy

rode by on a tractor and waved. He was the picture of my ideal man. A few days later, he rode by again, only this time he stopped. He gave me a beautiful rose. He asked me to dinner. I had no idea he was married.

"That night after dinner, he confessed that he was married. I never would have guessed. I feel that a married man shouldn't be asking anyone out, so it never occurred to me. He said he needed someone to talk to. Sex was lousy at home, and they never talked. As you know, one thing led to another and I was hooked."

Lee-Ann said that, after every date, her man would bring her a rose. They used to spend nights out while he delivered produce to grocery chains. She always went along for the ride. After a few months they took a weekend and went away.

"After that weekend his wife found out. She wanted a divorce. He agreed. I thought all my problems were over. Little did I know of all the heartache to come!"

Her man got the "guilties" and reconciled with his wife several times for the sake of the kids. He moved in and out of Lee-Ann's house and life for almost a year.

"I should have cut out then and there. I just kept hoping for Someday. I loved him more than life itself. I still do. Everything worked out eventually. He came and told me he wasn't happy. He hadn't wanted to reconcile all along, but he felt it was the right thing to do. After that realization, he was back with her again. I cried for days, quit eating and couldn't sleep. I got mad and how I hated him! I hated him with as much as I loved him. Then I got this huge bouquet of roses at work, telling me to leave the door open."

Lee-Ann was strong, but sabotaged by love. Her married man's pace of change was confusing. She was in a revolving door of love and hate, reunion and rejection. Her man finally did divorce. They were married in a quaint chapel that was full of roses.

Lee-Ann was happy, except for something inside. Jealousy was swelling inside her. It was like a thorn in her side.

"It's so hard trying to cope with his ex-wife. She wants him back. She's trying all sorts of things to get him. He feels obligated to her because of the kids. So he sets himself up for her games. Like when it snows, she calls and wants him to deliver groceries because she's snowbound. I have a wild imagination. And I'm jealous, and I know she wants him back. I'm even afraid of his attachment to his children sometimes. I'm still fearful that he'll go back to them like he did so many times in the past.

"Sometimes, I think I can't go on like this, with all this building up in me. It gets worse. How can I live with this for the rest of my life? I know I have it good now. I'm sure other people have more to complain about than me. I just want our lives to work out perfectly forever."

Lee-Ann's fears and jealousy are a legacy of her mistress past—an agonizing outgrowth of the eternal crisis. As a mistress she was scarred by her man's vacillation. She developed feelings of insecurity. Living in a triangle is living in a sort of competition with another woman. Part of the triangle is fear and envy.

You can go from mistress to wife overnight. However, your emotions cannot make the transformation so quickly. A marriage license is only a piece of paper. Promises, he's made them before and broken them too. Insecurity was a way of life as a mistress, sometimes for years. Insecurity breeds jealousy. The two are inextricably meshed and rarely deposited on the outside of the threshold.

Jealousy often seems to escalate after marriage. Why? Mistresses aren't allowed to be jealous. You knew he was married. Sharing is an expectation of triangular territory. Most mistresses repress their jealousy. After becoming the second wife, sometimes this feeling ignites to frightening proportions. You fear he'll go back to his family. Their past haunts you and torments you. Usually his first wife is not a real threat. It is in your mind. You shouldn't fear his ties to children. Or the few contacts with his ex. What you should fear is the quality of jealousy itself. It's powerful. Jealousy can destroy you, your love, your marriage, and your future.

Combating jealousy isn't going to be easy. For some the temptation will be strong. Others won't have such an ordeal with jealousy. You must eject any and every jealous thought and replace it with a reassuring one. Your man has married you and chosen a new life. Repeat that as often as you require.

Your struggle with jealousy and insecurity depends on your particular aptitude. Are you normally a jealous type? How many eternal crises have come your way? Has this mistress history increased your vulnerability? Has his past made you more prone to these traps?

Jealousy is not exclusive to mistress marriages, but they can increase your jealousy level. Your past wounds and his obligations can set you up for a battery of tests. You must learn to assess jealousy in yourself. The next few exercises will help you examine and isolate the green monster.

What is Your Threshold for Jealousy?

Ask anyone who is prone to jealousy, and they will tell you it's not easy being green! Are you a jealousy-prone person? How do you relate to that concept? Do you have a low threshold for jealousy? Or does it take a great deal of baiting to arouse envious behavior in you? Analyzing your capacity for jealousy and your threshold is a good idea if you are venturing from mistress to wife. The road you take from triangle territory to the second-marital abode will be specifically laced with temptations toward jealousy.

Knowing your jealousy threshold in advance can give you an edge on combating the green monster. Your reaction of jealousy, and the response you make to it, can have a significant effect on your future. I suggest you take the following test so you know your jealousy threshold. And I suggest you give it to your married man, too.

Directions: Read each of the following carefully. Circle the answer that best sums up your reaction, choosing from "always," "sometimes" or "never." Remember be honest or the test will be worthless to you. And don't be ashamed of your jealousy; it's only human.

1. You meet an old friend on the street or at a reunion. She brings up an old rival who stole the affections of someone you loved in the past. *Would you feel an*   always
intense rush of an old jealousy run   sometimes
through you?   never

2. Some women believe certain occupations, such as bartenders, musicians, or traveling salespersons, make bad husbands because these occupations teem with temptations toward other women. *Do you believe your man's occupation teems with temptations?*

always
sometimes
never

3. Jealousy means different things to different people. To some it means childishness. To others it means an important sign of true affection. *Does your concept of love include jealousy as a natural part of affection?*

always
sometimes
never

4. Suppose you are at a social gathering with your married man. Another woman begins flirtatious behavior. Would you be inclined to step in and claim your rights? *Are you possessive in a situation like that?*

always
sometimes
never

5. Nowadays, on jobs, in pursuit of hobbies, more men and women are beginning to become or try to become friends. Some say it's impossible for men and women to become friends without the onset of a chemistry between them. *Are male-female friendships dangerous chemically and biologically?*

always
sometimes
never

6. Suppose you happen to find some old love letters or poems written not to you but to his previous lover. *Would you be the kind of person who would be intensely hurt, angered, or crushed?*

always
sometimes
never

7. Almost everyone has a first love and a story about their first sexual experience. Oftentimes these tales are shared between lovers. Later these first love confessions are regretted. *Would you regret hearing his first love tales?*

always
sometimes
never

8. Suppose he is away on business and he misses calling at a time he promised to call. *Would you assume the worst, that some woman sidetracked him?*

   always
   sometimes
   never

9. You are invited to an evening of memories, watching old movies and looking through old year books and photo albums. Chances are there will be shots of him with someone else. *Would you rather not put yourself through it?*

   always
   sometimes
   never

10. For some an "I love you" isn't the best it could be. An improvement would be "I love you more than anyone I've ever known." *Would you prefer to always hear the latter version of the love declaration?*

    always
    sometimes
    never

Scoring:
For each "always" answer give yourself 15 points. For each "sometimes" answer give yourself 10 points. For each "never" answer give yourself 5 points. Now total your points.

Evaluation:
   50–80 Points: Leprechaun Luck. You are not a jealousy-prone person particularly. Another way of describing you is to say that you have a high threshold for jealousy. It takes a lot to make you green. In this regard you have the luck of the leprechauns. Your personality traits just don't lean toward the characteristics of envy, suspicion, or possessiveness. If someone were to flirt with your man, you would probably applaud her good taste rather than get the urge to scratch her eyes out. You think that jealousy is a wasted emotion that only hurts. You probably think it is unnecessary and not a sign of affection. Count your blessings on this green score. Having a high threshold for jealousy gives you an edge in the transition from mistress to wife.
   85–115 Points: Crocodile Armor. You are prone to jealousy at some times and at other times you are immune. Your threshold, in other words, is a medium one. You are like a crocodile with an armor that sometimes protects you from feeling the

pangs of jealousy. Go back to your answers and reread the "always" ones to see specifically where the armor fails you. Perhaps you aren't jealous of old movies, or old rivals, but you are touchy about a flirtatious woman or a missing phone call. Because your behavior is inconsistent where jealousy is concerned, you had better keep a close watch over your own greening. There may be times when feelings of insecurity bring on tidal waves of jealousy. Learn the signs and signals so you can master an attack of jealousy. In going from mistress to wife you will get lots of practice!

120–150 Points: Dragon Sickness. Unfortunately, you are very prone to feelings of jealousy. In other words you have a low threshold for jealousy. Even the slightest word, thought, or gesture can set off your reactions of suspicion and possessiveness. Chances are you have tried to look for some justification for jealous behavior by including this trait in the definition of love. You yearn for those love declarations that make you the superlative love in past, present, and future terms. There is so much potential everywhere to make you jealous that you have dragon sickness from the green monster. You could live happily ever after if you never had to see old photos, movies, or hear first-love tales. Unfortunately in going from mistress to wife, the road is rife with jealousy traps. So you had better start thinking about slaying your dragon sickness or else. You more than anyone understand it's not easy being green.

In Conclusion:

Don't despair over your threshold for jealousy. As I said, it is a human instinct for some of us. And the good thing about being human is that we can intellectualize. We can learn to see our green penchant, understand it, and hopefully get it under control. The future ahead of you, if you go from mistress to wife, will be much easier if you put your mind over matter here. It is true that jealousy only hurts. So arm yourself against all green enemies, dragons, or crocodiles, and cultivate leprechaun luck!

How often are you going to have to deal with jealousy? That depends on how jealous you are but also on how often the past pops up in your mind. Each of us thinks about the past with our own individual frequency. Some of us are very sensitive to the past and all the people, places, and things of yesteryear. Others of us hardly ever think of the past. Future-oriented people might consider dwelling on yesterday as backward-thinking. What I am leading to is your own time sensitivity. What time period are you oriented toward? The answer will have further bearing in the history tests.

Take the next test and learn where you fit.

What is Your Time Zone?

Time is a concept that all of us have in common. And yet, how we handle time depends upon our own individuality.

For example, take the appointment. Some of us pride ourselves on punctuality in keeping appointments. Others of us think punctuality is a hang-up. Some of us are always early. Some of us are always late. Time marches on while each of us finds our own pace in the parade.

Everyone has a preference in regard to past, present, or future time. What is your preference? In other words what is your time zone? Each of us prefers the time period in which we feel most comfortable. Take a look at your life and clues to your time zone will emerge.

The following test is designed to clarify your relationship with time. It will assist you in defining your own particular time zone. Once you can identify that time preference of yours, you can learn some new lessons about going from mistress to wife.

Directions: This is a multiple choice test. Therefore, you must read each of the statements or questions and choose one answer and one answer only. Fill in your answer in the space provided. Then proceed to the scoring section and the evaluation.

1. In what tense do you dream most frequently: (a) the present, (b) the past, (c) the future?

    1. _____

2. If you had to choose one philosophy that seems to replay in your experiences, which one pops up the most: (a) Those were the good old days, (b) My how time flys, (c) The best is yet to come.

    2. _____

3. When it comes to vacationing, the best part for you is (a) the planning—looking through brochures, deciding what would be the best and anticipating the vacation; (b) the reminiscences—recalling the vacation experiences, telling friends, showing slides or getting vacation photographs back; (c) the adventure of the vacation itself, the traveling, the sightseeing, the excitement of doing it all?

3. _____

4. Look at your taste in clothes. Do you have (a) nostalgic themes in your wardrobe—old-fashioned items or clothes handed down from another generation; (b) a wardrobe that is always in line with current fashion trends, a wardrobe you are always updating to keep it in style; (c) have a penchant for the avant-garde, the fashion item that is predicted for the future.

4. _____

5. Take stock of your conversation. Do you find yourself talking most about; (a) what will be with regard to career, social events, or family life; (b) what was with regard to happenings, events in your life, and accomplishments; (c) what is now, what's going on in your life in your career or in your relationships?

5. _____

6. Hobbies often reflect upon your preferences. If you had to generalize about what you do with your leisure time, which statement fits you most aptly: (a) My leisure is spent the same way it has been since childhood with a hobby that has grown along with me; (b) My hobbies change from time to time because I get bored with one and find a new leisure activity that is more appealing; (c) My leisure time is usually spent trying to achieve something, a new skill in a new sport, learning some new game, or discovering something.

6. _____

7. What subject do you think has the most educational value: (a) technology, (b) psychology, (c) sociology?

7. _____

8. Philosophically speaking for you, which are you most apt

to agree with: (a) We make our own destiny, (b) Life is best taken one day at a time, (c) Fate is a real force that predetermines many things?

8._____

9. If you were to design the perfect room, which statement includes your taste in furnishings: (a) The room would feature heirlooms, antiques, or collections, (b) The room would be smooth and bare with modern furniture and abstract lighting, (c) The room would be eclectic with a few favorite items and no one theme?

9._____

10. When it comes to your spending habits, do you tend to (a) spend so as to maintain your present standard of living, (b) invest in things that will be valuable at a later time, (c) save your money, hold onto things of value?

10._____

11. If you were sitting in a doctor's office and had to chose a paperback to read, which type would you choose: (a) an historical novel, (b) a science fiction fantasy, (c) a bestseller in current popularity?

11._____

12. Which movie would you be found watching: (a) a western saga, (b) a well-reviewed picture that you saw recently advertised, (c) an avant-garde foreign movie?

12._____

Scoring:
In the scoring table below, list all your answers from 1 to 12 in the column labeled *"Answers"*. Then look and see what point value each answer is worth in the table. Then list the point value from the column labeled *"Points"*. Add up your total number of points and fill it in the space marked *"Total"*. Then read the evaluation for a discussion of your score.

				Answers	Points
1.	(a) 10	(b) 5	(c) 15	1.____	1.____
2.	(a) 5	(b) 10	(c) 15	2.____	2.____
3.	(a) 15	(b) 5	(c) 10	3.____	3.____
4.	(a) 5	(b) 10	(c) 15	4.____	4.____

			Answers	*Points*
5. (a) 15	(b) 5	(c) 10	5._____	5._____
6. (a) 5	(b) 10	(c) 15	6._____	6._____
7. (a) 15	(b) 5	(c) 10	7._____	7._____
8. (a) 15	(b) 10	(c) 5	8._____	8._____
9. (a) 5	(b) 15	(c) 10	9._____	9._____
10. (a) 10	(b) 15	(c) 5	10._____	10._____
11. (a) 5	(b) 15	(c) 10	11._____	11._____
12. (a) 5	(b) 10	(c) 15	12._____	12._____
				Total_____

Evaluation:

Your score total can range anywhere from 60 to 180 Points. Find the category below that includes your particular score.

Time-Zone Yesterday: 60–95 Points. If you scored in this range, your own time preference is for the past. If you were a time machine you would be locked in yesterdays. You have a distinct liking for the past. The clues are all around you in your personal tastes, whether one looks at your wardrobe or your possessions. You value highly fond memories, nostalgic feelings, and all histories. You may find yourself attracted to collecting things and to that inability to ever throw old things away. The past as a concept is inextricably mixed into your identity. The past is always with you. You believe we are a sum of our pasts. The past is never far behind you, in conversation or anywhere else. Your time zone is the past.

Time-Zone Today: 100–140 Points. If you scored in this range, your own time preference is for the present. If you were a time machine you would never move from today. You strongly adhere to the philosophy that one must take one day at a time and that we must savor our present experiences because yesterday is gone and the future may never happen for us. For you the only reality is today. You are concerned with adapting to the ever-changing world around us. You have no chains from the past influencing you. You have no intruding vision focusing you always on tomorrows. Whether it's entertainment, fashion, philosophy or taste, the present is your theme. Your time zone is today.

Time-Zone Future: 145–180 Points. If you scored in this range, your own time preference is for the future. You are a time machine in the most progressive sense; you would only go forward! Your world view is always ten paces ahead. The thrill of living for you is anticipation, planning, and the promise of what can be. You are goal-oriented and your sense of achievement is never as sweet as sighting in the next goal. In your surroundings, in your conversation, in everything, you are giving off clues of the future and tomorrows. Take away a person's vision and for you that is snuffing out the very essence of life. Your time zone is the future.

In Conclusion:
What is your time zone? Now you know. We all have one. Once you know how to zero in on your time preference, the knowledge can be valuable. Our time orientation is easy to spot once you begin looking for it. The clues are everywhere. Knowing about your sense of timing is often the key to understanding things about yourself. Knowing your time zone is almost as important as knowing exactly what it can mean in your life!

If you go from mistress to wife, your sense of timing is very crucial. I deliberately included the test because mistresshood has a way of interrupting our normal time preferences. Why? Mistresses are usually present-oriented. They have to be. The future is one big question mark to which only your married man has answers. The past is an uncomfortable reminder of how long you have been playing this waiting game. The future and the past avoided, you are fixed on the present instead. Mistresses tend to feel capsulized in assorted passions of longing, anticipation, gloom, ecstacy. Mistresses tend to lead lives of one crisis after another played one day at a time. In that way years and sometimes decades rush by. Mistresses often lose many things along the way of loving a married man. One of those losses is your normal orientation to time, your own time zone.

Once you go from mistress to wife, you will be freed in a sense from your time prison of the present. You and your married man have more than a few stolen hours always in the present. You and he will have a life of presents and futures! How big a part of your new life is dedicated to dwelling on the past depends on your normal time preference.

Be wary of yourself if you are a person of the past time zone. The promise of your future and the joys of todays may be constantly interrupted by replays of past sadnesses and lonely nights. You must learn to replay only the positives from the past. It is going to be a necessity to practice the art of selection. Make sure if you find yourself reliving, rethinking, or retelling, the subjects are nice past things. Or else your past will spoil your happiness.

If you are one of those present-oriented persons or future-oriented types, the threat is not so great for you. Your time zone is an aptitude that will actually help you. Since the past isn't your preference, your inclinations time-wise will not lead you back to the days of mistress agony. You have an aptitude that is going to help you do quite well when it comes to testing and history.

Every woman that goes from mistress to wife must put her past and her married man's past into a proper perspective. If that doesn't happen automatically, then you are responsible for doing it a little bit at a time.

"Both my married man and I had been married before. In those first couple of years our pasts got in the way all the time. There were problems both with his ex-wife and my ex-husband. That brought on jealousies and fights and bad feelings. We seem to be working things out better now. We just had our fourth anniversary and our lives are really together. What happened between my husband and his ex-wife is the PAST! What we have with each other is what now counts, TODAY! Coming to that lesson has made our marriage great and we are going to work to keep it that way." *(Kennewick, Washington)*

"I was ashamed to admit to anyone how jealous I was at first. I wasn't allowed to say it as his mistress. Suddenly, as his second wife, my jealousy exploded and got all out of whack. When I saw his kids they just reminded me of his intimacy with his wife. Just the sight of them was almost excruciating for me. You can imagine how hard it was for me. I got to a breaking point though. I had to either beat this green monster or go from second wife to divorcée. Talking it out helped because Jack really understood. Love helped too, it really can conquer all." *(Winter Haven, Florida)*

"We have a running joke about our pasts. In our house we have a wall of accomplishments. It is decorated with our college degrees. His membership in ASCAP. The first dollar I made from marketing my creativity. We joke how his divorce should be put on the wall of accomplishments, too. Graduating from that experience deserves a prize. The past provides us with awards of excellence for surviving. Our joking and our philosophy has helped us survive and flourish too." *(Long Branch, New Jersey)*

Dealing with the past is going to be your challenge if you go from mistress to wife. I hope that you have had some helpful tips here. For those of you who are past-oriented and high in jealousy, that is going to be tantamount to a struggle. If you are one of the luckier ones, save your newfound knowledge because you may have to pass it along to your new husband, yesteryear's married man.

If you were a married mistress, your bouts with history and the tests ahead will be two-fold. You must triumph and so must he. Your married man will have to face all the history tests with regard to your past. At least now you can help him. You can give him the tests. You can alert him to the consequences of letting jealousy get the better of him and your relationship. You can foster him to look at all you have and the importance of that. You can stress the need for choosing and not being victimized by demoralizing emotions. You can find his time preferences and help him see how they really affect his behavior. It is but another gift you can give your married man.

"My married man told me everything about his marriage, his wife, his infidelities. I told him everything about me, all the details of my loves and my life. After we were married, we came to regret all those confidences. Now all those secrets hurt. We never should have told each other everything. Honesty isn't always the best policy. And yet in the telling of those confidences, we wove a confidential union that was responsible for our love and our eventual marriage. It's ironic, isn't it?" *(Deer Park, Illinois)*

I'll bet that previous quotation speaks for a great many mistresses. And especially for those who go on to become second wives. Revealing innermost thoughts and conflicts is a wonderful release and one that has its moments of regrets. However, that is essence of sharing and accepting one another.

If you go from mistress to married man's wife, you are going to have to accept him past and all. You are going to have to accept your mistress years and put them behind you as you move into new marital territory. Your attitude towards the past and your aptitudes for the past are going to be so significant. You are going to have to handle the history tests. Making peace with all that went before has to happen before you find new peace in your marriage.

As a second wife, the past will always be some part of your future. Memories, souvenirs, and mementos are as inevitable as seasons and holidays. In wedding that married man, you will pledge love through sickness and health, good times and bad. Silently add a pledge about overcoming past traumas, and the traumas the concept of the past can unleash. Loving each other in spite of what has gone before is a challenge. It is a test that you have to weather for better or for worse. History is a test but it is also a lesson in choice.

History can sour you or it can add a little Cinderella magic to your new life. You can remove your relationship from the triangle, but you can never remove the triangle from your relationship. You can't really erase the past. You can use it to your advantage with insight and practice. Not being able to handle the past can erase your chances for happiness. If you plan on graduating from mistress to wife, master history. If you cannot pass all the history tests, believe me you'll never make the grade as second wife. On the other hand, if you fare well in the history tests, your reward can be happy endings and happy beginnings. Once upon a time you were a mistress. You can be a second wife happily ever after, with a few lessons in history.

PART II

Strategies for Living

CHAPTER 5

Divorce—Judicial Monopoly

Divorce is a game of judicial monopoly. And like any game, there are moves, maneuvers, and mistakes. You and your married man, on the brink of his divorce, are now entering the gameboard. And before you begin there is much to learn. Certain players have distinct advantages and disadvantages. The game itself has traps and pitfalls. The stakes are indeed high. The playing of judicial monopoly requires skill. There are ways of managing the obstacles, of cutting your losses, and of expediting the process. That means strategy. You and your married man want to emerge at the end of judicial monopoly equipped for your new life. Therefore it is in your best interests to learn the rules of judicial monopoly thoroughly. Then develop the best possible strategy based on your own particular set of circumstances.

Some of you will find judicial monopoly a simple game. Others of you will find it a difficult challenge. Still others will find it an unfair travesty. However, after reading this chapter none of you will enter the game totally unprepared.

The purpose of this section is to educate you, the mistress, on the game so that you can educate your married man. You will learn to ascertain your man's psychological readiness and fitness. Then, you will learn how to arm him if necessary. You will be introduced to the subject of *the lawyer,* his or her role and selection. Then we will proceed to the problem areas of the divorce. We'll be looking at how to set your goals, filial and financial, and, perhaps most salient, how to terminate the game so that you and your married man can begin your new life.

Chances are divorce is a new frontier for you. If not, then you can probably benefit by your experience. Navigating the legal frontier can be trying. In fact it can range from trying to downright devastating! The legal process can be intimidating and confusing. The biggest drawback to you and your married man is naiveté. Once you've overcome that hurdle, you are on your way. Your strategy in playing judicial monopoly can significantly alter your chances for happiness in your new life.

But now is not the time to dwell upon the new life. Now is the time to sort out his old life. As you watch him in the final days of his marriage, what do you see? As he dismantles the family lifestyle and disengages from the family structure, who is this man right now? What is his mood? What is your reaction to his present state of affairs? Are you or he, or both of you, temporarily handicapped by "Marital Myopsis"?

What is marital myopsis? Is it dangerous? Answer a few questions and see. Are you scared to death by the impending divorce? Is he guilt-ridden about "abandoning" his children? Has he expressed anxiety about "walking out" on responsibilities? Do you both feel guilty because you have each other and "they" have nothing? Are either of you immobilized by this fear and conflict? Is he depressed for wanting "out" of that unhappy marriage and confused by this feeling? Does he seem like a man who is neither coming or going?

If you know these feelings of guilt, conflict, and anxiety, then you and he are vulnerable to marital myopsis. Marital myopsis means you are shortsighted, gripped by your present trauma. You and he see only the present pain, loss, and anguish of all. You feel your future is somehow unfair, if it means causing others heartbreak. Right now your psychological state is dangerous. It is highly subjective.

The following test is designed to help you understand the ramifications of your own and his psychological state. It is designed to assist you in getting pre-divorce anxieties into their proper perspective. Marital myopsis, or shortsightedness, is natural for many people in your situation. Yet it must be recognized and overcome. The end product of this is guilt with a capital G. And the impact of that guilt can be significant, as you will now see.

The Guilt Guillotine

In France, the instrument of capital punishment has been the guillotine. Many married men feel, perhaps unconsciously, that divorce is akin to some capital crime. Therefore they set themselves up for voluntary penalties and become naive victims of what I call the Guilt Guillotine. If there is a mistress mixed up in all this, she can be instrumental in either lowering the blade or saving her married man's neck. However, she must be aware of the Guilt Guillotine.

The following test is designed to help you help your married man from falling victim to the Guilt Guillotine. I have heard about this particular fate many times from married men, ex-mistresses, and second wives. Hopefully you and he can profit from others' losses. And if you can save his neck, you will in some ways be saving your own as you go from mistress to wife.

Directions: Answer each of the following statements with either True or False. For some of the responses you will be relying on your feelings. For some of the responses you will be relying on an assessment of his feelings. And I might add that giving him the test would be the best way to verify both of your feelings, so you will know well the Guilt Guillotine. After responding with your True or False selections, proceed to the scoring section and an evaluation of what that score means.

1. Choosing a lawyer is an arbitrary process because they are all legal experts.

   _____

2. The legal maneuvers in the divorce process are so complicated and aggravating that it is better to avoid involvement as much as possible.

   _____

3. It is more expedient and therefore better to take any deal that is being offered as a divorce settlement.

_____

4. Haggling over exact times, days, and places of your future visitation with the children is a waste of time.

_____

5. Trying to dictate to your lawyer the terms of your divorce regarding custody of the children is hopeless idealism.

_____

6. Alimony or "maintainence" is good because the kids need their mother at home.

_____

7. Giving the wife as much as possible is best so that the children don't have to change their home or lifestyle.

_____

8. Being financially generous is good for the kids because they already are suffering enough losses in divorce situations.

_____

9. It's not necessary to get everything in writing, since people mature as the pain of divorce subsides.

_____

10. Divorcing brings out feelings of failure and unworthiness in men, but that doesn't pose a problem in negotiating a divorce.

_____

Scoring:
Every True answer is worth 0 points. Every False answer is worth 10 points. Allot yourself the appropriate points for each answer and then add up all your points.

Evaluation:
All of the statements in the test are FALSE!!! The higher your score, the more vulnerable you and he are to the Guilt

Guillotine! If you scored any higher than 0, read the following carefully. Otherwise, your story may be a tale of two suicides!

Divorce can definitely make a man feel like a failure or like some unworthy deserter, regardless of the irrationality of these self-images. A mistress on his mind can make him feel worse guilt-wise. These feelings set your man up for bad judgements. He is not thinking or functioning logically, but rather emotionally and not with the healthiest emotions.

Watch for these common mistakes. Some married men will take any settlement, any deal, just to get this legal haggling over with fast. Some will give extravagant alimony so that Mom can stay home with the kids. Some will give hefty child support, too, throw in the house, car, and other possessions so as not to damage the children's lifestyle. The rationale is that perhaps generosity on Dad's part can redeem him, make restitution to the children, and prevent some of the suffering that goes along with divorce. A man's generosity inclinations are sometimes a direct measure of his guilt.

Some men pick a lawyer haphazardly, assuming they are all the same. They feel any lawyer who can handle this quickly is the best bet. A man must be careful in choosing a lawyer and take an active stance in all legal matters. Otherwise your married man winds up the loser with a settlement that makes his new life impossible. And you will lose too!

Custody arrangements must be carefully considered and scrupulously written out in the court papers. Joint custody is the ideal. Don't assume an ex-wife will naturally encourage fatherhood after divorce. Get custody and visitation details in print; every day, place, and time. Don't let his fatherhood wind up on the chopping block of the guillotine.

A man must be assertive in negotiating his divorce. *It is a permanent agreement.* It is the final arrangement of his past. It is a life sentence. Too many divorced men have told me that they would judge the guillotine easier than the fate they brought upon themselves with foolish, fast divorce deals!

Divorce can certainly cloud one's reason. A triangle can further muddle the issues. Next thing, he is standing in front of the Guilt Guillotine childless and penniless, helpless and hopeless. Remember his future is at stake and his future is your future. Don't let him cast himself like the fictional martyr, Sydney Carton from *A Tale of Two Cities*. Don't let him sign away his life to a sentence in some eternal Bastille. Don't let him put his neck on the chopping block. You and he can come out of the divorce bruised but not beaten, having been fair but not foolish.

Your psychological readiness and his is a point I cannot stress enough. Regardless of the present painful drama, you and he have a right to a future of love and happiness. If you and he feel villainous for your togetherness while his wife and children have only loss, realize *that is an inaccurate statement*. It is incomplete. You, and he too, have a sense and a reality of loss. And his wife has her relationship with the children, family, and friends. Her future is what she makes of it, not what either of you have "done" to it. You and your married man deserve your dreams. You are both entitled to the fruition of those dreams. You and he have a right to a second chance and to your love. Everyone in the triangle is getting a new chance at another life. The destiny of that new life is in the hands of each player.

Judicial monopoly is a game of transition. Yet it still will always have bearing on the years to come because relationships, both financial and family-oriented, will be set. Your psychological fitness is crucial. You must learn to see past the present traumas. You must bypass marital myopsis. You must cultivate strength. And you must realize that you are both good people who are sharing in a time of stress and heartbreak, hurting and being hurt; yet deserving better days.

Your decision-making capacity must be reliable. Your psychological state has to be realistic and positive to ensure that. One of the first decisions, and perhaps the most important one, will be in choosing a lawyer. Before we get to the pragmatic considerations of that selection process, let's look at the psychology implicit in that choice.

Do you or does your married man have an awe of professionals? Let me put it another way. Have you ever argued with a doctor about his or her diagnosis? Have you ever fired a doctor from your case? Have you ever scrutinized a dentist about his or her procedures, asked to see the X rays? Do you always seek second opinions from an unreferred professional before decision-making? Many of us have an awe of professionals. We don't question their judgements or their motives. We tend to think all professionals are excellent, be they doctors, dentists, psychiatrists, or lawyers. You know . . . a lawyer is a lawyer . . . with the same degree.

Stop and acknowledge one small fact. In every graduating class of professionals, there were A students and C students.

They had varying motivations and intellects. All professionals are not equal, not at graduation and not in their practices. Rid yourself of any professional awe. It is a tendency that puts you at a psychological disadvantage in choosing a lawyer and dealing with one.

The selection of a lawyer is the first investment in your new life with your married man. That lawyer will negotiate the terms of the divorce decree, terms that will become a living part of your second marriage. Once you overcome any awe of the professional, you are ready to begin.

Here are a few do's and don't's for choosing a lawyer:

1. Don't hire a lawyer because someone in the family used him/her once.
2. Do keep an ear out for good recommendations, but follow up.
3. Do interview several lawyers before paying anyone anything.
4. Do cross-examine his/her value structure. Prejudices can hurt a married man, be they feminist, sexist, or moralistic . . . beware.
5. Do inquire on his/her stand on father's rights. If they do not value fatherhood, they will not work for good visitation/custody arrangements.
6. Do make sure he/she is up-to-date with latest trends in divorce, such as temporary maintainence and joint custody.
7. Do assess his/her character and look for honesty, fairness, and diligence.
8. Do discuss your goals and get his/her appraisal of your odds for a successful settlement.
9. Don't hide the triangle or the mistress situation. Do make sure the lawyer also feels you deserve a second chance. Don't hire someone who may sympathize with the "deserted" wife.
10. Do discuss your finances and the method of payment and get an estimate.
11. Do hire someone who is willing to explain legal procedures, liabilities, and time frames.
12. Do hire a lawyer with experience and inquire about his/her experience with similar cases.

This selection process will not be quick. It will take extra effort. However, it is your first decision, your first future investment. Don't invest haphazardly. Choosing a good lawyer who is compatible with your circumstances is the beginning. You, your married man and the lawyer will develop all your moves through judicial monopoly.

We have covered the psychological aspects of the legal process. Let's proceed now to the concrete issues dealt with in judicial monopoly. Basically the stakes are children, property, and money. How these are shared after the divorce varies. Each and every settlement can be as individual as the individual players decide. Many couples will be able to rationally share the children and divide the assets. For many, this can be done quickly and without arguments in court. Settling any disagreements out of court is of course the easiest, the least expensive, and the least draining emotionally.

However, although the stakes are the same with varying degrees, the rules are the same legally speaking; not everyone playing judicial monopoly has the same motivation and technique. This is where the problem arises for many married men and their mistresses.

We are about to explore some of the problems that arise in the playing of judicial monopoly. Sincerely, I hope none of these experiences will become yours or your married man's. However, as part of your education, you should review them. They are some of the concrete disasters for which you and he should be prepared. The following pages will prime you and help you guide your legal representation.

In the playing of judicial monopoly, often there is foul play. Divorce proceedings occur in highly emotional territory. Some married people are graceful about the marital demise; some are not. For some married couples, instead of cooperating to separate themselves, they conspire in a battle of spite and bitterness. Oftentimes, it only takes *one* to tangle a divorce up into a game of vengeance.

This can be especially relevant to the married man with a mistress. Which comes first: a marriage on the rocks or a mistress? Most experts agree that a mistress is more likely to occur within a crumbling marriage. However, for the wife who discovers the mistress within her marriage, she can also discover a valuable scapegoat. Suddenly every problem in the marriage, every iota of blame, every failure of any kind is somehow channeled to the mistress and the bum (the husband). The wife postures herself as the "wronged" martyr, victimized by this other woman. This is the perfect rationale for her to become vengeance personified.

The vengeance works its way out in expressions of hostility and unreasonableness. Possessions become ammunition. Children become weapons. Property becomes the battlefield. Adultery becomes the justification. This can be a brief phase of anger and rejection. Or it can become a way of life that the married man is subjected to for years.

"His ex wanted everything. The couch she had always loathed, the house, even the china that had been in Sam's family for generations. He didn't care. Sam said they were only things and things could be replaced. So his ex zeroed in on the one thing that couldn't be replaced, the children. She refused to let Sam see them at all." *(Torrance, California)*

That comment brings us to the issue of father's and children's rights. This issue is one of the biggest dangers in judicial monopoly. Custody laws are changing, but slowly. Statistically nine out of ten mothers are still awarded custody of the children of divorce. Where can this leave the father? He usually has visitation rights spelled out in the divorce. However, are court orders realistic? And more importantly, are they enforceable in the face of an enraged ex-spouse?

Rights In Your Own Backyard

"We are sick and tired of hearing politicians talk about human rights [in foreign countries]. What about the need for human rights here in America! The right of a father to love his child and vice versa. What about that human right!

"I am a second wife. My husband hasn't been able to see his children for three years. He's had three court orders from State Supreme Court and has been denied visits fifty-six times. He's tried calling on the telephone, and the children are not allowed to come and talk. He has sent letters and they have come back unopened.

"I've watched him outside the children's house arguing with the police, court order in hand. The kids behind the windows unreachable, crying hysterically. The police write their report, and tell him to go back to court. He does; another order, another meaningless episode. Fathers have no rights.

"We keep up our end of the financial bargain, alimony and child support, but that doesn't matter. I have watched as his children claw at the windows and scream. Children have no rights either.

"There is no law in this land and no court and no judge to help you if you are a divorced Dad or a child. The father-child relationship is not guaranteed. It gets lost in legal jargon and bureaucracy. After our last court appearance, his ex exited laughing at us and we gave up.

"My husband came home and took all of the children's toys and put them in our basement. He closed up the room where the children were to stay during our visitation weekends. He padlocked the door. He took the clothes we bought for them and dumped them in the Salvation Army bins outside the A&P.

"The last thing he did was take the ceramic bold eagle off our mantlepiece and smash it on the floor. The eagle, he said, reminded him of justice, and there is no justice. There is no law to ensure your rights to see your children after divorce.

"I swept up the smithereens silently. What could I say? He was right. The laws are wrong. The courts are inadequate. And human rights? It is some slogan uttered by politicians for foreign shores. They should start working here for human rights and start in my backyard!"

The story of that triad is not an oddity. The annals of my research on second wives seem liberally seasoned with such tales.

"The worst torture for my married man was going to visit his children. He could hear them begging their mother to let them go. As she opened the door wide enough to yell and curse, they tried to squeeze their little bodies through the cracks. He just couldn't stand this after a while. One time his ex caught the son's arm in the door as she tried slamming it. That did it. My married man stopped trying. After a few trips to court, he stopped that too." *(Boulder, Colorado)*

"Where is the right of the child? Every child needs a mother and a father. Yet a child has no rights to a father after the divorce. By allowing one parent to withhold the child to punish the ex-spouse, we are destroying our children! If children are told Dad is a bum, we are teaching them that half of them is bad, too. What are we doing? Aren't children our greatest national resource?" *(Clearwater, Florida)*

What are these victims of the legal system talking about? Is there a climate in the courts that denies human rights? Legal custody proceedings are surrounded with language about the best interests of the child. When fathers say that is mere lip service, are they correct? How does the legal system tolerate this? Judicial monopoly is a very complicated game. It has some detours that are sexist and discriminatory.

Criminalized

In the game of judicial monopoly, Mark found the courts were not a man's world.

"My case is probably very typical. But when you go through it, it seems atypical. My wife and I couldn't make the marriage work. We both were unhappy for a long time. We had problems; money, affairs, and a basic philosophical conflict about raising our girls. We looked at life in totally different ways.

"My wife announced she was filing for divorce one night. She told me to pack my bags, and get out. I decided I didn't want to leave, the girls or the house. It was my home just as much as it was hers, or so I naively thought then. Two days later I came home and found the sheriff there to evict me forcibly like a common thug. He treated me like a criminal right in front of my daughters. The courts told me, after being thrown out, I still had to pay all the expenses, give up the car, and carry extra insurance. Worst of all, though, I was at my wife's mercy where seeing my daughters was concerned. My visitation seemed good at first. But by now I was beginning to learn that things are not always as they seem. I got to see my girls three weekends per month and one week night each week for dinner. However, my wife refused to cooperate. She didn't let the girls go with me. I was baffled because I paid her regularly in accordance with the court agreement. Anyway, to make a long story short, after six trips to court, and six unfair judges, I still found myself at her mercy. And at the mercy of a horrendous judicial system too. Neither were merciful!"

In the divorce process, it is usually the man who must leave his home and his possessions behind. He no longer lives with his children, seeing them by appointment only. This agreement definitely puts the man on the short end of the proverbial stick.

It is the man who has to assert his rights, negotiate for his property, and struggle to maintain relationships with children.

Add a mistress, and character assassination is rampant. Both physically and emotionally, the husband is at a distinct disadvantage in the legal game. One of the worst effects of this imbalance is that many a married man winds up internalizing this discrimination, thus feeling like a criminal or a villain. And many a man has to "pay" for his "crime."

Wally the Wallet

Wally is a divorcing husband, who was victimized by what I call the Wallet Syndrome. After divorcing his wife, Wally paid in a variety of ways. His ex-wife kept the house and all the contents therein. Wally had to pay alimony and child support for two children. He found he was also responsible for paying all the legal bills, for both his and his wife's lawyers. She did not work outside the home. Wally's new wife told me that was not the whole of it, though.

"Wally has to pay extraordinary medical, dental bills, prescription medicines, hospital bills, and even optical and orthodontic care for the children. Meeting our bills is hard, so we both work. The real problem is seeing the children. We would like to see them. The only time we hear anything about them is when we get a bill. That is a bad way to find out about your children.

"Wally's ex remarried and moved away. She wouldn't let Wally see the kids. And anyway, his visitation schedule wasn't based on her moving. So he hired his lawyer again and got a new schedule for visits. And the added expenses of paying the lawyer, long distance phone bills if he wanted to talk to the children, and air line tickets when they visited. The ex refused to acknowledge the new decree. She claimed she was in a new state, a new jurisdiction, and hired a new lawyer. Wally and I now had a barrage of bills and proceedings going in two states.

"Finally in exasperation, Wally cut off support payments as a tactic. In court, the judge always made him make up the back payments, but no one ever gave him back the time he had lost with his children. His ex-wife was just blotting Wally out of the life of those children, and filling in the blanks with her new husband. Except financially of course.

"The only right that Wally had was the ongoing right to pay. We went through a thousand emotions. Rage. Despair. In the end, we were numbed and broke. We could not afford any more revolving courtroom doors. We couldn't pay any more game-bills, even if it meant forfeiting the children for good."

Judicial monopoly can be frustrating and extremely expensive, financially as well as emotionally.

"The court places all the financial responsibility on the father. He is stripped of all rights except to pay bills. I understand why a lot of fathers walk away. The court doesn't leave a man much to lose." *(Biloxi, Mississippi)*

"Society is changing, but it is still not ready to treat men fairly, especially when there is a mistress marriage. When my married man divorced, what was his crime? Being unhappy? Not loving his wife? His court order gave his wife and two children $600 a month. Now he works seven days a week to keep up and I work too just to make ends meet. The court viewed me as a paramour, and stipulated that his children were not allowed in my presence. His wife made up all sorts of lewd tales and I guess the judge believed it. He got a raw deal, because he was treated like an immoral runaround, while his wife made out like a bandit. She played the lily-white martyr and succeeded in ruining our new marital years." *(Howard Beach, Queens)*

"I am a woman and I do not agree with the trend in this country of assuming women are always the angels and men are always the rats when it comes to divorce. I feel that men and women should be treated equally by the legal system. They should have an equal shot for custody, or joint custody. I believe that the parent who doesn't live with the children should be guaranteed time with them. If the parent refuses, then the sheriff should enforce the child's rights. Now men get screwed. If they have the money to, they go to court and get screwed again. If they have no money, they get taken to court and lose anyway. Sometimes I am ashamed to be a woman, when I see what some of them do in the name of motherhood." *(Elk Grove, Illinois)*

"I am a grandmother and I want to testify. My son married this girl and they had one child. He has divorced her and has been paying for the child and the mother. He has now married a lovely girl and has a new child. His first wife went to court and the judge treated my son like a bum. The mother brainwashed the child so that, when my son would go there, the child would commence this hysteria. My son gave up his right to see my grandchild. Who looked out for the rights of that child? It's like my grandchild died to me. My son is being tortured for a crime he didn't commit. He still has to pay her a lot of money. I feel like my heart is broken when I look at my son. He loves and can't see his own child. My heart breaks twice when I think of my grandchild. Can't the laws be changed somehow?" *(Florence, Alabama)*

"I want to tell you about my husband. I am now married to my former married boyfriend. Because of my husband's ex-wife, he has lost a terrific business, gone to jail three times, gone through five lawyers, and ended up bankrupt. He had a child from that marriage, was paying $130 a week and went to jail anyway! Believe me our marriage has been nothing but stress and strain and it's not our fault. It has changed me. I have no use for judges or the legal system. I know how it feels to be treated like an ignominious criminal, and a whipping post, because that says it for us. It all stinks." *(Trenton, New Jersey)*

Throughout these personal testimonies, there are examples of the wallet syndrome, the emotional child abuse of father deprivation, and discrimination against fathers. These are by-products of our legal system. They are on the gameboard of judicial monopoly.

How did they get there? These human injustices and obvious abuses of power do not seem consistent with our values of justice. The legal system is far from perfect. Basically, there are two areas that can pose serious problems.

Sexism is still prevalent in many courtrooms. The man is defined by his ability to pay. His ability or his capacity for parenting is less considered. This stems from stereotypes of the female mother/housewife and the male/breadwinner. Although society has changed drastically, the legal system has only changed minutely. However, there are things you can do. We'll get to that in a moment.

Accountability is perhaps the largest problem. There is a gap between what court orders say and what court orders can actually do. When the custodial parent (usually the mother but not always) violates a court order that allows visitation, there is no way to enforce that order. Law enforcement agencies in most states make it a policy not to get involved. They refer the parties back to the legal system. Unfortunately, for many fathers judges will not punish a mother for violating the orders. Vengeful women realize that they can break the law with impunity again and again. The legal network is therefore like a revolving door, catching only exasperated fathers and traumatized children in its spin.

Despite the fact that visitation is not safeguarded, the mother's rights to her alimony and child support are. There is now a national network to trace fathers who do not keep up with their court-ordered payments. Although this is a lengthy process and complex, the legal system has attempted to enforce the financial side of its court orders. However, there have been few attempts to enforce visitation rights and punish violations.

The climate of sexism, discrimination, and unaccountability creates a system that is complicated, redundant, and very expensive. Its implicit loopholes can be perfect breeding ground for a vengeful spouse to wreak havoc and bankruptcy interminably—that is, until the married man/divorced husband terminates the legal game.

And so again we get back to strategy. What can a married man and a mistress do to survive the dregs of judicial monopoly, if you see them in the offing? Briefly I can summarize a few basic points.

Know the limits of the judicial system. Lawyers can get you as many court orders as you and your married man can finance, but lawyers cannot enforce them. Lawyers are not mythical heros and heroines, on a quest to nobly save your world; they are business people. They are trained to represent clients. Oftentimes their ethics are their clients. They will represent a vengeful wife or an abusing mother. Don't forget lawyers defend the most despicable murderers. This is a job for them. To you, it may be a life and death drama: the life of a child, the death of fiscal solvency. But a lawyer sees scenarios like this daily. Numbness and insensitivity is an occupational hazard.

Judges were lawyers first. They have similar experiences and backgrounds. They sit before a parade of emotionally charged spouses daily and sort out fates. Judges can order justice, but judges cannot enforce it either. Too many still refuse to mete out punishment for visitation violations because motherhood is hallowed. Fatherhood is lower on the spectrum. Judges deal in compromise; usually everyone loses something.

Where does this leave you and your married man? It depends on your finances, his ex-spouse's spite capacity, and the laws in your state. Research the legal details with your lawyers. Develop realistic goals. If you run into dilemmas, set a limit on the number of court battles you are willing to wage. Know when to stop litigating. Some people think if they keep on fighting, justice will triumph in the end. That is not always accurate. If you keep on fighting, you may never win "justice" and you may lose all your savings and access to the children anyway, and gain only a legacy of bills and bitterness. A good lawyer will guide you and advise you. However, in the end you and your married man must dictate the strategy.

"I have been through a very long and expensive court battle to see my children. It lasted three years. I still don't know if I won or lost the case. For example, after my ex-wife defied two court orders for not letting me see the kids, the court fined her $500, rescinded the fine and I am now allowed to see the children for five and a half hours on the weekend, two hours less than the previous court order. I guess I lost but all I want now is for it to be over." *(Indiana)*

Judicial monopoly can be expensive, confounding, and self-defeating. So long as an ex-wife wants to harass, the legal system can accommodate her. Custody cases are never permanent. They can be fought again and again. Financial orders can be amended at every change of circumstance, and litigated over continually. Once you are well versed in these injustices, you can look for help.

Aside from your own sense of realism versus emotionalism, there are a number of men's rights groups that can be consulted. There are groups in every state for fathers and second wives. They can serve to advise you about legal procedures in your particular state and your specific case. They can also encourage you and your married man. They can help you both adjust to the changes in your lives and help you recover emotionally from traumas and losses.

You can also work for change. Take any energy, frustration, and rage you may feel and channel it into constructive efforts.

Work for the Equal Rights Amendment, which will equalize the divorce process. Work for joint custody legislation and for political candidates who share these views. If your married man is losing his children, encourage him to fight through an effort to change the system. Perhaps he will save another man's fatherhood. Fighting in court can only mean getting caught up in its revolving door sometimes. If you and your married man get into a legal ordeal, make your struggle worthwhile by trying to help future generations.

"I've prayed, worked, and cried out for divorced men to stand up and be counted. On television programs, in newspapers, community meetings, political rallies, books, any way at all to let people know what is happening to us, the divorced father and to our children." *(Spring Valley, California)*

"The media is full of the plights of the poor divorced woman, deserted by a runaround, impoverished, and raising her children alone. Let's give them the other side. The divorced woman keeps the children most of the time, keeps her life line and her security, and she is never alone. The divorced man is poor too, and twice as lonely. And he's dumped on with guilt, blame, and disorientation." *(Dover, Delaware)*

Judicial monopoly is a challenge. I cannot predict whether it will be a moderate challenge or an excruciating one for you and your married man. Only you and he can calculate your problems and your strategy. I can tell you, even at the writing of this book, I see changes in the system being made every day, slowly but surely. Still each divorce is different.

Recently a case in Virginia came to national attention. A divorced father was awarded $25,000 for the violation of his rights. Harold Memmer was prevented from seeing his three children by his ex-wife. He claimed that his mental state was severely hurt by this loss. He won the suit and $25,000 in damages. According to a reporter on the scene, his children shunned him outside the courtroom. Perhaps there are no clear cut victories. But this case will change things.

Once upon a time fathers entered the gameboard of judicial monopoly and gave up. They walked away leaving their children and their wallets behind. Now the consciousness of fathers has changed. Many are willing to fight for their rights for a new life, a fair settlement, and their relationships with their children. You and your married man can add to the changing trends and benefit from them.

Knowing the gameboard of judicial monopoly is a priming exercise. Hopefully, his divorce will be one of those that is mere paperwork with a minimum of anguish. However, you and he should be prepared for the danger zones. For some of you, judicial monopoly may seem like a gauntlet. You and your married man may feel like you are entering a Kafkaesque nightmare, laced with unjust bureaucrats and inhuman values. You may find guilt, moral indignation, debt, discrimination, sexism, and disillusionment plaguing you.

If your fate is one of those disastrous ones, remember this is a phase. Judicial monopoly may be akin to a gauntlet, but it will pass. Don't prolong the legal passage. Negotiate, settle, and move on. Your married man will not come out richer or unscarred. Divorce divides incomes, lifestyles, and families. However, the traumas can be temporary if you and he employed wise strategy. The gauntlet ends when the divorce is final and you and he put it behind you. On the other side of the gauntlet is your new life. You and he can begin your new life triumphing in your love and in surviving judicial monopoly. You can come out of it with your integrity intact. You and he can come out of it with confidence about your character, even in the face of personal losses. The legal passage is harrowing in varying degrees, but living with your married man is the end result. Freedom is sometimes worth facing any gauntlet. It was for me and my married man!

CHAPTER 6

Lodge-istics

If you go from mistress to wife, you are going to live happily ever after. What is the address of happily ever after? Where is its exact location? When he and you are man and wife at last, your dreams will be coming true, but where? Have you and your married man discussed lodge-istics?

By lodge-istics I simply mean your living arrangements for the future. Where are you and your married man planning to live after the divorce? Have you and he sat down and discussed homing prospects?

Sometimes a mistress gets wrapped up in daydreams. She thinks exclusively in terms of somedays, somehows, and some-wheres. The problem with fantasy-thinking is that the real facts of life are ignored. You, as a mistress, may see your future as an intangible romantic fantasy at the end of a rainbow. But, if you go to second wife, there has to be something concrete at the end of the rainbow.

You and your married man have to have a roof over your heads. That is reality. The purpose of this chapter is to help you build a foundation for your new life. The *where* of your new life together is one of the most important considerations in the Triangle Transition.

In this section we are going to explore all the aspects of lodge-istics. We are going to assess possible homing prospects, for you as well as him. We are going to outline potential dilemmas. There can be financial problems as well as emotional ones. We are going to pinpoint the most crucial considerations with regard to your future residence. Can you coordinate your life and his lodge-istically? In looking for answers to all these questions and dilemmas, we will begin to build the foundation for your new life.

Because only one out of ten married men emerge from divorce with child custody, this chapter is written with the assumption that only you and he will be living together. If children will be coming with him into your remarriage full-time, then read them into all the following plans. A whole chapter has been reserved for step-parenting, but here in this section just make sure you make room for them literally.

Perhaps I have underestimated your homing instincts. Perhaps you have gotten a headstart on planning your lodge-istics. Let's say you have given your future some thought, or a great deal of thought. What have you come up with?

The test that follows is the first step in translating your visions of the future into a real foundation.

Do You Have a Master or Mistress Plan?

If an architect were to design a home, surely he or she would have a master plan. In designing your future, you are in a sense your own architect. In planning your journey from mistress to wife, do you have a master plan, or in this case, a mistress plan? What kind of design are you drafting for your home?

I realize that's a big question. So before you answer, take the following test. It will help you collect your thoughts on the matter. And perhaps it will remind you of a few considerations you should be making. The test will also help you evaluate your mistress plan, that is, if you have one.

Directions: The following test is multiple choice and so you must read each question and choose only one answer from among the possible choices. Some of the questions may seem vague, but you must make a guess. Some of the questions may be new, so give them a bit of thought before answering. After you have completed all the questions go on to your scoring task.

1. Do you have a "dream house" concept? (a) Right now any house we'd share would be a dream come true. (b) Yes, I have a dream house picture in my mind but it's in the

distant future. (c) Our dream house is part of a plan, we'll start small and progress as we've agreed.

1._____

2. Could you and he live at your place? (a) We've decided on that already with job proximity, etc., in mind. (b) Absolutely, if only he'd say the word. (c) I haven't given it much thought really.

2._____

3. How close exactly have you and he discussed your living arrangements as a couple? (a) Living arrangements haven't been settled yet because he says, "First things first." (b) We've fantasized endlessly about where we would like to live, the neighborhood, the style of house, even the furniture. (c) We know exactly where we are going to live and try to build a life.

3._____

4. Have you considered living at his place? (a) That's in or out of the question because of his settlement. (b) Me live in her house—that's not exactly my fantasy. (c) It's too soon to tell about who will live in his house.

4._____

5. Have you and he been to a bank to seek mortgage advice? (a) Our dream house may be designed but financing is still in the realm of make-believe. (b) Yes, and we've come up with a plan. (c) No; to get mortgage advice is premature at this time.

5._____

6. Is there a down payment on hand for your living plan? (a) Not yet but we are both saving and meantime we have an alternative. (b) How can we talk financial investment before I know if his romantic investment is real enough? (c) I don't know what his financial plan is yet.

6._____

7. How would you feel if you and he as a couple just could never afford to own your own home? (a) Never say never, cause who knows? (b) We've talked of that possibility and how it makes us both feel. (c) That wouldn't matter be-

cause it's our love that counts not the love nest.

7._____

8. Have you planned the locale of your home with needs in mind? (a) He is my only need, so the where is up to him. (b) I suppose he will have to be near his job and children. (c) We've planned with proximities and needs in mind, mine and his.

8._____

9. Has the possibility of joint custody been written into your plan? (a) Yes, we have several options for different custody ruling. (b) Not yet, because if only he'd choose me I know things would work out. (c) No, I'm not sure what joint custody would mean or what his intentions for custody are.

9._____

10. Which of these sums up best your philosophy for the future? (a) The future is now and we are ready even if scared. (b) The future is up in the air waiting for the right time. (c) The future is someday when things work out.

10._____

Scoring:
Before we can see if your mistress plan is a good one or not, we must make sense out of your answers. So I have designed a scoring process. First write all your answers from 1 to 10 in the column marked *Answers*. Then look and see how much each answer is worth by referring to the point values. Then write in the number of points for each of your answers in the column marked *Points*. At the end total up your points and fill in the space next to *Total*. Then read whichever evaluation holds the range of your score.

				Answers	Points
1.	(a) 15	(b) 10	(c) 5	_____	_____
2.	(a) 5	(b) 15	(c) 10	_____	_____
3.	(a) 10	(b) 15	(c) 5	_____	_____
4.	(a) 5	(b) 15	(c) 10	_____	_____
5.	(a) 15	(b) 5	(c) 10	_____	_____
6.	(a) 5	(b) 15	(c) 10	_____	_____

			Answers	Points
7.	(a) 10	(b) 5	(c) 15	_____	_____
8.	(a) 15	(b) 10	(c) 5	_____	_____
9.	(a) 5	(b) 15	(c) 10	_____	_____
10.	(a) 5	(b) 10	(c) 15	_____	_____

Total _____

Evaluation:

Your score could range anywhere from 50 to 150 points. Choose the category below that encompasses your own score. It will tell you about your master or mistress plan and whether it is a good one or not.

120–150 Points: Fantasyland. According to the answers you chose, your next address is going to be fantasyland. Your mistress plan always opts for the answer that is romantic. You are preoccupied, not with the details of living arrangements, but with the fantasies you and he weave. Having a mistress plan that is made up of fantasies is almost like having no plan at all! Although you do make sense when you say it's the love not the love nest that counts, still you have to spend some time planning where the nest will be. The texture of your future is up to you. If you draft with nothing but daydreams, your design may never materialize!

85–115 Points: Tomorrowland. According to the answers you chose, your address is going to be tomorrowland. In your mistress plan everything is dated tomorrow. Concepts are all off in the distance or you haven't given the questions much thought. Your vocabulary is filled with references to "premature," "too soon," or "suppose this or that." You had better start designing a mistress plan that begins today, not tomorrow. If you don't start drafting your future, tell me, who will? Where you wind up is going to happen and if you don't plan for it, it may be a fate that you don't like. If you draft with nothing but evasions and postponements, is that saying that you have no plan because you have no future with him? Better to consider that now than tomorrow, because the answers will not be any easier or different. Tomorrowland may be never-neverland! If not, what are you waiting for?

50–80 Points: Frontierland. According to your answers, your next address may be a frontierland, but at least you have plans. One can never know all the details of the future, but one can do research and one can try and guess. Your mistress plan is best of all because you have a practical and thorough design. Your plan is based on his settlement, yours and his assets and needs, and not on whims or wishes. Your senses are in reality and your dwelling plans clearly show that. The texture of your future may be a new frontier to you and him, but you have a pioneer vision and are trying to equip yourselves as best you can. For you, frontierland may turn out to be utopia. Good luck!

In Conclusion:

You can't design your home of the future by concentrating on the stars or putting off the drafting process. You can only design your future home by starting with its foundations and planning out all the little mundane details. You must have a master plan of where you and he will live. Your mistress plan will be your guide. Work on yours, adjust it, update it, do whatever alterations are necessary. If you plan on traveling from mistress to wife, you had better have the route paved. The journey will be even more difficult if you have no master or mistress plan. I wish all of you an address in utopia.

From where you are now to utopia may seem like an impossible distance. If you take one step at a time, renovating your life and his will not seem so awesome. Let's look at your living arrangement and his right now. What have you and he to start with?

Houses and apartments must be discussed separately. They entail different plans of action. Apartments are not so difficult to deal with, because they are rented and not owned. The legalities and the trappings of leaving an apartment are relatively simple. If you have an apartment, is it suitable for the two of you? If so, then your lodge-istics may be simple. He can move in with you.

Does your married man live in an apartment with his wife and/or children? If so, then divorce will mean leaving his family in that apartment or seeing that they rent another without him. The most he has to lose is breaching a lease agreement. No property struggle looms.

If your married man is a home-owner, the picture is different. A house is a major investment. What will become of that house in the process of divorce? Has he discussed the house with his wife? Will she agree to sell? Is she determined to keep the house? If there are children, most judges will allow the wife to keep living in the house, providing she can make

the mortgage payments. This can tie up your married man's
assets indefinitely.

What happens to the house belonging to your married man
and his wife can become salient to your future if you and he
want a house of your own. Can your married man afford a
house for you, if his other house is not sold? Will a bank give
him a mortgage, if his name appears on the mortgage agreement
for the house his ex-wife keeps? If he winds up homeless after
divorce, have you a savings account that could become a down
payment on a new house?

All of these are weighty questions. Many of the ex-
mistresses with which I have spoken found the answers difficult
to cope with. Acknowledging these questions can help you find
solutions and, hopefully, answers. You can learn from the
lessons of others.

"My married man's ex-wife refused to cooperate in the
selling of the house. She knew, if she kept the house, Ray
would have no money to start again with me. Ray fought her
in court for the house; he wanted the court to order a sale.
Instead they said the ex-wife and the children could keep it.
The ex had to assume the payments on the mortgage. At the
point in the future when the house was sold, then Ray would
get his half. All of Ray's assets were on hold cause of this.
We had no down payment, no house, and no prospects. So we
had to put our dreams of a house on hold." *(Culver City,
Arizona)*

"His wife agreed to sell the house. But after selling and
paying the bank, he was left with a couple of thousand. That
wasn't enough for a down payment. I wish I had started saving
a few years ago so I had something too. We are renting a lovely
place now, but the rent is high and so our saving process is
very, very slow." *(Manhattan, New York)*

"When we went to the bank and applied for a mortgage it
was a real shock. We had pooled our savings and we had about
$10,000. We figured that would go down on a house, so all
we needed was a bank to give us the mortgage. We had a
perfect house in mind. The bank said that Hal couldn't afford
a second mortgage. Second mortgage? Yes, even though Hal
was divorced and not responsible for paying off his ex-house
according to his settlement, the bank still held him responsible.

We explained and even presented the divorce agreement. We tried three banks. We were refused three times for the same reason. It seems divorced men are still liable for the house they no longer live in, despite what legal papers say. We finally had to ask my parents to co-sign. It was the only way." *(Trenton, New Jersey)*

"His ex-wife got the house and then proceeded to not pay the mortgage. She figured my married man would pay rather than let the bank foreclose. We had to hire a lawyer and go to court to force a sale with the bank foreclosure proceedings right behind. We almost lost but finally the court agreed to let me buy the wife's half-share in the house. Lucky for me I had a nice sized account. Otherwise my married man would have lost his entire house investment." *(La Grande, Oregon)*

As you can see, the fate of the marital residence (as his house is called) can affect your future living plans. Disposal of that house should be thought about quite carefully. Buying a home in today's market is not the easy arrangement it once was. Real estate has skyrocketed. Mortgage rates fluctuate almost daily. Banks are strict when it comes to mortgage applications. You had better acquaint yourself with the real estate business. You should try to plan your fiscal affairs so that you can compensate for his special circumstances.

His house can become a battleground in more ways than one. It can be the turning point in your dream house plans. It can remain a stumbling block to your future even if you and your new husband have no legal responsibilities to it. It can become literally the prize in a tug of war between he and his wife, between your future and your past.

The House That Jack Built

The house that Jack built was in New Hampshire. It was his dream house. Ever since Jack was a kid, he dreamed of building his very own cedar home. As Jack grew up, he did well in business and he married well, he thought at first. The time came in his early thirties when he had the money, the time, and desire to build his dream house.

Piece by piece Jack built his house. It wasn't work for him. He thought about it constantly and spent every spare moment dedicated to it. Soon the house was assembled. There was just one slight problem. His marriage was in ruins.

"I met Jack because I was working for a masonry company. He was married and I knew it, but I knew that his relationship at home was a mess. And I couldn't just turn my heart off like a faucet. We became great friends and then lovers. His wife was always off to some social function, angry because all Jack wanted to do was work on the house."

Jack told his wife about his new mistress. She agreed to a separation. There were no children. Jack wasn't financially shaky and, besides, his wife worked. Alimony shouldn't be a possibility because they were only married four years and his wife was only twenty-nine. On the surface it looked like the kind of triangle that could be untangled easily.

"Jack's wife didn't flip over me. She had been dating some twenty-year-old from work anyway. It really was quite a Peyton Place. Then something happened. She decided that she didn't want to move out of the house, the house that Jack built board by board. Jack wouldn't move out either. It was his house. He offered to buy out her share but his wife said, 'No deal.' I couldn't believe it. They were going to wind up in court fighting over 'custody' of the house!"

Custody of a house? To Jack it wasn't just a house. He wasn't going to budge. His wife was just being stubborn. She had no feelings for the house, really. It was another of those cases where a person in a divorce situation cannot let go. And Jack was not going to let her have the house, just because she was the wife. He refused to move out and so did his wife.

"I love Jack and I understand what that house means to him. He wants for us to live there because I appreciate his dream. But still it's hard for me to cope with a separated man still living with his wife. What do I do? I see him dwindling because of this. His job is getting on his nerves. Insecurity is getting to me. The whole situation is getting on my nerves and that's an understatement. I try and give him encouragement, but I need some encouragement too."

So there you have it. An ideal house. An ideal married man

on the verge of divorce except for the house. An ideal love story with a nice future, except that the house is delaying everything. The house is the tug of war. The house is Jack's essence. Will the house that Jack built become the foundation for a new life? I hope so. For now it's all that remains from Jack's old life. The house that Jack built has a built-in dilemma for Jack's fiancée.

That is one example of how homing prospects can present problems. The loss of that house was a price Jack was unwilling to pay. The next story points up yet another possible dilemma. Suppose that your married man keeps his house and you move in. Would it give you a Rebecca-complex?

Seconds

"My name is Sarah, but it should be Rebecca! I feel like a revival of that old movie about Rebecca. It's about a new wife who moves into the house where the former wife lived. It's spooky. Only in my story the former wife isn't dead, just divorced. This house is still eerie for me."

So why did Sarah move into a house fully equipped with memories and ghosts? It doesn't exactly sound like a dream house.

"When Bob and I married he knew money was going to play a big part in our living plans. His ex-wife wanted to sell their house. Bob and I couldn't afford a new house. The interest rate, huge downpayment, etc. The only option for us was to buy out his ex-wife and move into their house. Then with our combined income we could afford the monthly expense. Bob promised we could redecorate and make the house ours."

As you can see the house was not a newlywed's fantasy. Sarah knew that she would have to leave the past on the outside of the threshold somehow. Their budget was the reality and they couldn't afford all the usual fantasies. Sarah was thrifty. She bought a lot of seconds—on wall papers, linoleum, panelling, and even a few nice pieces of furniture.

"It was traumatic for me in the beginning. The whole psychology of living in her house, even sleeping in their bedroom.

Eerie isn't even the word! Needless to say, redoing the bedroom was first. Then came the family room. Inside the house I was handling it, but what did I do about the neighbors?"

Sarah did everything with caution. A little at a time she gave the place a new personality. A new coat of wall paint covered up the memories forever. As she stripped the floors of carpets that were musty, she was stripping away bad vibrations too. With each new project Sarah found herself loving the house more. It was as if the house were responding to her care.

"It really is a lovely house. My negative feelings had nothing to do with the house, just with the past that lived in the house. Instead of house-hunting for a house, I had to hunt down all the ghosts in my house. See, I even said it . . . my house."

Seconds isn't always a preference. Sometimes a second wife gets a secondhand house. Some women can't handle seconds. Others, like Sarah, can overcome the psychological obstacles and make a first-rate life out of secondhand materials.

Second is a legacy that you may resent as a mistress. Beware: it can carry over after your marriage. Could you handle any challenges *seconds* may inflict? If your dwelling is from his past, will you dwell on that past? Are you willing to settle for redecorating an old life, rather than building anew with raw materials? Can you landscape with secondhand roses? If there is joint custody, will living in the same community with his ex make you continually feel second-rate? Will living nearby cast a shadow over your daily routine, as you look over your shoulder for his ex? Will you feel second-class in her old first-class neighborhood?

Think all these things through and make the necessary alterations in your psyche beforehand. There is another aspect for the mistress and married man to consider if they re-purchase his house. You may inherit a conflict over the concept of territoriality. This becomes more significant if you inherit stepchildren, either part-time or full-time. However, once you understand the territoriality concept, you can incorporate into your living design. You can apply it to everyone's well-being and advantage.

Surely you have seen a pet that favors certain areas in the household. The pet has its rug or its box and a place where food is always available. Most animals define favorite areas for themselves. Those areas become their territory. The study of animal behavior has always recognized this territoriality instinct.

Human beings, too, favor certain areas in a household. You may favor a certain chair in your living room. The kitchen may be your territory. When company comes, you gravitate to the company area. Do you get the gist of this territorial preference inside the home?

If you, as a second wife, move into his former dwelling, look for the territoriality patterns. You may want to change everything about his old house and erase all of its past unhappiness. However, perhaps in violating the territory of others, you can create more unhappy sensations. Your new husband may approve of any and all changes and adapt his territorial likes and dislikes. However, stepchildren may resent changes.

"When my stepchildren came on weekends their toys wound up strewn all over the living room. I reminded them that they had a room for all their toys. The living room was for entertaining adults. I didn't realize it but what I was doing was stripping them of their former rights. They had always had the living room for themselves. One night they told their Dad I was pushing them out, out of 'their' rooms and probably next out of the house. I felt awful. The solution came like a brainstorm. We did a lot of entertaining, so the living room was needed. In his old days there was no company and no pride in the appearance of the home. But there was an attic, perfect for conversion into a playroom just for them. It was a hit and made me a heroine for a change!" *(Philadelphia, Pennsylvania)*

"When we started out in his house, we hit a snag. After dinner he always went to the den. I had clean-up kitchen duty so I stayed there in the kitchen. We walked back and forth a hundred times to talk. Once I guess he liked the den's isolation, but not now. We realized the lonely division of the rooms and decided to knock out the wall between us. Now we each had our territory and each other." *(San Bernadino, California)*

"My married man got possession of his house and custody of his three kids. I moved in with my daughter. We were the invaders and felt like we didn't belong anywhere. We had no safe territory. The house wasn't that big, so bedrooms were going to have to be doubled up. To solve any gripes, we called a meeting, our own family board of zoning. All the kids got to participate in the rearranging. Giving them a say made all the changes easier. In time we all found new territories." *(Alva, Oklahoma)*

A little knowledge of territoriality can go a long way into incorporating ease into the new living scheme. It can help a new family get out of old family fragments and habits. Being aware of others is a good policy inside the house.

Next up, outsides. The location of a new house is crucial to lodge-istics. A new address must suit many needs, people, and factors. The accommodations must accommodate your life and his.

A lesson in geography is a must for you as a potential second wife. You must design your new life by mapping out all of the details and making sure your proximities are accessible.

By proximities I mean closenesses. Closeness to your job, if you work outside the home. Closeness to his job. Closeness to his children, if he has children and they will not be living with you. Closeness to your ex-husband, if you are a married mistress with children who will remain with you. You must take into consideration that fathers need access to their children and distance can be an obstacle. If you map out your new life without a thorough sense of geography, you are setting yourself up for problems.

Geography became a big problem for Patty, not that it was her fault. However, she still inherited the consequences.

By The Time I Get To Phoenix

"I met Russ at the airport. I was on a layover in Chicago; I am a flight attendant. He was on a business trip. He was there to meet an old friend of his. Instead of their friendship re-blooming, ours took over. We had a lot in common. We both lived in New Orleans. We both had unsatisfactory relationships, though only he was married at that time."

Russ and Patty's friendship took flight, right up to cloud nine. Their affair lasted five years before Russ finally opted for a divorce. He hesitated like many men do because of finance and family.

"Finally they were divorced. She soaked Russ dry, his ex-wife did. She bought a new car, and a new home. The worst part is she bought her new home in Phoenix, Arizona!"

Russ had a real hard time coping with that adjustment. His new visitation settlement was obsolete before it even came in the mail. His new marriage to Patty had a big axe thrown right into its center.

"Ever since his children have been away, Russ has become a different person. All he does is work sixty-eighty hours a week, Sundays and holidays. I can't seem to get through to him anymore. I have actually had to go to his office and drag him home so he could get some sleep. We are now going to a marriage counselor and we aren't even past being newlyweds. Russ admits it's not my fault; he misses his kids. The marriage counselor has helped me, but Russ stopped going because he says he hasn't got the time."

Patty gave me her philosophy. She said that Russ was punishing himself for divorcing. He is not happy without his children and so he will not even let himself be happy with Patty either. It's a real rut they are in. Geography isn't one of those problems that has an easy solution.

"I know that Russ and I would be fine if only he were closer to his children. Last night he was telling me that he was thinking of selling his business and moving to Phoenix. I suggested that to him many times and at last he is ready to consider it. I could easily transfer. My salary could keep us going until he did some business readjusting."

Patty and Russ sold everything and headed West. The last thing they bought was a smacking new van so they could drive cross-country and see America on the way. Lodge-istics was a real immobilizing reality for them, but it looks like they are on the right road now. By the time they get to Phoenix they will be closer again, closer to new beginnings and new proximities. By the time they get to Phoenix they will know what geography is all about, in more ways than one.

Going forward can be risky, but sometimes lodge-istics demand taking new chances. Going backward wasn't the philosophy Melanie ever entertained, until that piece of sculpture began giving her homing ideas.

Never Go Home Again?

Melanie's entire fate hung on the edge of a cliché. Could one ever go home again? How much could one gamble with? She was older now, about fifty-five; but why did she not feel proportionate wisdom?!

"It all began in 1952 when I made the choice of a lifetime. My fiancé then was in the Navy and sent overseas. We corresponded constantly and became engaged with the intention that we would marry when he returned. He sent me a money order to buy the ring. I moved to Washington, D.C., meantime to go to work. I felt a job in the Pentagon for the Navy Department would put me in closer touch with the man of my dreams. Instead of putting us closer, my new job exposed me to a new man. In a whirlwind courtship I sent my fiancé, Greg, a Dear John letter, married the other man, and moved to California. I have lived to regret that choice a long time."

Regrets came because the marriage failed. After two children and many bad years, Melanie divorced. She moved to her own place in northern California and began a new job. Her career progressed over the years and she soon found herself in administration. Through all the years she thought of Greg. and always kept a teak figurine that he sent her displayed prominently in her living room. The wooden sculpture showed two people wrapped in each other's arms. It was romantic. It became more romantic, more poignant, and more meaningful over the years to Melanie.

"Last year I went home for my thirtieth class reunion. Greg was there. He went from sailor to millionaire. I told him that we all have our crosses to bear! He visited my mother, at which time he learned all about my marriage, my divorce, and heaven knows what else my mother told him. When I first laid eyes on him at that reunion, I realized that the magic was still there. I melted into his arms. Since then I have lost twenty pounds, have trouble sleeping, and all those other silly symptoms that a silly teenager in love has to endure."

It doesn't take too much reading between these lines to see that Greg and Melanie began a passionate affair. Yet she had her life in northern California. She had a stable, excellent career. She had her two boys who were almost grown and settled into the California lifestyle. Greg, too, had his roots firmly planted in his hometown Southern soil. What would happen?

"It came down to this: this man has a sixteen-year-old son and feels duty-bound to stay home till his son goes to college in two years. I hear about his unhappy sex life at home and that he cares deeply for me. In his living room he has the teak coffee table that was supposed to be for me. All these years he has savored it as I have my figurine.

"Now he is 3000 miles away from me. Phone calls and pictures are all we have. All the years I have been divorced I have never had another man. Until now, I had no idea what I was saving myself for. As ridiculous as it sounds, I should have never let him go!"

And now Melanie is going to have to make that choice again. Should she let him go or should she move to her hometown and wait for him? It would cost her her job and her children's closeness. Will he come through on his promise of divorce and remarriage? Will the move back make her happy or will it cost her happiness?

"I am so confused. Is it true that one can never go home again? I think, all in all, that Greg is a virtuous man and I'm sure he's being honest with me. I fully realize that I have broken one of the commandments and am acting against my childhood training, but I feel a pinch of justification for this. I would do almost anything to have Greg back so that we could start again. After all, I knew him long before his wife did. And yet, with all these times between us, can we still blend our lives? I see myself clutching at the romantic figurine, and wonder if I'm being a romantic idiot. My feeling is that all's fair in love and war. This isn't war, but I'm fearful I'll wind up a casualty."

No, it isn't a war, but Melanie's fears are well-founded. The heart of her conflict is a lodge-istic problem. She will have to forfeit her lifestyle. Her career can not make the move; it is in northern California. Her children can not make the move, except on occasional trips. Melanie can't have it both ways. She can't incorporate her present and her past. One set of proximities is going to have to be abandoned. Could she erect a new life from remnants of yesterdays? Or would today's life block her future? Should the structure of a person's life be changed because of a piece of sculpture?

Melanie had a tough choice once again. Only she can decide which move to make. Melanie lived with a life of regrets already, but her new life with Greg may entail more regrets over other losses.

If marrying your married man will involve moving to another location, give it serious thought. Could you translate your career aspirations to another locale? Could you still have access to your family and friends? And if not, are you willing to make the adjustments? You will have to align your romanticism and your proximities somehow, beforehand. Right this moment, you, as a mistress, may be willing to go to the end of the earth with your married man so long as you can be together. Will the end of the earth be a place of fulfillment if that's where you wind up? Know where you are going before you get there.

Happily ever after is not the ending of a love story. Happily ever after is the beginning of a new story, your new life. Where the new edition takes place is very important. Here we have looked at real estate and the details of buying, selling, and acquiring homes. We have also looked at the financial and emotional standpoints. A few words about geography were added to give you an awareness of possible moving dilemmas. Lodge-istics is a strategy that you cannot afford to ignore.

Survey all the possibilities of your new life. Draft a life plan to the exact scale that you will arrive at after the marriage to your married man. While any house may not be a home, you cannot have a home without some kind of roof over your heads. If you plan on scaling the rainbow, make sure there is a landing strip on the other side and a building to go with it. Daydreams are not dwellings. Fantasies can give you a framework, but only reality can build the walls. In the Triangle Transition you will need a sturdy foundation in order to weather the structural strains. The knowledge of lodge-istics and its impact is a tool that will be instrumental in building your life as a second wife.

CHAPTER 7

Finance or Promise-ory Notes

Any marriage is a calculated risk in some measure. But in the scope of this book, we are not talking about any marriage. We are talking about your marriage to that married man. Because the mistress/married man marriage is special it has a special set of risks. You should calculate those risks thoroughly before you go from mistress to second wife. And when I say calculate, I mean it literally not figuratively. In this chapter get out your calculator! The risks we are going to concentrate on are the financial ones.

In many cases, when you sign that marriage license you are signing an invisible promissory note. For many married men their marriage contracts include financial liability clauses. Implicit in the wedding vows is the financial sacrifice he will have to make.

Are you finding this fiscal line of reasoning difficult to follow? Are you stumped by promissory notes and liability clauses? If you are, then you are like thousands of other mistresses and women. Don't be discouraged. By the end of this chapter you are going to learn a few lessons on money matters. And, most saliently of all, that money does indeed matter.

We are going to look step by step at the nature of financial solvency. We are going to see if you, and the two of you together can achieve fiscal *har-money!* Just why is it that we as women and we as mistresses shy away from the subject of accounting? What can the consequences of financial naiveté be? Why is your married man loaded with peculiar liabilities? What can you do that will balance your future?

Before you say "I do" to that married man, you should be thoroughly certain that you and he are compatible. Financial compatibility is just as important, if not more so, as all the other measures of compatibility. Yet sometimes it is the last type of compatibility we look at. Ignoring financial issues can leave you bankrupt in more ways than one. So get out your calculator, or pad and pen, and let's hit the accounting books.

In trying to assess the financial picture you and your married man will make up after your wedding, you have two disadvantages of your own. Your auditing skills may be hampered because, first, you are a woman and, second, you are a mistress!

Now perhaps you don't fit into this common mold, but you should be aware of it nevertheless. Why? Because most of us do fit and do have these auditing disadvantages.

Have you ever heard the term "math anxiety"? Math anxiety is a phenomenon that is very common to females. It means that women have problems studying, learning, and grasping mathematics. The reason is that females are not reared in this society to be mathematically competent. Mathematics is too often seen as a male expertise. You know the logic . . . females are good in English and males are good in science and mathematics. These role stereotyping tendencies in education lead to females fearing mathematics. Hence the term math anxiety.

If you give it some serious thought, math anxiety has probably touched your life. It has touched mine. Developing the term and focusing on it is one of the achievements of feminists. It is a valuable lesson and one we all must learn before we can even begin to grasp the subject of finance. Math anxiety is at the root of our reluctance as women to excel in the field of finance.

When I say the field of finance, I'm not talking about pursuing a professional career as a financier or an accountant. I'm talking about the personal sphere of finance. Were you brought up with an awareness of the need to structure a financial future for yourself? Were you reared to develop financial skills or aptitudes? I wasn't.

We women are usually brought up to spend our premarital money on clothes to attract the opposite sex, or travels to meet the opposite sex, or a new car. Even the very concept of premarital money says something. Our single years in the twenties or thirties are spent developing an education, or nowadays a career, but they are not spent on acquiring a financial philosophy or portfolio.

Some of us are taught to accumulate a trousseau, perhaps

the closest thing in our culture to a future investment. What's in a trousseau? Embroidered linens, bone china, Tupperware; not stocks or bonds. The point is that we are geared to think of our finances only up until the wedding day, and then some man is supposed to intervene and set the pace for the financial future.

No matter how liberated many of us are in some ways, financially we are still backward. How many women are taught the basic principles of investing? How many of us do our own tax filings? How many of us acquire a savings plan in our single days? How many of us think of buying a house or condominium for ourselves rather than renting an apartment? How many of us have a financial identity, a financial plan? How many of us think in terms of acquiring a financial estate? Are you getting the gist of our financial lack of education?

We as women are demanding equal pay for equal work, and equal opportunity, but are we rearing our daughters to be financially aware? Or are we still raising them as we were raised, and that is to let a man set the financial tone of life and future!

You, as a woman, must set sights financially. You must acquire a financial sense of responsibility. That doesn't mean necessarily the stock market and a trust fund, but it means a budget, a plan for now and the future.

If you are a mistress, financial astuteness is especially important. In marrying a married man who will divorce, you are going to encounter financial liabilities, and unfortunately most mistresses tend to have a special abhorrence for the entire subject of money. Their reasons are sound. However, the result is not quite so sound.

Historically speaking, the mistress was supposed to be a "kept" woman. That meant she was paid, in some sordid sense, for the love and/or the sex she lavished on her married man. The connotation was obviously cheap. The married man was seen as lasciviously paying for his erotic aberrations. Kept wasn't a pleasant description of the mistress/married man liaison.

Today's mistress isn't financially kept in ninety-eight percent of the case histories that I've surveyed. Yet many of today's mistresses have expressed great indignation at the historical concept of the kept woman. They have told me that "money is not exchanged," that their love cannot be bought, that they wouldn't take money if their man had it to give, and many similar variations.

It seems to bring up the word *money* in the same sentence with *mistress* is to do a disservice to the sacredness of the affair. It's as if that historical legacy must not be even alluded to by the mention of money. The mistress of today wants us to be 100 percent certain that her relationship with her married man is based on love and friendship, and not on a financial compromise.

The mistress of today is so adamant about her disinterest in monetary affairs that eventually it becomes her disadvantage. Now, that is not to say mistresses should look for money in an affair. However, the mistress who wants to go into the second-wife category should begin to consider the monetary possibilities. And the monetary impossibilities. As a mistress you may indeed be above the consideration of money. As a second-wife candidate, however, you had better take a stark look at money.

You, as a second-wife candidate, have two reasons why you avoid the financial picture. Your lack of fiscal training and your mistress dignity discourage calculating your future. Now is the time to outgrow both of those tendencies!

You must have financial wits about you for your own sake and for your married man's sake. The process of divorce and the aftermath of divorce are two liabilities that are peculiar to your potential mate. Your married man is going to feel as if he is emotionally bankrupt as he goes through the legal process. Just make sure he isn't stripped financially too. Considering the system, that is a tall order. Just look what happened to Sylvia and Stan.

Stan's Overhead

Sylvia was trained in psychology and still she got in over her head with Stan. She retraced it all for me, but it was therapy for her, too.

"I knew Stan as a friend. I saw him a lot. We live in a small town. I saw him not as a date, certainly not as a candidate for a husband. I was a professional counselor and for Stan I was a listening ear. There was no communication in Stan's marriage. There was no love for his wife, just for his children."

Sylvia was shocked when Stan proposed.

"One day I'm gonna marry you, Sylvia. I love you."

At first Sylvia didn't take him seriously. One day was almost as vague as someday.

"'Not me,' I told myself, 'I am not getting involved with a married man. My personal morals won't permit it.' But I realized that it had already happened. My feelings were already in a triangle and I didn't even know it was going on. Later myself as a whole, body and soul, was in the triangle."

Despite her training and her "smarts," Sylvia was in over her head. Sylvia was right in her evaluation of Stan's marriage. In less than a year, he filed for divorce. The divorce was fought, but granted. He was to pay alimony and child support. His ex-wife kept the house. The settlement was steep in her favor, but at least Stan was free.

"I thought this was the law, and the end! No. One of the things his ex-wife was awarded was the car. Since it was not nearly paid off, she was awarded the payments too. That seemed fair. A few months later the bank where the car was financed called. The payments were way behind. Stan explained the divorce settlement. The car company needed proof. We wrote the judge, who told us we would have to set up a hearing. A hearing meant more legal fees. We owed several thousands to the divorce lawyers and couldn't afford another $500 or more. We ended up paying for the car that his ex-wife kept anyway."

If that had been the worst of it, Sylvia and Stan could have just forgotten it. They were married and happy to finally be married. Then it became one nightmare down, and another on the rise.

"I went to the stores in town where Stan had charge accounts. I was going to add my name. His ex-wife had accumulated $2000 in several stores. I was astounded. We had never dreamed! Stan's alimony and child support certainly weren't paying any of the bills. We hadn't thought to close the accounts. After that revelation the bank told us it would be five years before our credit would ever be good again. How many years would it take us to pay up the $2,000 though!"

Needless to add, the arguments that Stan had with his ex-wife over these financial problems caused her to react angrily. She refused to let Stan see the kids.

"Now it was back to the lawyers again. Stan felt he had to fight for the kids. They were too young to fight for themselves. They deserved a father. So that meant a few thousand for a custody battle, court orders, and trauma."

Meanwhile, Sylvia worked at her counseling profession. Stan was a welder. They rented a small apartment and only could afford an old used car. Sylvia took the bus to work. It wasn't working out the way she had wanted.

"Stan and I were both so naive! He hadn't anticipated any of this. I never gave any thought to the financial sacrifices I would have to make. Stan's overhead was something I never realized. If our love and our outrage didn't bring us together so often, the money problems would have done us in long ago!"

Married men have huge overhead. Married men don't come cheaply. Someone is going to have to pay for the divorce, literally. Usually it is your married man. That often entails you, too! Your married man may be the best thing in life that ever happened to you. However, he is not one of those best things in life that are free. Your married man is going to be expensive for you. How expensive depends upon your own situation.

Divorce is a cruel lesson in economics. When one lifestyle is split in two, no one ever comes out richer. A man in the divorce process is defined in terms of his ability to pay. He is made to pay for the children and usually for the ex-wife too! The ex-wife usually keeps the house. The man pays for all the lawyers. Your married man's assets and his income will be divided. For many men that also means decimated.

The courts treat women as society treats women in general. Ex-wives are assumed to be financially inept. Therefore they are legally entitled to alimony or maintainance. Because a woman is assumed to be financially helpless and incapable, ex-wives are protected and helped. Many wives deserve this because of young children or their contribution to the marriage. Of that there is no doubt. However, many ex-wives use this financial label of helplessness. They trade on it. They build it into a racket. When this happens, the price of the divorce looks small when compared to the price of the aftermath of divorce!

Watch out for the ex-wife who is the potential racketeer! Don't underestimate the racket. Even if the marriage wasn't a wealthy one, a racket can still come out of it. Who profits? What is to be gained? Listen to the tales of a few second wives. Racketeering will become a clearer phenomenon.

"My husband divorced in 1973. We married soon afterwards. He faithfully paid his child support and alimony. Last year his ex-wife petitioned the court for more money. My husband had to hire a lawyer and submit W-2 forms. His ex sent a letter she, herself, drew up. The decision went in her favor. The court increased her support even though we have inflation to contend with too. I'm pregnant again and that ruling has taken a lot of joy out of me." (Bartow, Florida)

"We went through a very bitter divorce. It wasn't over money. My married man had no money, nor did I. His wife swore she'd take him to the cleaners. To the cleaners wasn't a far ride for us. Fighting her and for custody did us in. What she didn't think of, her lawyer did. Lawyers add fuel to the fires and stuff their wallets all the way to court and then to the bank. She didn't profit except in terms of revenge. We lost. Now we are financially bankrupt and emotionally bankrupt too." (St. Paul, Minnesota)

The court system can provide a wealthy arena for bankruptcy proceedings. Ex-wives can learn how to use the system to keep the legal bills escalating for years. Since they often don't have to pay lawyers, they have nothing to lose. This can be an eternal cross to bear financially.

The children can add to the ex-wives ability for racketeering. The children can be used to foment visitation battles and custody battles as a last resort. Or the children can be used to just milk your income a little at a time.

"We never had much money to begin our marriage with. We couldn't pay the $40 a week support money, and live on $60 that was left. His ex remarried and she didn't need the money anyway. Because we got behind on the payments, she wouldn't let my husband ever see his kids. We had no choice.

We couldn't afford the support so we couldn't hire a lawyer. My husband decided to drop the whole thing. He just asked her to send him pictures from time to time." *(Milwaukee, Wisconsin)*

In this case the children were used to strip the former married man of his esteem as a father. He couldn't be stripped financially, but there was obviously still something to be gained from the racket employed by the ex-wife.

"My husband pays an ungodly amount of child support in light of what he brings home. Don't ask me what she does with the support. Twice a month we get the kids and they look like ragamuffins. We buy them new things and never see them again. Next time it's ragamuffins again. She lives in an upper-class ranch while we live in a duplex in a low-rent district. She made as much money as my husband did last year yet we still ended up in court because she wanted more child support, and she got it! We got stuck with attorney's fees again too. Now she makes more money than my husband and I do together! It seems that the courts never leave you alone after the divorce. We spend on the support, on the kids, on the lawyers, on everyone but ourselves. We got wise to the ragamuffin game. Now we keep some good clothes here for when we take the kids somewhere. But there's no way to protect yourself all around." *(Champaign, Illinois)*

"I'm older—much older in three years. My husband's hair is now one-third gray and he's a young man. He was hospitalized for a bleeding ulcer a while back, after years of good health. It's some world we live in. Anything can happen. If anyone had told me ten years ago I'd be a mistress, then a second wife, then sole supporter of my husband and his five kids, I'd have told them they were crazy. But that's what happened.

"My ex-husband divorced me and married his secretary. I had an eleven-year-old son to care for, so I went to work for my father in his business. I fell in love with a married man in spite of myself. His wife was a real women's libber. She told me, 'You want him—you can have him—and take his five kids too!' She won't even visit the children. Now with my husband sick over a stressful divorce and five guilt-conflicted children, I find myself sole supporter of us all. I'm counting on my common sense, my education, and my love to see us through. And my dad is retiring so I can have the business to get us by. I hope we all make it, but I feel anything is possible!" *(Boulder, Colorado)*

There is an element of the extreme in most of those stories. However don't mistake extreme for bizarre. These financial upheavals really happened to these women. Something similar could happen to you! Would you be able to sacrifice and cope? Will you be lucky and find that your second marriage isn't riddled with financial crises?

Don't leave the answers up to fate. I have included extreme cases in this section just to familiarize you with some of the possibilities. Mainly, to provoke you to think financially. These kinds of fiscal disasters often do besiege married men after their divorce and remarriage. In general married men come with financial liabilities.

I want the generalities, the possibilities, to inspire you to zero in on your financial future. Assess your own situation. What kinds of fiscal goals do you have? Are you on your way to achieving them already? If you add your married man to your life, will he hamper your financial objectives or will he enhance your goals? Do you and he have the same priorities? Will your union entail financial sacrifice? Will you two add up to fiscal *har-money??*

If you've not given this subject much thought, here are a few exercises to get your accounting skills in shape.

What Is Your Money Mentality?

Each of us has a money mentality. What is yours? Do you daydream about mink coats or do you get a thrill when you clip out a 75¢ coupon from the newspaper on a double coupon week at the market? Do you skip the travel section in the Sunday paper or do you read it religiously and scout for good travel opportunities? Questions like these can sketch for you your monetary vision.

What money means to you and what you want money to do for your life are important considerations. Knowing your money mentality isn't mercenary as an endeavor. It is a step in personal honesty and growth. Your money mentality is a valuable part of you. Being true to your fiscal frame of mind will ensure your self-fulfillment. Stifling your financial framework may make you very frustrated and unhappy.

For these reasons we are going to explore your particular money mentality. Take the following test and you will get a true picture of where and how money fits into your scheme of things. Terms like rich and poor are all relative. However, your money mentality is very relevant to your future!

Directions: The next group of questions and statements are multiple choice. Choose the one answer with which you feel most comfortable. Then fill in your choice in the space provided at the end of each statement. After you have answered all questions proceed to the scoring table that follows. Good luck! Keep in mind that any money mentality is good as long as it really expresses you!!

1. Which of these statements best describes your wardrobe? (a) My wardrobe is but another extension of my image, my status, and my identity. (b) My wardrobe may be dated but it still reflects good taste and fashion awareness. (c) My wardrobe . . . is just clothes which fulfill the basic need to be dressed and that's all.

                                               1._____

2. What kind of car would you be seen driving? (a) An old heap. (b) An economy model. (c) An expensive car that reflects my personality.

                                               2._____

3. What best describes a week of your spending habits? (a) Groceries, drug store items, transportation costs, and with that there is little left for fluff. (b) I go through a lot of money a week and am not sure where it even goes. (c) Every week is an exercise in creative frugality.

                                               3._____

4. Given a rundown of the type of food you consume on a weekly basis, which describes your eating habits? (a) Home cooked meals, with one meatless dish per week. (b) My lifestyle affords restaurants during the week when I'm busy and quick steak and salad meals when I entertain.

(c) My weekly menu is well planned and thought out so that the budget guarantees pleasant meals.

4._____

5. What's in your jewelry box? (a) Nothing valuable really, just baubles and costume things that look pretty. (b) A good watch, a gold pair of earrings and some costume jewelry. (c) Diamond earrings, gold chains, valuable heirlooms, and purchases.

5._____

6. Is there a correlation in your mind between family and money and, if so, which do you relate to? (a) My family has money and there probably will always be money in any family of which I am a part. (b) Money should be a determining factor in the number of children one plans in a family. (c) Family and money don't really have any connection so far as I can say for me.

6._____

7. What's your magazine preference? (a) *Woman's Day* and *Family Circle*. (b) *True Romance* and *The Star*. (c) *Vogue* and *Bazaar*.

7._____

8. What kind of a consumer are you? (a) A bargain hunter. (b) An examiner of quality, elegance, and fashion. (c) A smart shopper.

8._____

9. If someone told you that they were going to take you on a weekend away, what would you expect? (a) A plane ride to some place exciting like Las Vegas or San Francisco or maybe Acapulco. (b) A nice automobile trip to some lovely city not too far away, or some local attraction. (c) A simple camping trip anywhere as long as it was away from home.

9._____

10. When you buy someone a gift, which of these best describes you? (a) You select with their preferences and your budget in mind. (b) You go all-out, spurred on by your generosity or liking for the recipient. (c) You search for

something suitable, relying on your craft abilities or creative talents.

10. _____

Scoring:
Copy all your answers from 1–10 in the column below labeled *Answers*. Then select the points allotted for each selection. Put the number of points in the column labeled *Points*. Total your number of points and read the evaluation that includes your total.

					Answers	Points
1.	(a) 15	(b) 10	(c) 5	1.	_____	_____
2.	(a) 5	(b) 10	(c) 15	2.	_____	_____
3.	(a) 10	(b) 15	(c) 5	3.	_____	_____
4.	(a) 5	(b) 15	(c) 10	4.	_____	_____
5.	(a) 5	(b) 10	(c) 15	5.	_____	_____
6.	(a) 15	(b) 10	(c) 5	6.	_____	_____
7.	(a) 10	(b) 5	(c) 15	7.	_____	_____
8.	(a) 5	(b) 15	(c) 10	8.	_____	_____
9.	(a) 15	(b) 10	(c) 5	9.	_____	_____
10.	(a) 10	(b) 15	(c) 5	10.	_____	_____
				Total	_____	

Evaluation:
As you answered these questions about yourself, in all likelihood the test seemed easy. If it did, you have a definite money personality, whichever it is! Once you start defining it, yours becomes obvious. Which money mentality are you?

50–80 Points: The Nonmaterialist. If you scored in this range, money isn't that much a part of your life. It could be because you haven't a lot of money at your disposal or it could be that you don't value money regardless. Your clothes, your food, your entertainments, your visions are not defined in terms of expense. Some things in your world view just do not have any connection with money. You must think about your tendency to be unmaterialistic. Are you satisfied with your non-materialistic stance? Or is it a function of necessity? Having a basically low money mentality can be good. You are in a sense carefree where status and keeping up are concerned. However, if your money mentality is something you want to change, then beware. Will marrying your married man allow for change, or will it seal your fate as a nonmaterialist?

85-115 Points: The Moderate Monetarian. If you scored in this range, you are basically a moderate. Money is a part of your life in the typical middle-class sense. You use it to maintain an appropriate lifestyle, one with moderation in all things. Your world neither reflects poverty nor affluence. Money doesn't cause you great stress nor does it afford you great luxuries. Chances are you are hard-working, also an ethical middle-class characteristic. You like to have a few nice things but you are willing to wait, work, bargain, and save in order to attain them. The moderate stance is a sensible one with regard to money. However, you as a moderate are also on the borderline. If you marry your married man, will you be able to stay middle class? If you go up the financial ladder, that you could handle. But if you find yourself plummeted down a few steps, will that ruin your happiness? Your money mentality now is satisfied because you are in control of saving and spending. Will his financial liabilities upset your middle ground?

120-150 Points: The Materialist. If you scored in this range, you are materialistic in your money matters. There is nothing wrong with being materialistic. Our entire capitalistic system is based on rewards and excelling. Perhaps you are well-to-do because of your own achievements and proud of it. You deserve expensive things that reflect your position. Perhaps you have been reared in a wealthy world and there's nothing wrong in that. Restaurants and *Vogue,* designer labels and the best things in life are a part of your particular lifestyle. A materialistic way of life sets you above the struggling masses. You are fortunate. Money has its place in your life and that place is important. If you are a materialist, be sure that your married man and you can maintain your standard of living after his divorce. Don't get yourself into a romantic fog, telling yourself that love is more important than money. You are used to money and, if your love has to exist without it, you may find frugality ruins the result!

In Conclusion:
The test here on your money mentality isn't so you can judge yourself too materialistic or too frugal. The test was to put

before you exactly how important money is in your life. Each of us has a money mentality. It may be diamonds and charge cards. It may be scrimping and saving. Regardless of what your fiscal frame of reference is, know it. In going from mistress to wife, your money mentality is an important gauge. If your second marriage forces you to change your monetary vision, make sure that change is one to which you can adjust.

The idea of analyzing your money mentality is to show you what your financial expectations are. You have financial goals that are reflected in how money fits into your life. And how money should fit into your future, if you are to be happy. If your money mentality is materialistic, then your married man's assets should be examined carefully. If you are not materialistic, money isn't going to be that important. So examine his liabilities and see how much you can handle and supplement.

Now you know your financial desires, your money personality. Is there a way you can predict the financial future of your second marriage? Can you tell if the fiscal future is bright or grim? Read on. The answer is yes!

Can You Make a Confidential Statement?

Naturally, you as a mistress and your married man have a very confidential relationship. Just how inclusive is that confidentiality? Does it carry over into financial matters? Have you ever sat down with pen in hand and calculated a confidential financial statement?

If not, now is the time. We are going to construct a financial picture of you and him and then both of you as a couple. Why? Because neither man nor woman can live on bread or kisses alone. And if you are not prudent financially, you may wind up with neither bread nor kisses in your marriage!

Directions: You must fill in the blanks in this exercise. Don't despair if accounting is not your forte. It isn't mine either. Therefore, I have kept this test simple and straightforward.

Let me point out here that some of the data will come from your affairs, some from his. This is a guide and so at times you will have to make personal adjustments, additions, or omissions. For instance, if you are still married, mark your answers in two columns; "pre-divorce" and "post-divorce." The same goes for your married man. Mark his answers in two columns: "pre-divorce" and "post-divorce." And remember, if your relationship hasn't been financially confidential up until this point, that will change right here and now.

	Pre-divorce	Post-divorce
1. What is your salary?	———	———
2. How much is in your savings account?	———	———
3. On a separate sheet or pad, list your assets and the approximate worth of each item. Enter the total worth here.	———	———
4. Do you have any other income that is not included in "salary" (commissions, alimony, dividends, etc.)? How much?	———	———
5. Do you have a trust fund? If so, list worth.	———	———
6. Does your salary guarantee financial escalation? If so, how much and at what rate?	———	———
7. Do you have extra money each month after necessities are paid for? How much?	———	———
8. How is your credit rating?	———	———
9. If you have paid off any loans, list for what and how much.	———	———
10. Do you have any outstanding loans (car, college, home, etc.)? What is the balance?	———	———

The next set of questions apply to your married man.

	Pre-divorce	Post-divorce
1. What is his salary?	———	———
2. How much is in his savings account?	———	———
3. On a separate sheet, list his assets and approximate worth of each. Enter the total worth here.	———	———

Pre-divorce Post-divorce

4. Does he have income other than
   salary? What? How much?   _____   _____

5. Does he have dependents? How
   many?   _____   _____

6. Does his wife work? Her
   salary?   _____   _____

7. Is his salary stationary or will it
   go up significantly?   _____   _____

8. How is his credit rating?   _____   _____

9. Does he have any outstanding
   loans? What?   _____   _____

10. Does he have extra money after
    meeting monthly expenses?
    How much?   _____   _____

Now for your answers as a couple. Answer the following from
his post-divorce column and yours if you have one. If settlement
terms are not final, then make an educated guess.

1. What is your combined salary?   _____

2. What are your cumulative savings?   _____

3. What are your combined assets?   _____

4. What is the extra income, if any, other than
   salary?   _____

5. Any trust funds for either of you?   _____

6. How is your collective credit rating?   _____

7. What are your outstanding loans?   _____

8. How many dependents will you as a couple
   be financially responsible for?   _____

9. List child support and alimony figures, if any,
   for each of you or both.   _____

10. Estimate your future salary by assessing po-
    tential for raises, promotions, etc. Is it sig-
    nificantly higher?   _____

In Conclusion:
Drafting a confidential statement may be dull, tedious, and
frightening. It can be depressing or encouraging, but always

enlightening. And that is the point. Once you construct a green print such as this, you have a blueprint for your financial future. You will know exactly where you and your married man stand with regard to fiscal probabilities.

You can make a million confidential statements with regard to your married man. However, until you can make the confidential financial statement, you are just biding romantic time. Remember we all need kisses and bread, too, no pun intended!

So now you have it, a picture of the financial future of your second marriage. And you have acknowledged your money personality too. Now think of the two together. Can you handle any debits? Will you be sacrificing financially? And if so, will you be willing to sacrifice? If the financial picture is promising, you can relax. Congratulations! If the fiscal future is not so promising, you can start to supplement it now. Don't despair. You have time now to give yourself the financial edge that just might pull you two through!

As a sort of mistress expert, people have always asked me for advice, especially because my married man and I found the happy ending. And people ask my husband for advice too. One of the best pieces of advice we both give is a financial tip. SAVE! If a mistress has a little money of her own, it can make or break your relationship. If a married man has to face a financial decimation and an emotional war, it's easier to bear if he knows his mistress can help emotionally and financially!

Save! Save on your salary! I can almost hear the collective gasp. I can almost see the doom enveloping you, as you assess your married man's liabilities. Don't forget the assets. He is an asset and so is your love. It's important to keep a balance. And don't forget that in today's economy most couples find that husband and wife must work. So if your contribution is a must, it isn't that much of an exception anyway.

Where do you begin? That's easy to answer. If you realize that financial compatibility is crucial and if that means you must pitch in, start with nickels and dimes.

Nickels and Dimes

When Sandra first started seeing Hank he was dissatisfied with every part of his life. That included his marriage and his business. He was then driving a truck long-distance hauling merchandise. He hated it. His real ambition was woodworking.

Sitting around at Sandra's one evening, he said, "If someone would give me a nickel, I'd quit trucking and go back to woodworking."

Sandra said, as she told me her story, "You know what? I reached into my pocket and gave him a nickel. He took the nickel, quit his job and went into his own business. That was the turning point in our affair."

Sandra knew that Hank wasn't going to have it easy financially for a long time. The divorce that happened soon after the nickel wasn't going to help any. A private joke soon became an institution with Sandra and Hank. They would often say to each other, "I'll give you a nickel if [this or that]." Then the nickel would be produced.

"One night I was sitting around missing Hank and very depressed over the state of our finances. The bills were everywhere. I was afraid that Hank would just give up and go back to trucking and his wife. I began telling myself that, if I had a dime for every time I was panicky about Hank, I'd be rich. Then I got an idea. Every time I thought that, I put a dime in my piggy bank. And I added all those nickels that we joked about. In a few months, we didn't have a fortune but we had something. That's how I learned to save."

Sandra was a waitress, so she always had a lot of change around. Her income wasn't much and yet it still provided her with something to put away every week. She didn't tell Hank about the panic and the dimes, the nickels and the piggy bank. It seemed rather silly. But she just kept on doing it.

Sandra opened a savings account and when she had $100 it felt like a million. There was no reason for her to panic over Hank anymore. He was feeling more like a million every day, since he put his life in order.

"While I was worrying about Hank, he was too busy to worry. He worked day and night. It was a good escape, I guess. He told me all the time I had saved his life, even when he seemed so tired I hardly believed it. But I guess I had. That nickel did it."

Sandra gave Hank $500 for their wedding as a present so that they could have a real honeymoon. He was getting a partner this time and a very resourceful one and he knew it. His business was picking up and everything was looking brighter than he had ever dreamed.

It's not that Hank and Sandra didn't have the bills, the legal fees, the child support, etc., it's just that they realized that sometimes in life it's the nickels and the dimes that can save you!

The way you handle nickels and dimes can be significant. Significant to you, as a person, in developing a financial personality. Significant to your married man as he assesses you as a mate. Don't forget that while you are sizing him up as a husband, he is sizing you up, too, as a wife. Adding financial sense to your list of assets is bound to impress him. Whether he needs your financial contribution or not, your married man is going to be more careful the second time around choosing a partner. Make sure you are not the kind of woman that seems like a luxury he will never be able to afford!

Financial compatibility should be a major consideration if you are going from mistress to wife. You and your married man should have compatibility in financial priorities. And the economics of your new life together should be worked out on paper long before the marriage license is purchased. The outcome of your combined income is your responsibility. Because, in the end, you will live on the budget that survives the triangle. Make certain you can balance your daydreams and your fantasies with that new joint account.

Right now you, as a mistress, will promise your married man many things. Loyalty. Friendship. Communication. Romance. I could go on and on. If you go from mistress to wife you will enunciate those promises in your wedding vows. Then as his second wife you will be called upon to live out those promises. Sometimes that will mean putting your money where your mouth is. Time will call in those promissory notes that so many married men acquire. If you calculate now, before the wedding, those promissory notes won't sour your promises. If you proceed in a fiscal fog, you may resent your new life, your man, and any children because of what they will cost your lifestyle.

Calculating the risks, the debits, and the liabilities can help you balance the budget in your new life. Any marriage is a gamble in some respects. Don't gamble with economics in the odds! Make certain that you know what your married man will cost. Make sure that you know what you'll be expected to contribute to that cost. Above all, make absolutely certain that your married man is worth it! Few married men are a bargain, but some of them are well worth the price!

CHAPTER 8

Outlaws and In-Laws

A mistress is an outlaw. Think about it for a moment. She may not wear six-guns on her hips, or have her photo tacked up on the wall in the post office, but a mistress is still an outlaw. Her triangular behavior makes her an outlaw morally. Her way of life is guided by a different code of ethics. Just like the outlaws of the Old West, a mistress is often seen as glamorous, elusive, and dangerous. A mistress is usually presumed to have a reputation of sorts and she is preceded by that reputation wherever she goes. And mistresses, like outlaws, create rustles in the air when they come into town.

What happens when the mistress comes into town as the second wife? Yesterday as a mistress you were defined as an outlaw. Then in a sudden flash of ceremony you are a wife and an in-law! The transformation is so ironic and so quick that in all likelihood it is a shock. It will probably be a shock not only to you, but to your married man, both sets of your parents, and to your collective extended families. If you are a married mistress, when you become a second wife, multiply the shock waves.

Going from mistress to wife, going from outlaw to in-law, means problems. Whether you decide to handle the in-laws or whether you decide not to bother, either way there are going to be problematic repercussions. The extended family will bring extended crises, confusing protocol, and pressures. You can ride off into the sunset with only your married man sometimes or you can stay in town and make your place. Either way you will be confronted with some decisions, some situations, and some conflicts that we will explore in this chapter. Consider this, though, at the outset. If you have weathered the tough triangle terrain, if you survived the transition to second wife, surely you can adjust the sights and get the family picture into focus.

There are really three perspectives to look at here. First and foremost it is *your* dilemma that concerns me. What will it be like for you when you go from outlaw to in-law? Secondly it is very useful to look at things from the other side of the family tree. What is expected of your in-laws and how will they react to an outlaw in their midst? And thirdly you must look at things from the point of view of your married man, now your new husband. Considering his feelings will probably affect your actions and your views. And as a mistress you are inclined to consider his feelings often, even if it means sacrificing and compromising.

Before we get started, there is one more observation I would like to make. You as a mistress will usually be seen as more of an outlaw than any married man. In some sense your parents may feel put off by him, but not with the same moral outrage that will be directed at you. You will probably see him fit into your family with more ease. Your fitting into his family on the other hand will be more difficult.

Why is it that the mistress is more the eternal outlaw, even after she becomes a legitimate in-law? Society is sexist. The scarlet A was for female adulterers only! As a mistress, you probably tend to introduce your married man into your family circles even if you represent him only as a friend or acquaintance. So your married man is a person first and maybe as time goes on, a scandal. You, on the other hand, are most likely the scandal first. You as a mistress are the outsider coming in, the outlaw taking over. Your reputation as such will act as a barrier to people getting to know the real you. Don't forget that your introduction into the family means a divorce has taken place. That leaves scars on a family, scars that are associated with you.

Finding your place as a wife and an in-law in his family is often a matter of dissolving the reputation, restoring order and peace among the relatives, and helping them face a new frontier of relationships. It is also a matter of choosing who is worth the trouble in his family. It can be as hard a job as any outlaw-turned-sheriff found in the Old West!

Let's get back to the first perspective now . . . yours. Since you are at the outset of the Triangle Transition, you may not be able to relate your own feelings. But if we look at a second wife who has made the outlaw to in-law switch, the dilemma will be clear.

Stacy, Grafting onto the Family Tree

Stacy wasn't a farmer or even a professional gardener. She did enjoy planting things, though. She tried to make her garden out back bloom with flowers in the summertime. Every spring she put in a few packets of vegetable seeds and a couple of tomato plants. For her effort she usually got enough flowers for a few bouquets and some vegetables. Stacy didn't try anything really complicated in her garden. She had a couple of fruit trees, which her neighbors told her would be perfect for grafting. That sounded too hard for Stacy. However, in time she found herself grafting all over the place!

"To be honest, I wasn't looking forward to ever meeting Paul's family. The thought of all those new people scared me. After hearing Paul's stories I was afraid to. They sounded so self-righteous and weren't any help to Paul after they found out he was divorcing. But the time came when we were invited to a wedding, not really 'we,' but Paul and his date. But I knew they were all waiting to see this little homewrecker of his."

Stacy knew that she had to begin handling the relatives sooner or later. She and Paul would be married soon and it was inevitable. Soon her cultivating skills would be tested, and this time not in any garden. She would have to learn to cultivate new relationships, weed out the people that bore them ill will, and somehow graft herself onto a new family tree.

"I'll never forget that wedding. Paul never let go of my hand the entire evening. He introduced me to everyone. Oh they were all cordial, don't get me wrong. But no one said more than they had to after the initial, 'I'd like you to meet so and so.' Only the bride's father came over to us and sat with us for a while. He was the only one in the room who came to get to know me. I thought all night, How was I ever going to adjust myself to this new group? I wasn't sure I even wanted to!"

The strangest part of that entire evening was that Stacy caught the bridal bouquet. She was more surprised than anyone. The flowers just fell right into her hands. Paul was delighted, if no one else seemed to be. Stacy took home her bouquet, dried its seeds, and saved them for spring planting.

"Our marriage is good now. We have our ups and downs. His folks are in and out of our lives. I'm planning to become pregnant soon. That makes me think of his family more. I wish we all got along better. But we don't. Some hard feelings are still there because of his decision to divorce. I still have a lot of resentments. I guess it takes years to get used to each other the way we all are, not the way we wish each other could be."

The thing about families is that they are always there. Members come and go, fight and reconcile. Families don't go away. The family tree grows and it changes. A few new branches are added here. A few old branches die there. Grafting onto the family tree isn't always easy or pleasant. It's like grafting on an old fruit tree. The new graft takes time, sunlight, and still its survival is unpredictable. Stacy and Paul were surviving as a family and flourishing. The extended family tree? The future was hard to predict. But Stacy's garden and the grafting looked better with each passing year.

Finding your place in his family tree is difficult for you because of your outlaw status. Chances are, you are trying to establish yourself in the face of family prejudice. You are trying to cultivate new relationships under duress. Duress because his family may have an unkind vision of you. Duress because you may not like any of them because of their behavior or reactions. The point is that, as an outlaw turning in-law, don't expect things to go smoothly at first. When you come into a room full of family, don't be surprised at the rustles of conversation. You are not the ordinary marriage candidate.

Just how difficult getting along with his in-laws is going to be depends on several things. First, is his family close geographically or emotionally? How open are they to changing times? How strong is their love for your married man? The answers will affect your adapting process. Any web of inter-relationships is complicated. The extended family is bound to be complex too. Just remember that and don't be surprised at the conflicts and the questions. As an outlaw they may all want to challenge you, just like they all challenged the fast guns back then.

Suppose you don't want to be a part of all these challenges, all these shoot-outs. Suppose you don't want to be wary of ambushes, instantly ready to defend yourself all the time. Can you avoid the whole family mess of pressures?

Yes you can. Surely you have heard that old adage, "You can pick your friends but not your relatives." Well, I don't buy that for a moment. Family membership is a given, yes. You don't choose your relations or your in-laws. However, just because you share blood lines or in-law lines, that doesn't destine you to share your life with these people. I believe family is like friends. They have to earn a place in your life. You can pick and choose which relatives you want to get involved with and how often and to what extent. You are very much in control of your family. You can define who in his family you want to include in your future. And you can eliminate those in-laws that are offensive for whatever reason. *You can pick your friends and you can pick your relatives and in-laws!*

Before you do, there are a few things that you should consider. Your relationships with your in-laws are very much your domain, but don't ignore their positions totally. Don't evaluate them too fast or judge them too harshly at the outset. Why? Because of your married man. Keep his best interests at heart. Use his best interests as a gauge and a tool.

In order to give you an example of the in-law perspective, here is a profile that points up their dilemma too.

Anchors Away

Lisa and Frank were married by a captain in a ceremony that took place on a hill overlooking the sea. It was a romantic triumph for them. They honeymooned quietly in that same Maine seaport. The salt air felt good. The salty seafood tasted good. Salt was finally taking on a new meaning, leaving behind all those salty tears of yesterday.

Being alone suited both of them well. Lisa didn't have much of a family. Her parents had died long ago. She had one brother on the West Coast. Frank had a family, but they couldn't seem to make the adjustments to his new way of life. They seemed to be weighted down by the past.

"Frank's parents and his whole family loved his first wife. They thought she was God's gift. She was the daughter they never had. Apart from Frank, they had their own relationship with her. After the grandchildren, they grew even closer. It was as if they had a son, and they had a daughter. When the two fought they jumped in to make peace, not taking sides, just trying to stop some kind of sibling rivalry. You can see the problem, can't you?"

To make a long story short, Frank's parents loved his wife a great deal more than Frank did. He became resentful because they always butted in and took her side more than his. He knew the marriage was a failure in its sixth year. He complained often to his parents, but they didn't hear what he was saying. So when he announced the divorce, they were devastated, but they should have seen it coming.

"Frank was on a guilt trip for a long time. His parents exerted as much pressure as they could to get him to go back. He did a few times but he always left again. Finally he told them, 'You go live with her if you love her so much; I can't.' When they heard from his wife that he had a mistress, he was a Cad with a capital C. I was just an expletive."

So Frank and Lisa went about their plans minus the family blessing. For the present time, Frank's parents had chosen sides. They chose to stand by his wife, commiserate, and blame Frank. Their decision was costing them their son in plain simple English.

"I think that his parents kept hoping that Frank would return and reestablish the family dream. When they realized that their 'daughter' and their son were a thing of the past, they really were nonplussed. They're not bad people really, just old-fashioned. This was the first divorce in the family. To them a mistress meant some kind of devil."

Frank and Lisa got a picturesque apartment on the water, like something out of a magazine. He gained ten pounds from her tender loving care and never looked better. Two weekends a month were spent with his children and that was moving along, if slowly. But despite any transitional problems they were both happier than ever.

"Frank missed his parents, but he told me that they would have to change. His ex was the past. We were the future. It was going to be hard for them, like losing a daughter. But if they didn't leave the past behind, they couldn't be a part of the future."

Lisa felt sorry for them in a way. She watched them slowly trying to understand their son. She was willing to overlook much of their behavior. They were victims too. They were being victimized by tradition and transition. They would have to cast off their anchors of the past and set sail on a new course.

The in-laws in Lisa's story personify the in-law perspective in several ways. In them you can see the traumas and the reactions that are often common to parents of triangle players.

Your married man's parents may have a strong relationship with his wife, their daughter-in-law. Even if they didn't like her at first, over the years they have adapted and accepted her as a family member. Children solidify the family bonds. Their daughter-in-law may have a special place in their hearts, as did Frank's wife. But special place or not-so-special place, she is a legitimate part of their family. A divorce shatters the family structure. Suddenly parents have to leave parts of the family behind and out. Some parents adjust better than others. Lisa's case is one where the parents found a problem adjusting. They were encountering a real loss, the loss of their daughter-in-law. From their point of view it was hard. From anyone's point of view it was sad.

The weights of the past and the ties established in the past are not easy to break for some in-laws. Their sense of loss clouds their view. It can make them villainize their own son and blame him for this filial holocaust. It can cause them to brand the mistress.

If they are old-fashioned people to begin with, they probably have stereotypical feelings about divorce. In their day divorce was not a viable option. Dealing with the mistress concept is hard even for liberal parents, so accepting a mistress into the family is traumatic for most. Many parents-in-law react harshly and coldly to the outlaw coming into their lives. Traditionally they are unprepared for this kind of triangle transition. Watching their family dissolve is painful and the transition is demanding for all.

Taking a look at things from the in-laws' point of view is wise. It can add compassion and understanding to your handling of them. But how much understanding should you give? How much aggravation and alienation from them should you tolerate as you go from outlaw to in-law? Where do you draw the line? Laurie wondered about that. The next profile will answer some of these questions.

Benedict Arnolds Slept Here

Laurie often mused to herself that Shaun couldn't really have come out of that family. Shaun was warm and wonderful. His parents were obnoxious, unkind, ignorant, and destructive ... for starters.

"His parents knew he was miserable in that marriage. And yet their philosophy was the old *'You made your bed, now you lie in it.'* Their grandchildren were at stake. Shaun simply had to give up his rights for happiness and stay married for the sake of those children. Well, it made me furious. How could they claim so much love for their grandchildren at the expense of their only son!"

Laurie often told Shaun he lived in some kind of macabre conspiracy. He was supposed to be cast as the family sacrifice. His whole world, except for his two daughters, was populated with Benedict Arnolds.

"It wasn't any surprise when Shaun told me I was his best friend. With friends like he had, he couldn't afford any enemies. He used to say that after the divorce I would be his whole family. I was the only one on his side. I was the only one who really had his best interests at heart. All the others just had a role he was expected to fit in, like it or not."

Laurie was seen as the homewrecker, the usual scapegoat. She couldn't have cared less what these traitors thought of her. But she cared when they started to malign her. They harassed her by phone and on the street a few times. They then told Shaun things that she supposedly said, things that were untrue.

"Someone was lying to Shaun and it wasn't me. They used any means to justify their end, which was to keep Shaun married. I had to show Shaun that his parents were liars, sneaky and deceitful. At first I felt really guilty about it. But hell, they should be the ones to feel guilty for what they were doing, not me, not Shaun."

Laurie was outraged by Shaun's parents. Outraged because of the way they acted. But outraged the most because of how they tried to cruelly manipulate Shaun's life. They often planned and plotted, used and abused Shaun.

"Like when Christmas rolled around. The whole family had a tradition of gathering on Christmas Eve. Each year at someone else's home. Well, the year of Shaun's separation, guess where they had it? At his wife's of course. They figured that Shaun would have to go and probably counted on the spirit of Christmas and family to woo him back home. I was really furious. They could have held it elsewhere so Shaun could have participated without the trimmings. Well, he declined."

Well, that is only one incident. Laurie couldn't condense it all here. She would have had to write a book and title it *Benedict Arnolds Slept Here*. Shaun told her often that she had saved his life. And indeed she had. She had saved him from a family conspiracy. And at least he was not sleeping with all the Benedict Arnolds anymore.

"I feel bad for Shaun because he lost his family. But the only other alternative was to lose himself and his right to happiness."

Cutting off the in-laws is a drastic move. However, in some cases, that's the way it goes. Laurie seemed justified by what she told me. Apparently his parents did not have Shaun's best interests at heart. In all their maneuvering, they had lost sight of their son somehow. Families aren't always wonderful. In this case Shaun was better off without them.

The best gauge to help you decide whether to include or exclude your in-laws is to focus on your married man's best interests. You must try and decide if his parents are worth it or not, if they love their son and deserve to be part of his new life or not.

Some men's parents are temporarily insane, so to speak, in the first days of their son's divorce and then his marriage to the mistress. Perhaps they have made heavy emotional investments into that first marriage and it's hard coping with the changes going on. Perhaps they are too crushed and numb to immediately throw out their arms and embrace you, the second wife. But if they basically love their son and are willing to put his happiness up front, in time they will adjust. After they have grown to love and unlove the first wife, they may be reluctant to reach out and become emotionally involved again with you. Again if they see you and him happy, if they see you making their son happy, for his sake they should come around.

Some in-laws, however, will hold on to their stand of moral outrage. They will hold their grudge against you. They will constantly interfere in your new marriage, deliberately trying to control the fate of their son. If they meddle at his expense, and they persist long after the transitional stage, then you are correct in eliminating them. If they cannot embrace his new life without trying to destroy it, then they deserve to be left out.

Before permanently writing off unsympathetic in-laws, there is one final consideration. Look at your married man's perspective. How does he feel about his parents? Has he always been close to them? Have they been a daily part of his life up until this turn of affairs? Will it be more difficult for him to ostracize them or to deal with their disapproval? Only your married man can provide you with the answers to these questions. You should explore his attitudes and discuss in-law strategy, before acting on your instincts alone.

Even if you dislike them for valid reasons and they obviously dislike you, your married man may still want to maintain a family relationship. What could be his reasoning for wanting these emotional stalemates?

Perhaps your married man wants to retain a sense of family continuity. Going through a divorce has put him in a front-row seat watching the explosion of his nuclear family. In the post-divorce period, he may need the sense of the extended family. He may want his children to have the security of the extended family to buttress them through the immediate family breakup. By the way, the stability of grandparents is very good for children of divorce. It is important for children to see that their relationships with grandparents stay the same even if their relationships with parents are changing. Your married man may rely on you to help him keep the family intact by tolerating extended family members. You may be asked to put your feelings aside for the sake of the other family members.

Perhaps your married man wants to bind the family wounds too. He may be very proud of you and he may want his parents to see just how wonderful you are. They can't go from disapproval to approval if they are never with you. So for his sake you may have to participate in his negotiating schemes. He may expect you to have them around and even go out of your way to make them comfortable. How much of a sacrifice this entails depends on each family. If you go from mistress to wife, will you be willing to compromise your judgements to keep peace or even to make peace in his family? Your new husband may want his parents to get to know the woman beneath the myth. If you love him, you'll cooperate.

Then there are some circumstances when the second wives wonder if they should take the peace initiative. The following letter is a good example.

"I need some advice. My married man and I have been married for seven years. We live in Florida and his parents live in Minnesota. They are religious people and they disowned him emotionally after finding out about me. Ever since his divorce they have had nothing to do with him or his children. We have a four-year-old girl that they have never even seen. I know he feels badly about this. But he is as stubborn as they are. We've talked about it often, but he won't make the first move. Obviously they won't either. I'm wondering, should I? It's not fair to the grandchildren to miss out on these relationships. I think if they could just visit and we could all spend some time together, the myths and the grudges could be put aside. What do you think?"

In a situation like this one, I think this second wife should go with her instincts and make a move to reconcile the extended family. There are times when you may be called on to be the peacemaker. You, as a second wife, should try to keep the lines of communication open among relatives. A bit of flexibility and a dash of forgiveness can be healthy characteristics to cultivate. If you sacrifice a little in ways that will benefit your man and all the children, the dividends will be worth the compromise.

Most of the advice in this chapter has dealt with the in-laws in particular. However, the same applies to dealing with the rest of his family, be it brothers, sisters, cousins, etc. There will be decisions with regard to many of them. You will have to decide whom to pick out as relatives worth having and whom to discard. In your decision-making, keep the three perspectives in mind—yours, theirs, and his.

It is impossible for me to give you a set of steadfast rules with regard to the extended family. Each family is individual in its own way. Each outlaw to in-law transition is unique because it will be yours. Only you can orchestrate your relationships given the demands and the compromises you are willing to make. Listening to second wives gives you examples of how different each situation is, but each situation is under your control.

"My married man has been quite close to his brothers all his life. However, after our marriage that way of life became increasingly difficult. They begrudged him his second chance. When we visited them with his kids from his first marriage, they would go out of their way to talk about his ex in front of me. Things like, 'How is your mother?' 'Tell her I'll call her next week.' Now, these things might sound harmless, but we had a hostile divorce. These people were deliberately adding fuel to the fires. Their fondness for the ex and their friendships should not be flaunted in front of us. My husband and I found it rude and infuriating. We decided to see them less and less." *(Lowell, Massachusetts)*

"When we started our new life as man and wife, we started to find new friends to replace the old relatives. You see, we felt like his brothers and sisters and even his parents were playing a game at our expense. At every family gathering, his ex would show up and then gums would be flapping and phones ringing for weeks. Who needs that? Not us!" *(Wilmington, Vermont)*

"I had no high hopes about my new in-laws, but they fooled me! They adored his first wife. But as time went on, she showed her true colors. Now his family adores me even more. They're always saying to each other, 'Just look what Tara brought him through!' And everybody tells me that they've never seen Tim so happy and smiling all the time. That's the nicest compliment of all." *(Battle Ground, Washington)*

"Just the other day I said to my mother-in-law, 'We've come a long way, haven't we?' There was a time we loathed each other. There were fights and feuds. I don't know how it all worked out, but it did. We have one thing in common, we both love the same guy. So for him we buried the hatchet and found out we even like each other. Surprising, but true!" *(Troy, New York)*

The transition from outlaw to in-law is usually the hardest in the beginning. The period of the divorce and the remarriage is full of change and myths, full of emotional pain and confusions. The best thing to remember is to maintain your integrity. If the entire family behaves scandalously as they react to your "scandal," keep your own dignity. Focus on your new husband and on your new life.

It was exactly that philosophy that steered Mary through a maze of family circles. Mary's story brings us to the special category of the married mistress who goes to second wife, with a divorce of her own in between. Sometimes that means double trouble, but not for Mary.

Family Circles

Mary has a new life and a new husband. Mary has a new old house and some new and some old relatives. It is a complicated story, so bear with me and pay attention.

"I was forty-five when I divorced my first husband. It was a shock to everyone who knew me. My teenage children were furious with me. My parents were aghast. I don't really know what my in-laws thought, but I'm sure it wasn't pleasant. It was easier for them to blame me than their son. I decided to divorce for several reasons. I became a mistress, the least likely candidate according to town gossip. I loved my married man. I was no longer in love with my husband nor he with me. We had one of those joyless marriages. I was middle-aged and I wanted a second chance. I wanted the last half of my life to have the best I could put into it."

Mary said she was determined to divorce with dignity. Her husband was rational after a while and felt the same. They agreed on nearly everything.

"I wanted joint custody. The children had a wonderful relationship with their father, and I didn't want to change that. We split all our assets right down the middle, including the house, which went up for sale. I was about to complete art school and so I didn't ask for alimony. I was fair and so was my husband. We were civilized. Divorce was not an emotional fiasco for us, it was a business deal."

So while Mary's relatives and in-laws swapped labels and tales, fault and blame, Mary was silent. She held her head high. She stood behind her married man as he approached his crisis. Although Mary's whole world was going round in circles, she had her feet in the middle maybe, but firmly on the ground.

Mary's married man, Adam, had more trouble changing partners. His children were younger. His wife was less than cooperative.

"Adam had a joyless marriage too. But his wife liked it that way. She wanted security, not a divorce and she did everything she could to gum up the works. Especially when it came to the kids. She wouldn't let Adam see them. Well, I'd seen this routine before. I told Adam not to play her game. I told him to tell her, 'If you don't want me to see the kids, fine. When you change your mind, call me.' Then she had no weapon. It was a gamble, but Adam took it. After a few months of not seeing the kids at all, he never pleaded with her; she came round."

Adam's family couldn't handle his paternal nonchalance, his mistress, his adultery, or his divorce. Mary's attitude was, so be it. She and Adam married as soon as both divorces were final. They bought an old house on the outskirts of town and took to refinishing antiques.

"We both wanted our new life. Taking all that old furniture, stripping it and refinishing it, was like a symbol to us. It was therapy. It proved that new lives could be made out of furniture and out of dreams. Little by little things improved. All the kids got used to us. Even the family circles mended."

Life goes on and around in circles. I loved Mary's story because she took a doubly complicated situation and created a beautiful new life. She did it with style and polish.

A mistress who is married goes from in-law to outlaw and then outlaw to in-law again. There are confrontations on three battlefields: your family, your first set of in-laws, and your new in-laws. Where there are children, add another potential battlefield. A married mistress can be a scapegoat, a home-wrecker, an in-law, and an outlaw simultaneously. Her married man can also be seen as a homewrecker and an outlaw.

A married mistress can also be judged more harshly than any other kind of mistress by others. Not only is she "immoral," but she is "betraying" a husband and probably "neglecting" her children. The theme, of course, is that she is a terrible person. This line of reasoning can be going on in the minds of her own relatives, so imagine what can be buzzing around the house-holds of her new in-laws.

The married mistress who becomes the second wife has a larger web of relationships, past and future. She has more room for problems. She must pick and choose relatives with many perspectives in mind. She should allow her children to maintain all their past ties with their father and paternal relatives. She can still move ahead herself and break with the past.

Perhaps the married mistress will have a greater understanding for the in-law challenge because she is experienced in dealing with extended families. She can bring more complications to a second marriage, but possibly more patience and wisdom.

Changing families and changing partners bring confusions in protocol. Mistresses, married before or not, have to face the family network and adapt. They can't rely on guaranteed prec-edents or standard etiquette. Mistress marriages are a new breed. Triangle transitions and the difficulties that result aren't dealt with often in the syndicated columns in the newspapers. What I'm getting around to is a test for you, the mistress, on etiquette. In many ways it will serve as a review of this chapter. Take the test and see if you have gotten the gist of the family questions and answers that lie ahead.

Is There a Mistress Etiquette?

Is there a mistress etiquette? You won't find the answer to that question either in Emily Post or Ann Landers. However, in these times of family affairs and family affairs, questions regarding etiquette do come up. No one goes smoothly from mistress to wife overnight and the Triangle Transition holds many sticky situations.

How does a woman handle herself in the process of going from mistress to wife? And even after the mistress becomes the second wife, many awkward situations continue to plague her. Are there a set of rules she can rely on to guide her conduct? Would you be able to instinctively feel out the proper way to act?

I've designed a test to help you learn a little bit about mistress etiquette. It's not black and white like table manners. However, with a little practice and understanding you can learn to conduct yourself admirably through even the most unadmirable situations.

Directions: What follows is a list of situations. After reading each situation, you will be asked to answer Yes or No. Do your best. After scoring yourself you will see just how much you know about mistress etiquette and just how much there really is to know on the subject!

1. Coincidently you know his family. His divorce is giving him a rough time. Should you enlist his family's support? Should you visit or call them, explain his problems, and ask them to give him more support? Would you involve his family? Yes or No. _____

2. You have received a telephone call or letter from a member of his family telling you to butt out. It also includes references to his reconciliation attempts, some tidbits about how happy his marriage once was. You could just ignore it or you could confront him with this information. Would you tell him? Yes or No. _____

3. Even though he has separated and is in the process of divorce, his parents invite him and his ex-wife and their children for a holiday dinner. He asks you to give him some advice. Should he attend for the sake of the family and his children? Or should he refuse to go because they were inconsiderate in inviting his ex? Would you advise him to go? Yes or No. _____

4. It's common knowledge that his parents think you are immoral, to put it mildly. He has told you on a number

of occasions about their less-than-pleasant remarks about your character. Now there is a family function and he wants you to accompany him. Would you refuse to go? Yes or No.   _____

5. In spite of his unhappy marriage, his parents continue to pressure him to reconcile. To you they seem more concerned with order, public opinion, and their grandchildren, than they do with their own son. Is it fair to judge them on this criteria? Are they showing their true colors? Would you judge them on their own behavior? Yes or No_____

6. His divorce isn't final yet, but you are certain of his intentions and his sincerity. You have introduced him to your family. Now there is a family function you must attend. Is it the right time to bring him? Even at the risk of whispers of scandal, would you attend with him at your side? What would you do? Go to the gala with your married man? Yes or No.   _____

7. He's told you a great deal about his parents. They seem to be a close family. They strongly disapprove of his family breakup. You're inclined to think that they are not all bad. He suggests that you all have dinner even though his divorce isn't final. He suggests that you invite them to your house so that you can show them how wonderful you are. Would you invite them? Yes or No.   _____

8. His parents have been hostile, meddlesome, harassing, and ugly. This has been directed at you as well as at him. He finds it all very upsetting. Should you encourage him to just cut them off and agree never to let them set foot in your house? Should you hold them accountable for their obnoxious behavior and let them pay the price of losing their son? What would you do? Tell him to forget them? Yes or No.   _____

9. You and he are planning a simple civil wedding ceremony. Neither set of parents are wild about your union. Should you go out of your way and include them in your plans? Even though they never made any kind of congratulatory overtures, should you be forgiving and invite them to the ceremony and whatever party may follow? Yes or No.   _____

10. He reports that his parents have said some rather untruthful things about you. Either it could be gossip that they heard through the grapevine or some negative opinion that is clearly unfounded. You feel so slandered and outraged you are inclined to call them up and set them straight. Should you be assertive and let them have it? Would you blast them? Yes or No.   _____

Scoring:
In the column below labeled *Answers,* fill in all your answers from 1 to 10. Then look to the left and see what each answer is worth. Write the number of points in the column labeled *Points.* Add your total score and see what it all means in the following evaluation section.

	Yes	No	Answers	Points
1.	5	10	_____	_____
2.	10	5	_____	_____
3.	5	10	_____	_____
4.	5	10	_____	_____
5.	5	10	_____	_____
6.	10	5	_____	_____
7.	5	10	_____	_____
8.	5	10	_____	_____
9.	5	10	_____	_____
10.	5	10	_____	_____
			Total _____	

Evaluation:
First of all, let me say that no one fails this test. If your score doesn't measure up, it may not be your fault but the strain of being a mistress in a society that unfairly discriminates against you. With that word of caution, read the category that includes your score.

50–65 Points: Etiquette, Impossible! If your score fell here, for you mistress etiquette is impossible. You may ask, how can you be civilized in an uncivilized world? Your situation most likely has had a heavy dose of harassment, meddling, anger, and bitterness. Perhaps his parents are leading a campaign to slur you in his eyes and everyone else's and at the same time are trying to patch up his marriage. While you have a right to see it like it is, and avoid them, try to retain your dignity. Don't stoop to their level. Refrain from scenes that would compromise your integrity. Remember, as hard as it may be to, that divorce brings out the worst in people. Had you dealt with his family in a non-scandalous period they might have been quite different. You don't have to patronize them or invite them to ruin your wedding, but you do have to remember they are his only parents. And his problem, not yours. Give it time, give them time, and you will look better all around for it.

70–85 Points: Etiquette, Confused! If your score fell here, for you the matter of etiquette is confusing. You are justified to feel this way because the rules for the mistress are new, and, yes, complicated. Your score indicates conflicting instincts. So for you, here are a few guidelines in a nutshell. Try to take his family with a grain of salt at first. That means don't enlist their help or listen to their advice or insults. Don't encourage him to participate in matchmaking schemes or allow yourself to be baited into defending yourself. Concentrate on you and him and in time things will settle. Regardless of his family's initial consensus on his divorce, don't be too harsh on them. Don't cut them off forever. Know when to stand firm and when to give them a chance to redeem themselves. When you are sure of him, then introduce him into your family scheme. There are no steadfast rules regarding when things will be "right" before or after the divorce. Some divorces take years, for valid reasons. Just be proud of yourself and his love and hold your head high. And remember this situation too will pass.

90–100 Points: Etiquette Expertise! If your score fell here, for you mistress etiquette is a breeze. You have a natural feel for situations and handling yourself and others. You are most likely mature, compassionate, and assertive. You are secure enough not to be or feel threatened by other people's gossip, opinion of you, or behavior. You and he have it all together and are just biding your time until people realize that that is the reality they must deal with. You realize that the Triangle Transition is a difficult time for him and his family, and that you will reserve judgement until some future date. You don't need other people's approval and so you are not inclined to get wound up in schemes or scenes of bitterness or pettiness. You are expert at maintaining your dignity and integrity and that is why in time he and everyone else will look up to you. And if not, it will be no loss to you.

In Conclusion:

Mistress etiquette? Sounds bizarre, unconventional, and complex. It is a maze of choices and temptations. Triangles do unleash extreme emotions and difficult situations. You, as a mistress who could go to second wife, will have to handle situations that Emily and Ann and Abby never imagined. But I know you can do it!

The mistress/married man marriage is a new frontier. It holds for you new horizons. It holds opportunities for new relationships with your new family of in-laws. And it holds a transition period where you will be treated like the outlaw. The outlaw to in-law transition can be a showdown with some tough times. It can also be a time for you to scan his family and pan for the potential relatives that can add to your new life.

So what if you are an outlaw? You can become a redeemed in-law, if you so desire. You can pick your relatives as you pick your friends. In a way, your mistress history was a proving ground. If you go on to become a second wife, you have beat the odds. So you can master any challenge, any family circle!

PART III

Strategies for Parenting

CHAPTER 9

Paternity—Bind, Bond, and Booster

A mistress is usually not in love with an ordinary man. A mistress is also likely to be in love with a father. Most married men have children. Their paternal commitment to their children is the No. 1 obstacle to many when they contemplate divorce. As a mistress you probably know that fact all too well.

For a married man the decision to divorce implies the change of a lifetime. In that change nine out of ten fathers lose custody of their children, no matter what you read about changing trends. It is a huge price for a father to pay. He will no longer be a daily part of his children's lives. He will no longer be in control of decisions about them. It is a price that generates a monumental crisis in paternity. It makes the divorce decision dreadful.

Watching your married man planning his divorce is no picnic. He will begin to dismantle the lifestyle he has worked hard to achieve. He will divide the assets and the property. But when it comes to the children, then what? They can't be cut in half. So it is the married man who feels like he is being torn in two, torn between his love for you and his love for his children.

When your married man finally decides to divorce his wife, and not his children, you may think he has finally resolved his paternal crisis. What you may not realize is that the father in your married man may be destined to a lifetime of hurdles. In the wake of divorce, the father's crisis isn't over. In reality, it is then that his paternal crisis is just beginning. The dilemma he and his children will face trying to hold on to each other is in its infancy.

Why is the paternal crisis so traumatic after divorce? You might argue that a married man doesn't lose his children when he leaves his wife. You might argue that he just has to readjust his schedule and adapt his relationships with them. The crux of a father's crisis, however, is not simply the whens and the wheres of meeting his children. The crux of the paternal crisis is inside him. It is not found in the tangibles of life, but in the intangible concept of his own self-image.

When the married man opts for a better life with you, his mistress, it takes a toll on his paternal self-image. He can't escape that shudder of conscience that says he is "leaving" his children. Let's backtrack a bit.

A man who has a child adds "father" to his self-definition. He gives himself a new set of expectations as a father. He takes on responsibility for his child, adding a new dimension to his self-concept. A divorce will affect his child, even a smooth divorce. Knowing the trauma that he is inflicting on his child with a divorce produces monumental guilt. A married man sees himself as hurting his child in this move. Even if it is best in the long run, the guilt of the initial impact cannot be totally erased. A man sees divorcing as unfatherly. Even if he is more committed to being a good father than ever before, he still pays for divorce with a portion of his self-love. The father part of his self-esteem suffers.

Unfortunately, trying to be a father after divorce adds a constant drama affecting paternity. Trying to maintain a relationship with his children after divorce puts myriads of men in a paternal bond. Yet the paternal bind destines them toward this crisis. You will witness firsthand this paternal crisis and what it does to your man. You will have to be his booster. Sometimes that will mean the only tie he has to good feelings about his fatherhood. You'll see that as we go along later.

What I am saying is that his bind is your bind. His paternal crisis, and the struggle to cope with it, will affect your life as a second wife. How exactly depends on your situation. It can dump myriads of problems in your marriage, and yet these can make your love stronger. It depends on you, on him, and how you both handle paternity. On *The Phil Donahue Show*, not so long ago, my husband Michael spoke about the paternity crisis. He said, "There are no divorced fathers, there are only divorced husbands. Yet society doesn't see it that way." There should be no divorced fathers, but there are, and not by their choice. As a second wife, paternity becomes a crucial issue, even more so than it was when you were a mistress.

Throughout this chapter we are going to hear from second wives about their experiences. As they unfold, you will see specifically what I mean by paternal binds. Through it all you will see the bond that cannot be stifled easily. And most importantly you will see the challenge and the commitment it will take from you, when as a second wife you are called on to bolster your new husband.

Are you suited to meet the challenges of his paternity crisis? Are you equipped to master the commitment you will be called upon to make to his fatherhood? Before we go any further, let's examine you in particular and how you will react as a second wife. How you will feel about his fatherhood is in many ways predetermined by your feelings now. What are they?

Take the following test and see.

How Do You Rate Fatherhood?

M-O-T-H-E-R spells mother. We all know the song and we all know what motherhood means. Motherhood, like apple pie, is woven thoroughly into the fabric of our culture. Mothers regularly get their due in terms of homage, esteem, and publicity. Motherhood is universally venerated and respected on many more occasions in our society than once a year on Mother's Day. We speak of the maternal drive, the maternal instinct, and maternal fulfillment.

In contrast, what does F-A-T-H-E-R mean? As a concept, what does fatherhood mean to you? As a mistress you probably know what it means to your married man, but let's talk about you. How do you rate fatherhood? How does your rating of fatherhood relate to your married man?

The following test will provide some interesting answers about you and about him and about how you will fare if you go from mistress to wife.

Directions: This is a multiple choice test. After reading each of the questions or statements, you must select one answer from among the choices. List the letter in the space provided for each statement or question. Then proceed to the scoring table and an evaluation of your answers.

1. The best parent is usually (a) the father,(b) the mother, (c) not necessarily either one.

    1._____

2. In the last several decades, custody was based on the "tender years" doctrine, which said that mothers are better equipped to tend children in their formative years. That doctrine became the basis for maternal custody. What is your reaction? (a) It's true. (b) It was logical then because of women's social role as homemaker. (c) Then and now it was overly simplistic and biased.

    2._____

3. Men are basically (a) discriminated against when we speak of emotional capacities; (b) unemotional and more work-oriented than women; (c) emotional creatures who express or deal with their emotions differently than women do.

    3._____

4. The sense we have of fatherhood is derived from the historical view. Historically speaking fatherhood has been (a) underrated; (b) depicted accurately; (c) eclipsed by motherhood.

    4._____

5. Women are natural nurturers. (a) I agree with that statement. (b) I disagree because men can be nurturers too. (c) I disagree because the statement is sexist; men have nurtured, can nurture, and do nurture.

    5._____

6. After divorce a child would find it easiest to (a) live in the framework of a joint custody agreement, part of the time with Mom and part with Dad; (b) live with Mom who can give continuity and security; (c) live with the best parent depending on each situation.

    6._____

7. Which parent has more influence on a child's later experiences in career, marriage, and sex? (a) Generalizations are inadequate; it could be either. (b) Of course the mother; that has always been known from Oedipus onwards. (c)

The father, according to a new body of knowledge, often determines ambition, and marital and sexual partners.

7._____

8. Men who fight for custody of their children are usually (a) vengeful in their motivation; (b) assertive and honest; (c) unique.

8._____

9. Do you feel that your married man (a) has an inherent need to have custody, as do most men; (b) overreacts to the prospect of losing his child after divorce; (c) should try for custody if he so desires.

9._____

10. How do you explain those fathers who lose contact with their children after divorce? (a) They are acting in a natural tradition. (b) You have no explanation. (c) They have problems and sufferings that are unknown and historically unheard.

10._____

11. Mothers tend to "hog" the parent/child relationship. How do you feel about that statement? (a) That is true, expected, and standard. (b) That is ridiculous. (c) Fathers tend to accept the child being Mother's domain and accept isolation from the child.

11._____

12. Do you think that the nurturing ability is a (a) neuter trait, (b) feminine trait; (c) a relative trait.

12._____

13. When you look for a man who would make a "good father," what do you look for? (a) A man who is good with kids. (b) A man who is a reliable and stable provider financially and socially. (c) A man who is a good all-around person.

13._____

14. Is it easier for a man to go through life childless? (a) Yes, absolutely. (b) No, men are driven to procreate too. (c)

It depends on the person not their gender.

14._____

15. After the birth of a child, manuals often speak of a father's upset. In your opinion what causes this? (a) The man feels left out. (b) The man feels neglected by his wife. (c) The man encounters conflicts and confusions that have gone unnoticed.

15._____

Scoring:
Below is a scoring table. Each answer is worth a certain number of points. First list your letter selection for each question in the column marked *Answers*. Then refer to the table and list the·points attributed to your answer in the column marked *Points*. Total your points and proceed to the evaluation.

			Answers	Points
1.) (a) 5	(b) 0	(c) 10	_____	_____
2.) (a) 0	(b) 5	(c) 10	_____	_____
3.) (a) 5	(b) 0	(c) 10	_____	_____
4.) (a) 10	(b) 0	(c) 5	_____	_____
5.) (a) 0	(b) 5	(c) 10	_____	_____
6.) (a) 10	(b) 0	(c) 5	_____	_____
7.) (a) 5	(b) 0	(c) 10	_____	_____
8.) (a) 0	(b) 10	(c) 5	_____	_____
9.) (a) 10	(b) 0	(c) 5	_____	_____
10.) (a) 0	(b) 5	(c) 10	_____	_____
11.) (a) 5	(b) 0	(c) 10	_____	_____
12.) (a) 10	(b) 0	(c) 5	_____	_____
13.) (a) 5	(b) 0	(c) 10	_____	_____
14.) (a) 0	(b) 10	(c) 5	_____	_____
15.) (a) 10	(b) 0	(c) 5	_____	_____
		Total	_____	

Evaluation:
    0–50 Points: If your score fell into this range, you have a *momist* view of fatherhood. You characteristically underrate fatherhood. For you parenthood and motherhood are synonymous. You feel that mothers are natural nurturers, the best

parents, the only custodians for children. You feel that a man's place is outside the family except financially speaking. You are definitely prejudiced about a man's capacity for child-rearing, his emotional potential, and his motivation where parenthood is concerned. You are comfortable with maternal superiority, the maternal instinct, and the maternal drive and all theories that favor mothers.

Let me point out that a momist perspective toward fatherhood is common. However, if your married man is assertive about his fatherhood, watch out! Fatherhood is not high in your value structure or in your consciousness. You may not understand your married man as father and therefore not fathom or appreciate his paternal drive, his paternal instinct, and his paternal crisis.

55–100 Points: If your score fell into this range, you have a *confused* view of fatherhood. There are conflicts in your rating system. You are basically torn between the societal prejudices of momism and the struggle for equality in parenting. You definitely feel that some men have been discriminated against in the whole child-rearing issue. Some men nurture well. Motherhood has definitely eclipsed fatherhood. And yet sometimes the father is the best parent. You see parenthood and nurturing not as sex-related, but in more relative terms. Some men should try for custody. Some men are good with kids. For some men a childless life is empty. And yet you are still confused as to why some men and not others make "good fathers." You can't explain why some divorced men lose contact with their children. Fatherhood has a confused record in your view. You can't speak about all men as fathers, but it's for certain that some fathers have gotten a bad deal!

Your view of fatherhood is progressive. Therefore you will find it easier to adapt to a married man who is not going to give up his children without a struggle. However, beneath the progressive seeds of your views, you still harbor sexism. You still see parenthood as the norm for mothers and not the norm for fathers. Men who are driven to father are still unique, or the exception. As you see your married man's paternal dilemma and what fatherhood means to him, you will probably progress further toward equality in parenting.

105–150 Points: If your score fell into this range, you have an *equal* view of fatherhood and parenting. You do not underrate fatherhood or hold any of the momist prejudices that are so common. Reproduction is a human instinct as far as you are concerned, not a feminine drive or a relative drive. Nurturing is neuter. Every human being has the capacity to care for its young. Men have been discriminated against historically speaking and oftentimes shut out of the parenthood experience. Custody norms never took into account the father's view, the father's sense of loss, or the father's silent unacknowledged sorrows. You favor joint custody, equality down the line. Any man can be a good father, not only men who excel with kids. Fathers have been underrated long enough. Any man who fights for his children is honest and not some unique exception. Men and women are different, yes, but each gender brings something special to parenting and something each child should have. When we treat all men as fathers, all men will blossom in the parental role.

Your view of fatherhood is just beginning to get the attention it deserves. You are the best equipped to deal with your married man as he struggles through a time of great paternal crisis. In you he has found a real understanding partner. Your image of fatherhood will only strengthen him no matter what the outcome of his paternity. When it comes to the issue of fatherhood, speak out. Your views can help us all!

In Conclusion:
Hopefully we have all learned something from this test, regardless of the score you achieved. How you rate fatherhood will play quite an important role in your life as a mistress-to-wife. It might even determine whether or not you make the transition. Read this chapter carefully. Try to acquire new insights into fatherhood for yourself and your father; for your married man and his fatherhood; and for your own children. Paternity should be as important to you as it is to him.

The following story of Sally and Derrick will highlight just how important fatherhood can be. For them it became a matter of life and death!

The Dark Side of the Disneyland Dad

In his thirty-fifth year, Derrick became what is commonly known as the Disneyland Dad. His label had nothing to do with geography or California. Derrick lived in Burns Flat, Oklahoma, with his second wife, Sally. Even though Sally had been his mistress, his divorce wasn't as bitter as some he had seen. Not at first anyway.

Derrick told us, "I got standard visitation—Sundays. Now I realize I had the wrong lawyer. I should have fought for more. I just thought my ex-wife would cooperate if I wanted more time with our four kids."

But let's get back to Derrick's label. Every Sunday Derrick would pick up his children at 10 a.m. The drive to their home was two hours, so it was unfeasible to go back to his house and then make the round trip back by 6 p.m. when due home. So every Sunday Derrick had a logistics dilemma. To solve it he planned outings.

"I didn't know what to do with the kids at first. We had a mere eight hours, and a long drive to anywhere. So I took them somewhere each time we got together. Sometimes the movies. Or horseback riding. The local amusement park was a favorite and so was the new Mall."

Derrick didn't mean to become a social director. He didn't mean to spoil the kids with an overdose of popcorn, cotton candy, and trinkets. He was only trying to do his best in the measly eight hours into which his fatherhood was squeezed.

"My ex-wife got nastier all the time. She told me it was harder for her to take care of the kids because I was spoiling them. She felt she was always the heavy stuck with the laundry and the discipline while I got to dole out all the good times. Then she started telling me I couldn't see them this Sunday for this reason and that Sunday for another. It wasn't fair.

"Maybe I did overdo with the good times, but I was afraid the children would forget about me or not want to come with me. I wasn't exactly a big part of their daily life anymore. I had these bouts of depression every Sunday night after I made that long drive home alone."

Sally filled in a lot. She said Derrick usually came home in tears. He missed those kids terribly. He had spent twelve years rearing them and now he got eight hours a week, and less and less.

"Sure Derrick gave things to the kids. All week long, he'd

pick up a candy bar here, a toy there, socks, ribbons. It was his only way of still feeling like a father."

His ex taunted him, and called him a Disneyland Dad. The exact definition: a father who overindulges his children with gifts and good times on Sundays. Underline this with the ex-wife's jealousy and the fact that father's behavior makes mother's job at home harder.

"She envied me! What a joke!" Derrick said. "I hated this new role. I felt like a ringmaster at a circus. You know, 'Which sideshow is next, Dad?' I missed prayers at bedtime, midnight visitors in my bed."

Sally said that in time Derrick became a casualty of divorce. His visits with the kids were thwarted.

"We have been married six years now. He's been hospitalized four times by four different doctors, who have never found any medical reasons. They said it must be nerves. Nerves, no. Derrick was suffering from a broken heart. Fathers have hearts, you know. He was frustrated and worried sick. The unfairness of it all got to him."

Is a life-and-death situation too drastic an expression to use about Derrick? Was he worrying himself to death? Yes, literally. His health was going down the tubes. As his life as a father dwindled, a slow death of frustration and physical ailments took over.

There is such a dark side to being a Disneyland Dad. Time with the kids is so brief. There is guilt, fear of losing their love, worry, and loneliness. And aggravation from the exwife who blames her discipline problems on you. Disneyland Dads aren't fun and games. We chide them for trying to buy a child's love. We fail to recognize the desperation and the frustration that lies beneath their generosity. We don't see their bind. Darkness only comes out at night. For a father, the dark side of the Disneyland Dad prevails all the time.

Take away a man's children and he suffers an inconsolable loss. You can't be a parent one day and then the next lose your parenting instincts. Yet that is exactly what a father is expected to do. He is eliminated from that daily activity of loving and living with his child. That loss and loneliness is compounded by fear that his paternity will just slowly die as the children forget him.

That fear is not altogether irrational either. How many wives encourage fatherhood after divorce? We know what percentage of men renege on support payments, but does anyone know how many mothers cut fathers out of the lives of children?

"There are so many of us out here who can identify with losing children by divorce. I could tell you stories that would curl your hair regarding visitation problems, the constant battles in and out of court, and the toll this takes on fathers and second wives and of course the children." *(Hales Corners, Wisconsin)*

"My husband's ex-wife took the children to Florida, which means he only gets to see them for a few weeks in the summer and one holiday time a year. He doesn't want me to write to them or send them anything or do anything to assure their love when they are gone. He is afraid his ex-wife will move again and not tell us where the next time. By the way, he pays child support even though they are out of state. We wouldn't dare stop. Fear is a way of life." *(Bangor, Maine)*

In so many cases the divorce is followed by the ex-wife's moving, usually to another state. Some do it for spite; some for a job or a new marriage. Some just want a new life, not realizing that the children deserve some part of their old life—Dad.

"We've been married for eight years now. In that eight years my husband's ex-wife has moved six times, making my husband find her and his son. His ex has had boyfriends that have beat up on her and the boy. When my husband goes to pick up the boy, he has been threatened and shot at once by one of her crazy lovers. A lawyer has still told us we have no chance of gaining custody. She (his ex) has moved 200 miles away now. She won't allow his son on a bus because the child is only ten years old. My husband is literally afraid for his life to go there alone, so he doesn't make the trip a lot. We now have an infant and it's hard for me to pick up and go. It's getting to be such a hassle! I'm at the end of my rope and so is he. Only what's the answer?" *(Lynchburg, Virginia)*

Hassle is too mild a word. It is a crisis year-in and year-out for every father who goes through times like these. After divorce most men find themselves in a bind paternally. Visitation schedules are rarely fair or easy to work out. Custody is even rarer. What keeps them going?

Regardless of how difficult maintaining a relationship is with a child, fathers are driven. Regardless of how limited, shallow, or piecemeal the quality of that new relationship is, fathers are driven to participate. That parent-child bond is primal. No matter what the paternal bind, that bond makes the father hang in there. No matter how much heartache that bind inflicts on a father, the bond and the love that survives makes it all worthwhile.

The next story doesn't measure up to a fairy tale but it has a very happy ending.

Nights at the Round Table

The tale of Arthur was teeming with medieval imagery. He lives in New Castle. His wife had had many suitors, only not the chivalrous, platonic kind. Arthur didn't care after a while. He found Beverly.

One day his wife told him to leave, which he did gladly, save for their two children ages nine and twelve. Arthur decided he was going to arm himself and go after the dragon, in this case custody of the children. It was your basic impossible dream, common to modern fathers.

The custody proceeding took many years and in the meantime Arthur and Beverly were married. The adversary nature of this legal joust made his ex-wife impossible. He was rarely allowed visits with the children. So many nights Beverly and Arthur sat around the round table in their kitchen. Beverly characterized what it was like then.

"The point of my and my husband's personal experience is how much pain we went through; it's indescribable. We eventually lost the custody case. His ex-wife was living with other men constantly as always and has never married to this day. But the court claimed we needed three witnesses who were impartial to testify to her lifestyle. We could not get the witnesses. As for all the times the kids were withheld from us, no one really ever addressed that."

Arthur's reigning paternal crisis went on for years. He and Beverly still held vigils at the round table often. Mysteriously things worked out. How? There was no magician named Merlyn. There was no fairy godperson. What there was, was this parent-child bond.

"No matter how much brainwashing their mother threw at them, Arthur's children knew how much their Dad loved them. They knew I cared too. Oh, they always loved their mother. They never saw her the way we did, but that was best for them. They got closer to us as the years passed and the bitterness got less. Arthur has always been there when he was needed. He has never missed a support payment, whether he was allowed to visit them or not. Believe me there were months on end, at different times, when he never saw them. He was even thrown out of the house one Christmas when he brought gifts for the kids. That's all ancient history now. Last Thanksgiving we all got together, at last a happy family around that round table."

Is it ancient history for Arthur and Beverly, or should I say medieval history? What makes Arthur's tale a legend is this: His impossible dream of custody, his bravery against the system, his wounds, and his pain are common to fathers all over America.

We must not forget the happy ending though. That bond, if we all just help it along, will flourish and thrive. So strong is that bond that, even when we don't help, it survives. The following letter addressed to both me and my husband Michael provides a little proof.

"Hi, I'm a sixteen-year-old girl who hasn't seen her father since I was two. My father was put in jail several times for just trying to visit me. My mother keeps telling me my father was a bum who beat up on us, but I don't remember. He got lucky, I guess, he didn't have to pay child support if he would just leave us alone. I keep wondering all the time what he looks like, how he acts, and if he loves me even though he hasn't seen me in fourteen years! The courts won't let him call or write either; it's not fair! I saw you and your husband on *Donahue* talking about fathers and children and I just had to write." *(Cliffside Park, New Jersey)*

I only hope that someday soon that girl and her father can be reunited. He will be rejuvenated surely to see that love bonding him to a child he hasn't seen for years. I hope that happens before it's too late. The next entry here is from a daughter who didn't find such forgiveness in her heart, leastwise not in the beginning.

"I'm married now with a year-old son. I am a product of divorce. When my parents separated, it took Mom less than a month to make us hate our father. My father got standard visitation then, Sundays and one night a week for dinner. But who wanted to see a man who, as my mother said, 'cared so little for us as to leave us.' Seeing my father then was an uncomfortable chore.

"We were manipulated by a woman who needed her children around her to keep her own ego and her motherly role intact. We were emotionally bounced back and forth and became confused about all involved. It took me nine years to sort out the crap my mother had dished out. I wanted to live with my father. My mother would not allow us back then to have a healthy relationship with my father because I guess she thought it meant we loved her less. That was something she couldn't handle. I feel that many mothers feel this way and more often than not it cripples the children's relationship with the father. I hated mine for years. I put him through hell because of my mother's insecurities and I don't think I will ever forgive myself for that. I was able after a lot of work to develop a meaningful relationship with my Dad in spite of all we've gone through. My brothers and sisters never have and it hurts my father. You see, he used to back down in order to prevent putting us in the middle of himself and my mother. We always thought, because he didn't fight hard enough, he didn't love us enough. Hindsight is wonderful. I see all sides now. And I am very lucky to have found my father at last." *(San Diego, California)*

The point of all this is, for you, a second-wife candidate, to see the importance of that bond and the indestructible nature of it. The bond between your married man and his children will endure no matter what the stress. That bond may appear to falter or snap, but don't underestimate its resilience. That bond will figure strongly in your future. As a father, your married man will be driven to pay allegiance to that pull in his gut toward his children. That pull may take you into territory that you may find trying and strange. Handling his paternal bind and bond will test you. Yet, more than any other time, that is when your man will most need your help.

What kind of help will he need? Now, as a mistress, you say you will provide that help. Later, as a second wife, you will see that is easier said than done. For a better explanation, let's meet Pam and Nicholas.

Happy Holidays!

"When I was a mistress, I hated holidays. They upset me. I thought once Nicholas and I were married, holidays would change for me. They did, but they got worse."

That transition may sound impossible. After all, having your man at holiday time should make it alright. But, not if your man is suffering. Nick was suffering!

Nicholas's ex-wife was a vindictive maniac and a good one. By that I mean she directed all her energy in devising ways to torture Nick using his son and daughters in the game plan. I was introduced to this perverse genius by Nick's second wife, Pam. Pam was beside herself with rage and frustration.

"Nick was supposed to see his son, age two, and his twin daughters, age four for the Christmas vacation. We had been looking forward to it so much. We had a tree and loads of gifts. The icebox was full of turkey and candy canes. When Nick got to their house the children did not want to go with him. They had been told that if they went with Daddy they would miss Santa Claus. Nick tried to reason with them that that wasn't true. But can you reason with little kids after they have been brainwashed for four months by their trusted mother? No. So Nick came home devastated. There was no way we could enjoy Christmas."

So, needless to add, Nick and Pam had no peace on earth that December, but time passed. His ex moved farther away.

"We went to court a few times and got little accomplished. Brainwashing wasn't something the courts wanted to deal with."

There wasn't much that Pam could do except just suffer

along with Nick. He was helpless in his paternal bondage. She was equally helpless. Then came Father's Day.

"Nick was in tears by six o'clock on Father's Day. No call. Not even a card. I wanted to kill his ex-wife and those damn children who were hurting this wonderful man so much. Thank God he went to sleep early. I lay awake half the night praying to God to help me overcome this bitterness, this anger that I had. I had to watch all this pain and do nothing. It was driving me crazy!"

Holidays for a man without his children are hell. Holidays for his second wife accrue new rituals. That feeling of midnight madness when you harangue your god for allowing this. That feeling of being engulfed in a rage so powerful that it frightens you with its totality. That horrible knowledge of your help-lessness as you witness his loss. There is nothing so torturous as wanting to help and not being able to. The June calendar creeps up on Father's Day. His children are away or just off limits. What should you do? Ignore it or celebrate it? There is not an answer to that dilemma. Except to endure it along with him.

Sometimes you can talk to him and assure him that this is not his fault. Sometimes it's best to just hold him and say nothing. Your company and warmth can be assuring for him, assuring him he is still a good father. You have to be his booster because there are times when your sympathy and understanding are *all* that remain of his fatherhood.

Don't underestimate the true importance of your sympathy. Very often it is the second wife's assurances that keep a father going. A father can lose perspective alone and sink into a depression that is overpowering. He can wallow in guilt and blame. He can almost convince himself that all this is his fault somehow.

"My husband went through a very bad time over his daugh-ter. His ex allowed him to spend one weekend a month with Veronica. This was after much legal activity. Then his ex turned around and said this visitation was hurting Veronica. She claimed afterwards the child was upset for days. She moved to have visitation with the father eliminated forever. Veronica told us she cried when she got home because she missed her father and it was such a long time until she could see him again. But the ex-wife had a child psychologist on her side and a school record that showed emotional upset. My husband agreed to stop the visits rather than put Veronica through any-more. It nearly destroyed us, and him." *(Syracuse, New York)*

That incident can be summed up in a phrase, The Trauma Maneuver. The Trauma Maneuver is a strategy executed by the mother with precision. This can be conscious or unconscious. First the mother cuts the children off from their father almost totally. No phone calls. No regular contact. Then she allows a visit once in a while for a short time. In the meantime the mother fills the child's life with criticisms about the father, accusations, insecurities. Things like "Your father has a new wife, he's not interested in you anymore" or "He's a bum." The child gets the message that Mom hates Dad. Thus she gets the conflict that if I like Dad still, that's wrong in Mom's eyes. Compound that with the child missing her father. Throw in a short visit steeped with conflict and pressure and voila! You have a child with a trauma every time she sees her father. And you have a mother who says, "She gets upset every time she sees her father."

The Trauma Maneuver is very hard on fathers. Even though the mother is setting the child up for this trauma, the father does play a role. The father becomes poison, so to speak, for his own child. Blame becomes a clouded issue when the father focuses only on the trauma his visits inflict on the child.

You as a second wife must assure him that he is not the guilty party here. You may have to say it a hundred times. You will have to help him decide whether it is best to back off or best to hang in there and fight. The best advice varies with the situation. Some kids need to know that their father kept fight-ing. Some kids, however, are put through so much battling that more could be just too destructive.

A second wife must realize that once you marry your man, the triangle isn't over. You will still have to fight for him, for his self-image as a father. His ex-wife will be demeaning him paternally all the time. You must meet those attacks head on with all the encouragement he needs. His paternal image of himself depends on you convincing him over and over. This makes some second wives almost live-in therapists. One of their wifely duties becomes patching up the wounded image of their man as he muddles through the paternal crisis.

Bolstering with words is one way of helping. That technique

usually applies when the father is cut off from his children. Sometimes you have to bolster with more than words.

"Right after the separation, his ex moved out West. She told the kids they'd get horses and dirtbikes and so they wanted to go. This broke Larry's heart. He couldn't believe the kids wanted to leave him just like that. He fought the move legally but lost. All he got was summer visits. After a year, when the summer came, Larry tried to recapture his fatherhood with the children. It was a real letdown. The kids had become strangers. They seemed to be just like their mother and not at all like him. He had no input in their lives, so he had no influence. After a year alone, getting back into the swing of a family was horrible. It was bad for him and he was their father. As a stepmother it was horrible for me." *(Okemos, Missouri)*

Fathering children on a part-time basis is hard for him and harder for you. That is a whole other chapter really. But here let me insert that you must be committed to paternity because you have to play your part in it all. You have to help him cope when the children are gone. You have to help him cope and cope yourself when the children are with you.

The real test comes when you are called upon to stepmother, when he lives his fatherhood after your marriage. Will your feelings then be a help or a hindrance to his paternity? If your married man decides to go for full custody what will your reaction be? Will you encourage him or discourage him? Once he has his children on weekends and vacations, will your behavior help him father or will your behavior distract from his efforts?

As a mistress your commitment to his fatherhood is 100 percent. If it's not, it should be. Because his paternal crisis and his paternal bondage will demand much from you. Suppose you can't get along with his children? Will that alter your feelings about his wanting to spend as much time as possible with them?

"My new husband had two huge teenagers. They hated me. I was open at first. I tried to be understanding, but after a while I just hated them back. Then I found myself sulking before the weekend or hinting that we could do other things if it weren't for the kids. Without even realizing what I was doing, I was trying to chip away at my husband's fatherhood." *(New Tripoli, Pennsylvania)*

Even the nicest second wives find problems with his paternal commitment. You must learn to separate your relationship with the children from his. Stepmothering is different from your attitude toward his parenthood. You must learn to say, if this becomes your case temporarily or permanently "I love you, but I don't love your kids." He must learn to see that his fathering is a sphere unto itself. It's separate from your new family relationships. Despite how successfully or unsuccessfully your relationships go with his children, you must not invade his fatherhood.

You can back out, you can do things yourself while he is with the children, but you shouldn't force him to stop fathering on your account. Many second wives find the paternal bondage overwhelming and disheartening.

"I got my ideas about motherhood from *Redbook* ads with cuddly infants held by teary-eyed mothers. I got my ideas about fatherhood the same way. I was all sentimental about him and his poor kids being held apart for so long by our unjust system. Then he got them and the reality was harrowing. Now the roles were reversed, I needed all the understanding. I complained endlessly I think for two years, but we all came through it, his fatherhood still intact along with my sanity." *(Arlington, Texas)*

"I never wanted to be one of those selfish women who say it's me or the kids. I thought they were heartless. I still would never say it, but now I understand them more. It can get to you." *(Grand Rapids, Michigan)*

There are quite a large number of women who do give that kind of ultimatum for many reasons. They are not all monsters. However, they are doing a thing that can be monstrous. Destroying a man's fatherhood is a serious responsibility. You, as a second wife, can make or break his paternity. Your attitude can really make an impact on his paternal crisis. Children need their father. You will be called on to put their needs above your own. He can be the best father he can be only when you are behind him all the way.

Then there may be the misguided notion that you can redirect his fatherhood. If his ex-wife is making fathering his child difficult, perhaps he can transfer his fatherhood to your children or to a new baby of your own. That is fallacious reasoning. Fathers can't forget a child, no matter what. They can't transfer their love from one to another. A father can't fill the gap of a lost child with a new child. He can love the new child, but that love cannot erase that child he lost through divorce. Beware if you think you can eliminate his conflict-ridden children and make it all up to him with a baby. It's just not that easy.

"My husband is a beautiful caring father. I know because he is adopting my eight-year-old son. My former husband is out of the picture and not because of me. I let him see Johnny but he lives very far away and slowly their relationship ended. Johnny now loves my husband very much. The way Hal gets along with my son is as if he were born to him. Still, I can see that this isn't enough for Hal. He misses his own son, who lives out-of-state, very much. Sometimes I think fathering mine makes it harder on him." *(Lake Stevens, Washington)*

"When I found out I was pregnant, I used it as an excuse not to have his children stay with us as much. You see, I felt like I had half a husband because of his other responsibilities. I didn't want my baby to have half a father too. I wanted him just for us. I saw it working too. He became so involved with our baby, his were not in first place anymore. However, I realized how wrong I was. He was unhappy sometimes although he never said a word. I learned that fatherhood isn't a commodity that runs dry if there's too many hungry mouths. The more love we all ask for from him, the more he seems to have." *(Cleveland, Ohio)*

As you can see, your married man's paternal crisis is full of pitfalls for you. You may be tempted many times in the beginning to just try and wipe it out of your marriage. Don't.

I am going to leave you with one story about a child who grew up without her father.

"I'm writing this letter for your sake and especially for your children's sake. My husband and I had a terrible time with his ex-wife. He fought until all our money was gone and still we never got to see his daughter and son. The years went by and those children grew up with lies about their father and me and they both really never got to know us. My husband really suffered through this and even though we had children of our own, as you say, they cannot ever take the place of the other children. My husband's son never sought us out when he got older. He joined the service and we heard he died in Viet Nam. His daughter, however, did seek us out. She was messed up on drugs and came to us at sixteen and wanted to get to know us and live with us. We took her in at seventeen. She left at eighteen to go off on her own. She got to know us, especially her father, and the trauma of learning he was not the ogre he was made out to be all her life was too much for her I guess. She tried suicide once and overdosed on drugs several times. She knows we want to help her but she said in her own words, 'I love you, too, but I don't know how to handle it.'

"We feel so resentful because this child never got to know us and never felt our influence in the growing years. We truly believe, if she had, his daughter would not be on drugs and so confused and unable to cope with life. And his son would not have been so indifferent and lost to us forever. Maybe it all would have worked out the same anyway but we can't accept that. Children really do need their father." *(Tallahassee, Florida)*

How you cope with your man's paternal crisis is just that dramatic. How you adjust to his paternal bind and his fatherly bond will have significant impact on your life, your marriage, and all the children in your lives.

Now his paternity may be the main obstacle to your happiness together. That statement may remain true even after you and he marry. He can unmarry his wife, but never his offspring. His paternal instinct will persist, driving him into his own peculiar bind. You, too, will be driven along and asked to sacrifice. His paternity will always be a part of your marriage, regardless of the fate of his children. With them or without them he will need you to booster and bolster him. If you don't respect fatherhood immensely, if you don't think you can hack all his paternal tribulations, maybe you should think twice about going from mistress to wife.

If you are ready, committed, and think you are able, take heart.

"No matter what the heartache and pain, it's worth it. Through all our trials in this paternal mess in our life, we have grown closer and love each other more. It's not been easy. And it's not fair. But we're still here." *(Indianapolis, Indiana)*

Now as a mistress, you probably love the father in your married man. You sympathize with his plight. Keep all that love and empathy alive for his fatherhood. Because as my married man, now my husband, says, "Fathers are forever."

CHAPTER 10

Step-Parenting—On the Outside Looking In

A mistress is no newcomer to the feeling of being an outsider. Loving a married man means living on the outskirts of his life. A mistress lovingly builds her life around him and yet often has to watch him build his life around his family. You, as a mistress, may be his anchor, his life-support system, his breath of fresh air, but still you know that feeling of being the veteran outsider.

If you go from mistress to wife, will you penetrate the center of his life at last? Yes, in some ways. However, in one realm of his life you will still remain an outsider. As your married man's second wife you will probably enter into the world of step-parenting full-time or part-time. For most it will be part-time.

The days when you begin your new role as a step-parent will reintroduce you to that feeling of being the veteran outsider. As his children's stepmother you are not their real mother and yet you will assume parental responsibilities and parental situations. You are a parent and then again you are not. You are neither fish nor fowl. You will feel at times like someone watching a birthday party and not being let in on the fun.

Step-parenting is full of surprises. It is shocking, awesome, stimulating and rewarding. It is also gruesome in its way. None of us can really be prepared except for that recurring experience of being the outsider. And as we go along you will see why and how that feeling recurs.

Stepping out of the mistress shoes and into the stepmother

shoes will demand an adjustment. Until quite recently, divorce literature has dwelt on the plight of the children or the divorcing couple. The plight of the step-parent is only recently coming into the limelight. Add the mistress connection to that plight and the complexities intensify.

When you finally have that married man and you and he are planning your life together at last, does the picture include step-parenting expectations? Chances are you have met his children. Chances are you already have maternal feelings for them. After all, all during your affair his children have been discussed. You've heard about their childhood diseases, their ups and downs, and the secret conflicts your married man in particular felt. You knew how they were doing in school and who was having what problem, and you probably even gave advice. And so, you as a mistress got to know his children and care for them, even if you did all without ever spending time with them.

Now in the transition of your triangle, you will become their stepmother. You will be spending real time developing your own relationship with them and affecting their lives. How will all this work? Some of us have imagined scenarios of baking chocolate chip cookies with his children or solving their arithmetic homework, fantasies steeped with cooperation and love. Your expectations about his children are very important. Because keeping in step with your new step-parenting role will become a major part of that second marriage of your married man.

I have inserted a test here to prime you for your new role as a step-parent. The test is designed to bring into focus what you think being a step-parent is. Before we get into all the details, let's examine what you think lies ahead. As a step-parent you may be the new kid on the block, but I am determined to prepare you thoroughly. I can't protect you from that sense of still being the outsider looking in, but you won't be alone out there in no-man's-land.

You will be well versed in the new territory of the step-parent. From beginning the role to coping with its demands to surviving and triumphing, you will know what to expect. So let's get down to the first important lesson and see about your expectations. Are your notions about becoming a stepmother accurate? Take the following test and see.

Out-Of-Step Notions

How do you feel about becoming a stepmother? Chances are, if you do go from mistress to wife, you will inherit that role too. Have you given it any thought? Have you tried to imagine what you and he and the children will be like together? Have you given any thought to what kind of a stepmother you would be?

Many of us who are adventuring into the world of step-mothering have wondered about it. Very often we have come up with some notions of what it will be like. Do you have any preconceived notions? Take the following test and see. Then see what the preconceived notions can mean.

Directions: Read each of the statements below and answer either True or False. If necessary, use educated guesses. Then proceed to the scoring and the evaluation.

1. You will love his children naturally because they are a part of him.   _____

2. With some extra effort you can win their affections quickly.   _____

3. When they see how happy you make their Dad, they will be more inclined to accept you.   _____

4. You and your married man and his children will become one happy family in contrast to the unhappy family life his former bad marriage created.   _____

5. You will treat his children as if they were your own.   _____

6. His children will welcome the company of a new step-brother or stepsister.   _____

7. Your feelings for his ex-wife will not interfere with your feelings for his children.   _____

8. They are only children and so you will not mind making a few sacrifices for them.   _____

9. If you had raised them they would not have their faults. With your influence they will change.   _____

10. Showing you care will help them adjust.   _____

Scoring:
Each True answer is worth 10 points. Each False answer is worth 0 points. Give yourself points for each answer and total your score.

Evaluation:
The higher your score the more preconceived notions you have. And since preconceived notions really are expectations, what does your score say about your future?

0–30 Points: The Cautious Stepmother. If you scored in this low range, you are very alert to the conflicts involved in stepmothering. You have few out-of-step notions. You sense already that love, acceptance, and family harmony aren't going to happen overnight. Since you don't have romantic expectations, you are not going to be extremely disappointed from the start. You may not know what your role as a stepmother will be, but you do have an inkling of what it will not be. A cautious stance is a good one to take. You are as well prepared as can be for the adventure in stepmothering.

40–60 Points: The Confused Stepmother. If you scored in this middle range, your preconceived notions are very inconsistent. You have some notions and therefore some expectations. Review your True answers to see exactly where your notions are. It is in those areas where you will find your future difficulties and disappointments. Do you think loving, sacrificing, dealing with his children will come automatically to you? Do you think the response of his children to you will be predictable and easy to elicit? Do you think family cooperation will come as naturally as does the cooperation between you and your married man? The answers are all no. In your confusion lies your greatest strength. It will enable you to look for the conflicts which everyone will experience in the making of a new step-family. In your confusion you will see all sides as you adventure into stepmothering.

70–100 Points: The Misguided Stepmother. If you scored in this high range, watch out! You have too many of the preconceived notions that so many of us have. Each of these notions represents an expectation that is in all likelihood unrealistic. Having high hopes and trying too hard usually adds pressures and problems to stepmothering. Your misguided stance is directing you into danger. You may be devastated when things don't measure up to the love and harmony you are expecting to find. Stepmothering isn't going to be an adventure in automatic love and cohesion. So you had better prepare yourself and wipe away all those preconceived notions.

In Conclusion:

Reread all the statements and repeat "False" to yourself after each one. Ridding yourself of preconceived notions will help you. Sometimes for the new stepmother it's best to expect the worst and ask for nothing. Then you will appreciate the slow progress and the slow process that step-families involve. If I sound negative, don't be put off. Stepmothering can be a pleasant experience, but it takes time and understanding and patience. This chapter will help you understand the difference between out-of-step notions and keeping in step with your new role. Step-parenting is a new world and quite a different one. And very important if you go from mistress to second wife.

If you did poorly on the test, don't despair. The crucial point is that you are beginning to think about step-parenting and you. Now you will see it all firsthand through the experiences of some second wives. They will tell you now about the realities of child-rearing his children and what they have learned.

You are already one step ahead of Allyson. She learned the hard way that her preconceived notions worked against her. It took her a long time to comprehend the odd nature of a mistress's malaise that is really quite common.

Allyson's Honeymooning

Allyson started off her letter by telling me, "I found a copy of the book *A Stranger in A Strange Land* on an airplane. I had never read the book but that title haunted me for the longest time because that's exactly how I felt after marrying Johnny."

Allyson was a stewardess. When her apartment was burglarized, she called the police and they sent Johnny. That's how they met. One thing led to another as these stories often go, and soon Johnny and Allyson were married man/mistress and then husband/second wife. At the time of their marriage Allyson was twenty-nine and Johnny thirty-two. Allyson had never been married before, thus had never experienced marriage or parenthood.

Allyson had a lot of fantasies about their future. Actually that was odd. She knew traveling wasn't always like the pictures in the travel brochures. And Johnny didn't help dispel her fantasies, in spite of his seeing the dark side of things all the time on the police force. Allyson went along obsessed with bridal dreams, planning a fairy-tale wedding and a happily-ever-after marriage. It was going to be she and Johnny and his two boys and harmony.

"I bought books like *Feed Your Kids Right* and *838 Ways to Amuse a Child* and *Bride* magazine. I was going to be a supermom. I fixed up a room for the boys. I was so happy. Looking back I wasn't apprehensive about anything."

The weekend after their honeymoon, Allyson and Johnny settled down with the two boys, who would come foreverafter every weekend. Allyson shopped furiously and cooked elaborate, nutritious meals. Getting weekends off was no easy matter for either of them. They juggled their work schedules to get weekends off for the kids, which meant they had no time off alone together. They planned outings. And they found that they fought a lot.

"We fought over such stupid things. He would blow up about the carpet installation not being right. I would get hysterical at him for not putting oil in the car. We got so angry about little things, even though we weren't disappointed in each other. It was confusing and miserable.

"Married life was hectic. It seemed we never had a quiet night together. I was gone during the week nights and when I wasn't, Johnny had to go to bed early to get up at five. Weekends—forget it! The kids seemed to hate my cooking. Everybody had an incredibly short fuse. Nothing seemed to go as I thought it would."

Poor Allyson. Life wasn't measuring up to the fantasies she had about newlyweds and one big happy family. What Allyson failed to realize was that she wasn't your ordinary bride. She was an ex-mistress going into a second marriage that was a package deal.

The point of Allyson's letter and her story came at the bottom of the sixth page.

"After two years I realized something. I was angry at Johnny. We were never newlyweds. From the first weekend we had his children and all the hassles of a full-fledged family. We had no privacy and no time for romance. I fought with him 'cause I was mourning never feeling like a newlywed."

Allyson's mooning, or mourning, was a natural reaction. Reality shattered her fantasies. It all happened so fast she couldn't grasp, for two years, the real life of a second wife. She was a stranger in a strange land.

Allyson's story illuminates a few points about being a second wife. When you marry a package deal, a man with children, you become an instant family. There is no privacy, depending on the visitation schedule of the children, that is. Allyson was unprepared for the invasion of children into her life, with all the responsibilities and chaos. Her expectations were unrealistic. Her attempts at being a supermom were unappreciated. All she did was add to her frustration level. Hence the tension.

The transition from mistress to second wife is not like going from fiancée to wife. The conflicts, the pressures, the demands are different. Allyson epitomized the shock and a hidden malaise that are characteristic for the second wife. For a closer look at the conflicts in progress, let's look into the life of Cathy.

Color Me Eggshell

Cathy described her affair this way: "I was Larry's listening post. His first marriage went down the tubes before he met me. By the time we went into our marriage, we both wanted it to work desperately."

Cathy had been married once too and had a child, hence her strong desire to make the second time work. Larry's ex-wife finally gave him custody, which is another story in itself. What that meant is that with Cathy's one and Larry's five, they had a blended family of six children ranging in age from four to seventeen.

Cathy was a free-lance interior designer. Larry was a successful businessman. They lived in South Carolina. Both Cathy and Larry were attuned to all the conflicts that they all would begin to feel.

"The first year every time I designed a room for someone, the color scheme was eggshell. Now I know why. I walked on eggshells. So I dreamed about eggshell walls. You see, I knew that Larry's kids would have a hard time adjusting to me and their new situation. After visits with their Mom they returned with a loyalty conflict you could cut with a knife. I guess they felt being nice to me was in some way disloyal to their own mother. I tried to give them lots of space. Being a decorator helped me a lot. I knew the importance of space and time. We all needed it as we tried to muddle through our new experience."

Things ran smoothly, according to Cathy, only because everyone was so polite and careful. She tried not to over-mother Larry's children. He tried not to interfere in Cathy's raising her child. The children's visits with their other parent were adhered to religiously. Holidays were carefully measured and planned so that no one would feel pressured into anything.

"Discipline was a real hard one for me to handle. I didn't want to be accused of playing favorites. I didn't want to yell and risk their disapproval. It was a slow road just being accepted. I lived in fear of their telling me things like 'I don't have to listen to you, you're not my mother!' Larry and I had discipline conferences on a regular basis behind closed doors. We were all confused about what we were to each other and what we were supposed to be."

Cathy listed a million little problems that make for uncomfortable moments. Like what Larry's children should call her parents. They weren't biological grandchildren, but they couldn't call her parents "step-grandpa" could they? They shouldn't call her mother. Who should they have attend parents' night at school? Who gave good-night kisses to whom? Cathy was exactly right when she said to "color me eggshell."

Step-parenting is often one long list of confusions. Roles are unclear. How much love should a step-parent show? How much discipline should a step-parent give? Too much affection can only add to the stepchild's loyalty conflicts. Too little discipline can only make situations harder to handle. Steadfast rules are difficult to establish from step-family to step-family. Each mix is made up of different individuals with differing needs and conflicts. Cathy's case can't clarify the rules for step-parents. The only rule is to expect confusion and conflicts.

From Cathy's case one can see the value of caution. Blended families need space and time. You as a second wife and stepmother should give yourself the sense of the future. In time all the confusion will work itself out. You and your stepchildren will find a way of relating to each other, and, as time goes on, of liking each other—as we'll see in a few pages. Stepping on eggshells can be a good way to approach the entire experience of step-parenting his children.

A step-parent is not a parent. A stepmother must learn to adjust and act outside of the usual parental norm. You are outside the nuclear family in your role. It takes practice to learn how to blend your role as an outsider and your role inside the new blended family. Living outside these one-big-happy-family fantasies is requisite.

Betsy, the next second wife we are going to meet, felt more like a leper than a mere outsider. Her tale points up the worst aspects of step-parenting. Unfortunately her story combines many of these pitfalls.

Betsy—The Invisible Maid

"At the time I became involved with Stan, my present husband, I was a Sunday school teacher and organist for my church. I was and still am a Christian woman. I was one of those women who said it could never happen to me. I had a good husband but still something was missing in my marriage for both of us. I became involved with Stan after knowing him for eight years as a dear friend's husband. To make a long and painful story short, we both divorced and are now married."

So far Betsy's tale isn't all that unusual.

"I found what I was looking for in a man and a marriage, but I also found misery with Stan's three daughters. His ex couldn't accept any of the blame for their marriage ending, so I got all the blame from everyone. Stan's three daughters are spending the summer with us and their hostility is everywhere."

Betsy went on to tell me this has been the worst summer in all her forty-one years. She is cooking three meals a day, doing daily laundry loads, ironing all the clothes, sewing, shopping, cleaning, making beds, etc. Never having had children of her own, this amount of housework is new to her.

"It's not even the endless chores, they are almost a kind of refuge. It's that I get no thank yous, no appreciation. No one even talks to me unless I ask a question. Stan's youngest loathes me. I can't even touch her. If I do by mistake—say we rub shoulders in the car or I fix her collar—she touches her shoulder or collar and smells her fingers. It's as if I'm diseased to a point that I have a foul odor she's sniffing for. The hostility escalates, the chores pile up. I feel like an invisible maid."

Writing all this out was wonderful therapy for Betsy. She admitted to me that she hated Stan's daughters. She called them "spoiled, ungrateful little tarts." She said that she is glad she didn't have children if this is what it's like.

"I give out 100 percent and get nothing back. Not even a kind word. I look out the window and see Stan hugging one of them and I resent it. I do all the hard work and he gets all the goodies. They are going out and having all the good times all summer and I'm excluded even if I'm along."

Betsy was upset with herself for being this way and that made her feel worse.

"I am angry and hurt and I can't stand living with these girls. Then I feel like a child, because they're only children and I'm supposed to behave like an adult. So I keep all this bottled up till I'm ready to explode."

It was obvious to me that Betsy was having second thoughts about being a second wife. At this point, if she had to do it over, she wouldn't. Who would sentence themselves to become an invisible maid in a hostile household?!

Betsy's misery stems from compounded problems. She has a right to her feelings of anger. Step-parenting, even part-time, demands a great deal of work; chores, planning, organization, and compromising. It means bearing the brunt of the stepchild's bruises from the divorce. Add the mistress connection and all those bruises are compounded. There's hostility, subtle or open. There's jealousy. If you make their dad happy sometimes that can make a child more jealous and insecure. There's the blame that you are given as the homewrecker or the dad-stealer. There's the guilt you take on, justified or not. Step-parenting propels you into emotionally draining head trips. The commitment looks endless as the permanence of his children in your life hits home. It all seems to be a long sentence of eternal messes. So during the initiation period, expect some depression. Know that these trials and tribulations are going to have a significant impact on your happiness and your life.

Every stepmother wants to be a supermom. That's normal. Most stepmothers find that they can't be a supermom. That's normal too. Yet when the second wife finds she can't face things all smiles and maternal warmth, she goes through a failure complex that shakes her to primal depths. I call this *The Maternal Doubt Syndrome*.

The Maternal Doubt Syndrome begins when you figuratively look in the mirror and see a grown woman welling up with enmity over the machinations of little divorce-scarred children. You see yourself, supposedly the adult, behaving like a petty, jealous, ill-tempered child. It is a diminishing image of yourself! It fills you with feelings of maternal inadequacy and failure, and unleashes grave doubts about your capacity to mother. Thoughts like "If I can't handle his children, maybe I am not cut out for parenthood" reverberate. You find yourself thinking that "they are only children and his children, and if I can't love them, what is wrong with me?" And so you begin to cast yourself as unfit as a mother. You begin to think you have no maternal potential or capacity because here, where your maternal instinct should rise up, it seems lacking. The Maternal Doubt Syndrome hits women who have no children the hardest. Second wives with children from prior marriages don't find this one so debilitating.

Watch out for and don't become self-victimized by the Maternal Doubt Syndrome. First of all, even though they are children, their rejection can scar you. Even though they are children their demands take their toll unless you are 100 percent martyr. They are not your own flesh and blood, so don't expect yourself to respond instantaneously as if you are their natural mother. You will not be able to treat them as your own right off, if ever. Many mistresses have the misguided view that love will spring up naturally and immediately between themselves and his children. That is inaccurate and oversimplistic. A bond will come but it will take years. Remember you are a stepmother not a mother. You are an outsider trying to cement yourself into his nuclear family. Failings are not yours. When you react with anger, jealousy, etc., it is not a sure sign of your inadequacy, or unfitness. It is a reaction to the difficulties of stepmothering. Commend yourself for trying, for hanging in there and sacrificing.

You must not lose sight of the motivation. You are doing this for your man, not for the kids. Look to him for the thank-you part. Realize that in time the stepmother/stepchild role can even have a peculiar advantage. The next profile will show you the beginnings of what I mean.

First Sign of Spring

Sheila went from mistress to wife expecting the worst. She had good reason.

"Jim had one of those disaster-bound marriages. It was on and off long before me. But when his wife found out about us, then everything was my fault. She tried to make Jim stay married, but he was happy for the first time in his life with me. So she swore he'd pay . . . and he did."

Sheila told me all about the contested divorce, the court battles, the legal fees, the broken court orders regarding visitation, etc. In addition to all that, for two years Jim's children had been told that Sheila was the cause of Daddy leaving. Sheila had good cause for worry when it came to thinking about stepmothering.

A close friend of hers had cautioned her. She'd heard about the difficulties of step-parenting even when there was no triangle before the divorce. She was aware of the usual pitfalls.

"I knew I wasn't going to try to mother them. They needed their father during the little time allotted to them, not me. So I held back and made myself scarce during those first few weekends after Jim and I were married and the court finally allowed us to have the children at our new house. I decided to approach step-parenting as an experiment. I would look at their behavior as if we were a textbook case, look for the usual conflicts, outbursts, and hostility. I was guarded. I was going to coat myself with a thick skin."

Expecting the worst, Sheila was totally unprepared for what followed in less than a year's time. Jim had two girls, ages five and seven, and one son, age nine. Some weekends Jim planned outings for all of them and sometimes Jim would take only his son on errands and leave the girls with Sheila. The girls told Sheila, "My Mom doesn't like you." Yet, they all delighted in playing beauty parlor. In their way they were making a place in their life for Sheila despite their mother's attitude. If Sheila wasn't attending an outing, they pleaded for her to change her mind.

"It got to be weird for me. The two little girls began following me around all weekend into the kitchen, the laundry room, the supermarket. Still they wouldn't kiss me good-bye or good-night or offer me candy like they did their dad. It was like they had this private taboo system about our relationship. Then one afternoon, they were on the run with their grandparents and stopped in for a moment. They were overflowing with stories and rushing out the door. They each hugged and kissed Dad and then lo and behold they reached out to me. Arms outstretched, lips puckered, eyes closed, as if they did this daily. I swallowed my shock and kissed them nonchalantly. It was our first kiss. Jim almost went through the floor. I was choked up. I had never expected this moment or the emotion it would inspire in my heart. It was a moment I will never forget. It erased so much of the hassles and the conflicts instantaneously."

Sheila and her stepchildren had been through several rounds of seasons. She had felt the coldness of them along with winter's chill. She had seen the hard times heat up like the summer days. She had witnessed changing emotions along with the leaves changing color in autumn. And now with those first kisses she had seen the first sign of spring.

Sheila's touching moment brings us to the beginning of that bond that establishes itself between stepmother and stepchild. Your step-relationship will be outside the norm, as family affairs go. Yet that gives an advantage. You and your stepchildren can be friends, just people. You are not mother/daughter or mother/son. Sometimes your relationship benefits from that. Not being the natural parent places you outside the usual parent/child struggles. Rebellion or identity crises aren't aimed at step-parents usually. Your stepchildren may not be afraid of you, in awe of you, as they are toward natural parents. No blood tie can actually set the pace and tenor for a friendship that is different and special.

If you go from mistress to wife, count on the stepchildren making a place in your new married life. What kind of place? That is as individual as you and those children. However, there are certain generalities, as I have tried to establish.

It's ironic really. When you are a mistress at times you feel like excess baggage. You are outside his daily life. You fear that, in a bind, you, the extra piece of luggage, will be the first to go. Yet once you step out of the mistress role and become his second wife, he is the one who conjures up metaphors of excess baggage. Unlike a newlywed to a never-married man, you as a second-wife-newlywed, take on his excess baggage in the person of his children. Some second wives find this extra load odious. Others find it an eventual blessing. On the spectrum from one extreme to the other, where will your feelings wind up? Will you echo some of these comments?

"It is very hard the second time around, under these circumstances. The children blame me for everything that has happened and because they don't have Daddy at home anymore. I love my husband very much, but it is hard trying to cope with the problems of being a second wife and stepmother. It is the pure bliss that we experience when everything is settled down that keeps me going." *(Lyons, New York)*

"Before getting married to my married man I had presentiments—they were *his* kids and I liked them. After getting married I had post-sentiments—suddenly they were *her* kids full of her faults and I couldn't stand them." *(Portland, Oregon)*

"As a mistress I used to scream at him about how I didn't want to be a martyr for his kids while he stayed married. Now as a second wife I am a real martyr for his kids. It's not a manner of speech. I am actively sacrificing for their welfare in a thousand ways." *(Eastlake, Ohio)*

"He keeps telling me to hold on every weekend we spend with his kids. He says that they're getting older all the time. I have one comment for him, we're getting older too." *(Seattle, Washington)*

"His kids made me feel like a dirty object. I had no name. I was referred to as 'her.' After nine months they began calling me Sandy. After two years they actually liked talking to me. And now, you know, I really look forward to their visits! I thought it would never happen." *(Belmont, California)*

As you can see it is a long hard road to becoming comfortable with his children. Being on the outside of that family and trying to find a place is no easy task. You must really give it all thought. You must try and find out if you have what it takes, if you think your married man and his love justifies the struggle. Are you the kind of person that can stick out all the trials until you see the first signs of spring?

Some mistresses who became second wives have only good things to say about their step-experiences. Some of them were just plain lucky. Some of them coped well with the hard times and quickly forgot them when the rewards started rolling in.

"My married man and I were afraid of divorce, but we risked everything and went for it. Now I see that none of the changes have hurt us permanently. If anything, his business is more prosperous. No one, and this is a small town, has made any rude comments to either of us. In fact, I have received nothing but praise and good words from people saying how wonderful I was to take on his seven children and what a wonderful job I am doing. We have had the kids for four years now and have had nothing but joy with them. Just because a mother gives birth does not make her a good mother. I never had any children and I can give *my* children more than any mother could. And now they have a father who's happy too. I thank God for my darling and our happy family." *(Olympia, Washington)*

"It's been over two years now since we've been married. We have a great life together, but we still have our problems, mostly his ex-wife. His son loves me more, more than anyone, including his father and I think that must hurt my man. But I'm his son's idol, because I spend every single minute of my time caring about him when he's with us. My man and his ex-wife are too distracted and not very good parents at this point. I feel they don't know how to raise a child. They don't know how to treat their son, to realize he is a person. Maybe it's just that he and I are friends and can have fun that way. But anyway the three of us have an excellent relationship." *(San Jose, California)*

"Our marriage is good and our bonds grow stronger every day. I mean the love between me and my husband and the love between me and my stepchildren. We've stuck by our stepchildren and hung in for five years trying to keep up contact no matter how hard their mother made things for us. Now it's paid off. They're all big now. Recently my husband got a job offer which meant moving to another state. It took a lot of love for those seven kids to say, 'Dad, do it.' They said, 'It's time you did something for yourself and your wife.' They are truly great kids! We've all never been closer than now. We get letters and phone calls all the time. The oldest and his wife are making plans to visit and show us my first step-grandchild. I wonder, are my husband and I lucky people? We think we are. We have fought hard for the love and admiration of these kids. It's really paid off for us. Just knowing how much they care is a small price to get, considering the hell we've gone through together. But it's worth it. I'd do it again and so would he." *(Athens, Georgia)*

Not every second wife can say that. In fact two-thirds of second marriage failures have been caused by the stresses of rearing stepchildren. That may seem a high figure but remember that statistic refers to all second marriages, not just mistress/married man marriages. However, because of your mistress history, you bring added pressures to your odds, as you have seen throughout the pages of this book. It's not that I'm trying to scare you or to depress you, it's that I want you to be sure of yourself. As a mistress you've gone through enough unhappiness. I don't want you going from the frying pan into the fire. And step-parenting can burn some irreparably. Your love can go up in smoke and your dreams and fantasies can be reduced to burning embers.

I hope now you have developed an awareness for the demands of step-parenting. You can start assessing his kids and anticipating how they will react to you. There are no steadfast rules. Teenagers can be terrible but infants can be hard to handle too. You have to decide how you will cope. More importantly you have to decide if you are willing to cope. If your married man is worth it, if you and he are meant for each other, then welcome this challenge.

I've given you a heavy dose of the negatives to test you. And as you've seen, the negatives tend to come in the beginning of your new role as step-parent. If these negatives didn't change your mind about a second marriage, that's a good sign.

The positives can far outweigh your initiation trials. Your stepchildren can become friends for life. And even if your step-relationship never reaches perfection, your new husband will love you even more for trying. He will see a new dimension to you and, in all likelihood, commend you for it.

As a mistress you are an outsider. That is good experience in an ironic way. You are used to looking in at his life. Now look in at what lies ahead for you as a stepmother. Take consolation in the fact that being an outsider has coated you with a sticktuitiveness. That friendship insurance has given you an advantage as a parent. Being an outsider is a feeling that may be with you for a long time, but there are worse feelings. Once you are married to your married man you won't be an outsider where he is concerned and that's what counts!

Take advantage of your status as an outsider. Put it to good use before you get inside your marriage with that married man. You are marrying into a family and make sure you are cut out for that long road to a cohesive step-family. At first you may feel exiled from the birthday party going on, but in time you and your new step-family will hold parties and celebrations that make it all worthwhile.

CHAPTER 11

Maternity—To Be or Not To Be?

Married men get you in the womb! Time and again, mistresses have told me that not only did their married man sabotage their heart, monopolize their mind, but he kindled a primal urge to bear his child. Affairs of the heart are captivating. Fantasies of the mind are immobilizing. However, once the maternal stirrings begin, no other conflict is so overwhelming.

The Maternal Seed

Carol's letter unfolds the beginnings of the maternal crisis for the mistress.

"I am single, never married, although I have been in a couple of cohabitation situations. Until I got involved with my married man, I was convinced that marriage and children were not my goals. I think deep down inside I knew that there would be a man around and perhaps I'd marry him, but I was pretty sure that children were not for me. Now I'm not so sure. Now I want desperately to have his baby. Now it's all a jumble."

What was responsible for Carol's change of heart, change of mind, and, most importantly, her change in the womb? Being an introspective soul by nature, Carol reviewed the possible reasons behind her new maternal awakening.

"Perhaps this shift in goals is the result of my being less than six months away from my thirtieth birthday and my growing awareness that time is getting away from me. The day is not far off when I will realize that time itself has decided the maternal matter for me.

"Perhaps I'm looking for a root system. I am a recent transplant to New York City from Syracuse, where I grew up and went to college. As I type this, I realize I've been here nearly two years and I still feel like a newcomer. Maybe I'm trying to put down roots for the future.

"Or is it that this is the real thing? Am I really in love with the right man and is my desire to have his child the natural outgrowth of that love? I wish I could know for sure.

"I was a lifelong atheist. God to me seems like some of the men I've known; they want you to surrender your life to them in return for the promise that they will provide! And they or he asks you to be a good little girl in exchange for the promise of eternal whatever in some hereafter. I just couldn't stand the sexism, the hypocrisy and the self-aggrandizement of religions. But suddenly, that feeling too is a jumble. Now I feel a bit more agnostic. If there is a god, maybe it is he or she that can help."

Carol's self-inquisition covered the usual forces in maternal questions: age, human nature, love, immortality, and security. However, none of her explorations gave her definite answers. From where does the maternal seed come and when is it right to sow it?

I don't have the exact answer for Carol either; only she does ultimately. However, the purpose of this chapter is to delve into the issue of motherhood and what it means for you.

Just like Carol, many women are introduced to maternal inklings as part of their mistressing experience. Myself included. I never thought much about having children until I saw the possibilities mirrored in my married man's eyes. Mistressing can catapult a woman into a world whirling with new traumas and emotions. The maternal decision, and the indecision that can surround it, can be the biggest trauma of all.

To be a mother or not to be a mother . . . that is the question. The question is awesome and profound. It touches upon the issues of humanity, femininity, and immortality. Maternity is said to be the essence and fulfillment of womanhood.

Years ago, motherhood wasn't an intellectual issue. No one thought about having children; they just happened. However, today that is not the case for thousands of women. To be or not to be is a question that quizzes many of us emotionally and intellectually. While you are still a mistress, maternity is postponed until the triangle is sorted out. However, what happens when you go from mistress to wife?

To be a mother or not to be a mother plagues the second wife who, heretofore, was childless. It also plagues the second wife who has children already, because she has not mothered that married man's child.

Will you, fueled by his love, go from mistress to mother? Will you find the decision easy to make? I have found that many second wives have great difficulty with the maternal crisis. The Triangle Transition seems to complicate an already complicated issue for the modern woman.

Going from mistress to wife, not only will you have conflicts regarding career and age. In addition to standard maternal doubts, you will have a host of other conflicts. In all likelihood your mistress marriage will interfere with the usual progression of marriage-to-maternity. In this chapter we are going to explore those potential conflicts. Will his paternity overshadow your own maternity? Will stepmothering his children be too much or will it be enough to satiate the maternal drive? Can you literally afford maternity with the financial strains of a package deal? Can you afford not to mother? Are your married man's aspirations in line with your own concerning parenting anew? And is there a right time to answer the maternal question? Time itself is one of the most crucial elements in the maternal question.

In a previous chapter we delved into your man's paternal passage and the trauma that is often experienced. I stressed the need for every second wife to be sensitive to paternal crises. But can you be too sensitive? Can oversensitivity to your man's parental dilemma create a new dilemma for you? The answer is yes. Paternity has a way of monopolizing many a mistress marriage.

Horror-scope

Tanya began by telling me a little about herself.

"My occupation is a little hard to explain. I'm an enthusiastic craftsperson, I write, and I do horoscopes. I am fascinated by assassinations and dictators. I have a degree in journalism and I went to Katharine Gibbs, which as you can see from my typing was not a total success.

"When I met Jeffrey, I had no idea he was married. You see, I don't believe in doing my own horoscope. After he told me, I didn't care at first. I resented the way some men expect you to drop everything and change your schedule for them. I thought a married man wouldn't make those demands. Little did I know then!"

Tanya learned what many mistresses do. That is that their whole life soon revolves around the married man. Not only her schedule, but her dreams, her emotional moods, and everything soon was determined by Jeffrey.

"Jeffrey divorced after a year. He said he and his wife were like two mismatched roommates who woke up to find that they had nothing in common. Except, of course, a son. That son became the star in our own nightmare. It began when his ex-wife disappeared with the child. Jeff was anguish personified. He launched a custody battle. He hired a detective. We weren't wealthy, so you can imagine the strain. Somewhere along the way we were married. But nothing in our lives compared to the headlines of his fatherly suffering."

A few years flipped by. The legal system has the pace of a turtle and a heart of stone. The years seemed slow because they were hard and because nothing happened to change Jeff's situation.

"Now I was thirty-two and Jeff was thirty-nine. Despite all his trials and efforts, he never found out his ex-wife's location. I wanted to have a child of our own and I knew that my time was running out. He was so preoccupied and torn about the entire subject of children that he didn't want another one. He told me he felt it was unfair to the son he lost.

"I was now getting progressively crazy about it. I went to have my tarot cards read almost daily, hoping for some revelation. As for horoscopes, I knew ours. We had been living a horror-scope for years. It was time to change the signs.

"Jeffrey and I had it out. He said a new child would be like salt in a wound, only a constant reminder of his pain. I told him he was being unfair to us both. He was playing right into the hands of his ex-wife's malicious desires. He was asking me to sacrifice my maternity for his paternal obsessions. That was illogical and too much to ask. Of course another child wouldn't be a replacement, but my maternal desire was unique and had nothing to do with our past or our hardships."

As a postscript, Jeffrey and Tanya had a daughter, an Aquarius. It was a new era for them. It didn't eliminate Jeff's paternal loss, but it did add a positive dimension to his fatherhood.

"We named her Joy, that says it all. And to think I almost postponed away having a baby because we were so trapped in pain. We should have had her three years ago. In time I hope Jeffrey finds his son. In the meantime, though, Joy at least distracts him and we both deserved a reprieve from our horror-scope."

The paternal anguish that many a divorced father is subjected to can monopolize his life for years and even decades. He can lose a child and become heartbroken. His paternal feelings dry up as a self-defense mechanism. Or he can be subjected to so much difficulty in the visiting arrangements that bitterness and downright frustration can become the theme of his life.

The second wife, as his companion, gets as preoccupied as he does with this paternal passage. His paternity, living it out or living through the court battles, can take preference over everything. A divorced man who suffers the loss of his children goes into a mourning period. For some it can be a lifetime. And as his paternity squirms, writhes, gasps for breath, and dies, maternity seems an inappropriate topic. The second wife's maternal hopes are martyred to the memory of his lost or out-of-reach children.

"My husband sees his sons, although infrequently. I think that can be even worse sometimes. He sees all their faults inbred by too much mother and he has no influence to change them. He feels their lack of attachment to him. He suffers every time they forget his birthday or refuse to come out when he calls them. This has soured him on fathering. When I bring up a child of our own, he goes into a tantrum. His children have ruined his life, his peace of mind, and his chance for happiness. The thought of setting himself up again for more of that is anathema. But I just don't feel that way at all. It's either his misery or my fulfillment. What a choice!" *(Celina, Ohio)*

Every second wife has to make some kind of choice. Each mistress marriage is different. Each paternal crisis is unique. Some fathers are scarred more than others. Some men are more resilient. But in every case, a second wife must be sensitive to her maternal desires as well as being sensitive to his paternal passage. It is a grave mistake to spend a lifetime obsessed with his paternity, especially when it brings only anxiety. You must learn when to accept life's injustices and move ahead. The issue of parenting is a prime example.

If your new husband is dead set against parenting anew, then the choice is excruciating. Someone is going to have to compromise. But his paternal aspirations should be explored and respected before the wedding day.

If your new husband is totally preoccupied with his loss and yet designed to father well, then it might help if you try hard to make him look at the future rather than only the past. He has a lifetime to father the children he already has and any new ones. Times will perhaps not always be so rough. The children will not always be small. An ex-wife will not be able to ex-communicate Dad from the curiosity of his children forever. Someday he will have an opportunity to explain things to his children. Where there's a will, there's a way.

The Triangle Transition has a way of locking us into immediate episodes. Its traumas and emotions are so captivating that we forget all of these problems will pass in time. A sense of the future is crucial. Valuing time is crucial. Don't allow his paternity to overshadow the potential joy of a new child of your mutual making.

The fact that he has children gives paternity a significant bearing on your maternal future. It also works in a different way upon you. Stepmothering has a complicated effect upon many second wives. Stepmothering is a mutation of maternity. For some second wives it can be a tease. For others it can be a turnoff. And for some it can be a seesaw, spurring them toward maternity one minute and chasing them away the next. That's what it was like for Penny.

T-Shirt Telepathy

In the sixties, people unveiled their values and their desires on placards. In the seventies, the screening material became custom T-shirts. The slogans printed on T-shirts were too numerous to count, too intimate for some, and yet necessary for thousands.

T-shirts became central to Penny for a number of reasons.

First, they were the business of Penny's married man, now her husband. They provided the coup de grace and the rendezvous, according to Penny.

"Larry owns a small business producing custom-ordered T-shirts. I am the whole staff. That's how we became lovers. It was a hectic Saturday and I was selling our wares at a storefront. Children were running around, parents were screaming, the temperature was in the high nineties, and I had counted to at least ten thousand. Just as I was about to burst, Larry breezed in with some stock, charmed all the customers and their brats, took some money, and reappeared with lunch along with a huge bucket of beer for us. Between his charm, his thoughtfulness, and his boy scout act, I fell like a rock for him.

"His being married didn't prove to be a lasting obstacle. His wife was always out of town. He told me he was impossible to live with in her presence. I think they were doing these things to each other in an escalating cycle to aggravate one another. I was only another symptom of their impending divorce."

Up to this point you may not see any problems in this tale. Neither did Penny at first.

"Larry had two teenage sons. He worked out joint custody. I don't even know if I can explain all the changes this has put me through. All I can say is it has inspired a whole new line of T-shirts. One day I wear a tee saying 'Baby . . . never' because his kids drive me nuts sometimes. The next week I wear one saying 'Baby . . . trying.' I've designed T-shirts saying, 'Stepmother . . . Help!'

The source of Penny's creativity is also the source of an impending crisis about mothering. Stepmothering is exposing her to fears, to strong maternal inclinations, and to loving and hating Larry's children all in the same week. His children are whetting her appetite to reproduce. Yet almost simultaneously they are signaling doubts about the wisdom of another child.

"Originally Larry wasn't planning on any more children. It's not that he was firmly opposed; he just didn't think I was so inclined. I wasn't, but now it's different. He tells me parenthood is no rose garden. I see that, but you can't have the roses without the thorns. He says it's my choice, he'll go either way. I can't find the confidence to decide. Where am I now? Just read the shirt I'm wearing, but every day my mind and my shirt changes. Meantime I fill my nights with TV movies and Stelladoros to distract me."

The window to Penny's soul is not her eyes, but the message on the T-shirt. Parenthood is a difficult choice. For a stepparent it becomes more difficult as a choice. Stepmothers find his children a tease, an inspiration, and a turnoff.

"Some moments I see how close my stepdaughter and I are getting and I get all emotional. It makes me think how wonderful having my own daughter would be. So I'm saving every cent of my salary so I can afford to stay home in a year or so and have that baby." *(Springfield, Missouri)*

"I've never had children of my own. I'm thirty-four and I must decide once and for all. Each time I get close to retiring my birth control pills I have a bad weekend with my step-kids and I think NO WAY! Children can be so demanding, trying, and monopolizing. Are all children like that? Or is it different when they are yours? Some people say yes and others say no, and I don't know what to think anymore!" *(Manhattan Beach, California)*

Fortunately, step-parenting isn't seen as a double-edged sword by everyone. For some second wives having stepchildren is the best of both worlds maternally speaking.

Setting Her Pace

Beverly was in her twelfth year of teaching elementary school, third grade to be exact. She was in her second marriage, which was a result of her first affair. Her former married man is now her husband. Beverly is in her third year of running. She found she was a natural at running. She is in her first experience with parenthood. Her first marriage was childless. Her second has part-time stepchildren, a boy thirteen and a girl eleven.

"I've never been happier than I am now. I look forward to every day, every year, because my life couldn't be happier or fuller. My job was beginning to bore me when I found running. It gave me a focus for my energy and a new way to find goals. Adam gave love and marriage a whole new meaning for me. And best of all his children have enriched my life enormously."

Sometimes teaching puts teachers off about having a family of their own. When children are your business, sometimes that's enough for one life. And yet for many teachers, men and women, who opt for childlessness, sometimes a faint doubt or regret lingers about that decision. Beverly didn't have that problem.

"I knew I didn't want to be a full-time mother. My life was full of work, and children, and activities. But I had this tinge of indecision. Then I became a step-parent. That solved all my maternal doubts. I loved mothering this way. It's part-time. I have the pleasure of my stepchildren's company sometimes and I have my own life too. I'm part of rearing them and yet I don't have the entire burden of being responsible for them all the time. I see our friendships growing and I see my influences and I'm relieved to get rid of them on Sunday nights. I can't think of a better arrangement!"

Beverly is a lucky woman. But it is not all a matter of luck. Beverly knows her goals and her limits, when she's running and when she's running her life and her new family. Every now and then I see Beverly out running with her stepson. The two of them seem so comfortable with each other, so at ease as they jog past. It's wonderful to see a second wife setting her own pace and winning all across the board!

The point of this profile is that step-parenting can be enough for some second wives. It is an opportunity to participate in parenting, an opportunity that some find satiating. Stepchildren can bring joy as well as conflicts. They can make some lives full enough so that childlessness isn't a barren decision. For a woman like Beverly, her stepchildren are her children. She will never feel she is childless. Stepchildren aren't really your "own," but for some people that is advantageous. It depends upon your maternal ideas, your temperament, and your own situation.

I have found that the step-parenting experience is one of the most diversified experiences of living. It is diversifying in its impact upon each and every couple. It is diversifying in the number of ways it is reported. The reactions of step-parents are varied. The combinations of step-parents and the blended families they head are the most diversified of all. Blended families are confusing. Being a member and a potential mother again can be most confusing. In the next story you will get the picture. That is if you can follow the plot.

Rocking the Boat

Nowadays, with divorce and remarriage, families grow in arithmetic progressions. What was once a simple family tree can overnight become an unfathomable family of strangers. The family of strangers is called the blended family. Here is how one was formed.

Andrea was an unhappily married woman who became a happy mistress to Dave. Andrea divorced her husband and retained custody of their two sons. Dave divorced his wife and married Andrea. Dave had two daughters that remained in his ex-wife's household. After the honeymoon Andrea was a stepmother and Dave was a stepfather. In time their ex-spouses both remarried. So each set of children had four sets of parents. See the confusion? Let's concentrate on Andrea and Dave and their two full-time sons and their two part-time daughters.

"Blended families are so hard on everybody. My two sons miss their real father even though they see him regularly. They had a real conflict getting used to Dave being around the house and to being with their Mom. Poor Dave, though, his daughters seem to prefer my company. Even though I'm a stepmother they really have more in common with me. We shop, I let them cook. I am trying hard to help them develop a close rapport with their Dad but it's a slow process. I think they blame him for the divorce."

This blended family sounds harrowing, which it is. However, it is not so different from other blended families. Each blended family is a blend of conflicts and adjustments. A blend of new relationships and old loyalties. But now there is a new conflict brewing in the house!

"I can't get the thought out of my mind of having Dave's baby. I know that it's absolutely crazy, but still I want his baby. I love my sons and Dave is getting along better with them as they let their guard down. And I'm growing to love my new part-time stepdaughters. But still I want a child of ours. I dream about the smell of a new infant. I fantasize about what our baby would look like and be like. I'm not too old for a new child. I know Dave feels this too. But we are not the problem. It's the kids. My sons might be driven to mutiny. Dave's daughters might get jealous and never want to come to us. Would Dave and I play favorites with ours? We're so conscious of all the complications of raising all these blended children, we have become insecure as parents. Should we parent again? My friends tell me not to rock the boat, but this family of ours is always in a state of hurricane anyway."

Andrea and Dave did a lot of worrying and weighing and then they got her pregnant. Things would never be dull around that house! That is the only certainty they could guarantee.

"I am feeling better all the time. I used to feel guilty about my family problems. If only I'd met Dave years ago, our situations would be different. I didn't. So what! What's done is done. Our family is wild, but then we are not the only blended family in America. I can't change the past, but I can't let the past stop me from having a future that is all we want it to be. I won't wallow in what might have been. That's what finally decided the issue. We wanted another child and so we will have it. The baby will be one solution to regrets. Who'll have time to regret or reason."

I'm very happy for Andrea and Dave. In time I hope all the children will be too. They will be because children are resilient. For some, life is smooth sailing. For others, it's always a rocking boat.

A second wife who is a mother and a stepmother, too, can find maternal inclination unbelievably complicated. If she has her own and his from another marriage, how can she justify wanting another child? It's easy to understand when you are a woman in love. It may be simple to want the new baby, but hard to inflict your choice on the rest of your family.

Basically a new child can stimulate jealousies among siblings. The child can unleash guilts and loyalty conflicts for everyone too. But is fear of the possible conflicts good reason to pass on a child that you desperately want? Andrea and Dave thought not and I have to agree. But it is not an easy decision. In this instance, not only step-parenting and parenting, but the blended family also made the *to mother or not to mother* question more complex.

Each second wife has to face the choice, whether she is childless or a step-parent or a parent from a previous marriage. To mother or not to mother is always a weighty question. Just how weighty, is a relative issue. We have surveyed the conflicts basically from an emotional standpoint. Now let's take the question literally: Can you afford to mother?

Finance seems so mundane an issue compared to the profound territory of procreation. However, it has its place and a very important place indeed! I am not going to labor the point of whether or not you and your husband can afford a child. But I am going to file a directive that you give it serious thought. His past can be expensive. Your income may be a necessity to your mutual lifestyle. Will a child strain the finances and just how much? Can you afford to give up your job to mother? Can you make adjustments? Can you afford to give your child enough of what any child deserves?

The main object of these financial questions is not to deter your maternity per se. If you want a baby, then plan for it. Family planning should be part of everyone's education. There are ways to change your life and prepare yourself so that maternity can fit into your life. If necessary, you should reread the earlier chapter dedicated to finance. Then incorporate your parenthood plans into the budget.

In these tenuous financial times, each new generation is not going to automatically grow up in an upwardly mobile fashion. As a culture it seems our progression of affluence is slowing down. Does that foreshadow gloom? Not necessarily. But it does mean that we must assess our values and our attitudes toward living. A second wife inherits usually a package deal with financial strings that bind for years. Is this a financial miscalculation? It depends upon which sacrifices you make and how much you resent the sacrifices. Maternity must be viewed in a financial way because in today's world it is an expense. However, like every other aspect of the fiscal reality, it can be handled with a little juggling and a lot of preparing.

I have purposely linked maternity and money. I have deliberately dealt with stepmothering and mothering anew in conjunction. I have warned you about how paternity can eclipse maternity. Why? You must be aware of these pitfalls because they can determine your choice. Consciously or unconsciously, they will influence your maternal decision. Pragmatically, they may rule out motherhood. Psychologically, they may inhibit you maternally. In spite of them all, you must not forget that the choice is yours.

Sometimes a second wife blames her maternal obstacles on others, especially her new husband. Although she married a package deal and knew the ramifications, she can be sorry. When years pass by and a new child is impossible, and stepchildren are incorrigible, she can blame it all on her husband. Or herself. Either way, the regrets escalate.

"I loved my married man. I married him, I divorced him, too, three years ago. I felt terrible, but I just couldn't take it. I thought all I ever wanted in life was this man. But in time having him meant having poverty, harassment, and worst— childlessness. His wife dragged us in and out of court till we were broke. We couldn't afford a baby because we needed my income. And I didn't feel it was fair to bring a child into lives as chaotic as ours. I became bitter, resentful. I tried to cope, but I wanted a child more than anything, even him. Being a second wife wasn't for me. I hope I can find a man who can help me build a family, not simply survive. I know I failed, but I wonder how many women can hold up and go on sacrificing in a mess like mine. And forfeit their maternal rights too!" *(Jersey City, New Jersey)*

"I wanted to be his wife, lover, confidante, companion, but most of all I wanted to have his baby. That's where it went all wrong. You see, he had had enough of parenthood already. I felt the opposite. I felt I hadn't begun. Children demand a different set of priorities in terms of money, time, freedom, and more. I wanted it and he didn't. We grew apart because of this and now we are separated." *(Baldwin, New York)*

Childlessness does not necessarily go along with becoming a second wife. However, in the past that is what usually happened. Presently, you must look closely at your financial future, your married man, and yourself and determine the issue before the marriage.

There is only one more question that is equal to the question "Can I afford to mother?" That is "Can I afford not to mother?" If going from mistress to wife means you cannot go from mistress to mother, be wary. People change. The maternal drive may be invisible within you now, but will it remain silent forever?

Childlessness is a choice that many couples are opting for in this society. It is a viable choice and can make some couples very happy. However, if childlessness is a condition that is unchangeable in the union of you and this married man, make certain it's a condition that will satisfy you for a lifetime. In ten or twenty years don't blame him or his stepchildren for preventing you from maternal fulfillment. Don't trade motherhood for marriage. Now it may seem unimportant, but time has a way of germinating the maternal seed.

The Natural Sciences

"I told Ethan that my career was like a baby. I have nurtured it for years. It was blossoming. I was satisfied being a career person. I wanted marriage, but I didn't ever want children."

Ethan was a bit skeptical. It's not that he didn't love Clair. He loved her for ten years before he got his divorce and married her. It's just that he didn't trust women. His first wife had snuck a child in, right in the middle of medical school. He never forgave her for that trickery. His divorce had cost him dearly. He rarely went to see his son and it was even rarer that he ever talked about it.

Clair was a researcher. She had studied hard and worked hard. Her success was very rewarding to her. Success and marriage too, what more could she ever hope for?

"Ethan and I agreed that childlessness was best for us. We had our careers, which left us little time as it was. His being a doctor and my being a researcher made juggling work and love hard enough. Then, his whole episode with parenting was some mystery to me. I knew he was torn up about his son, but

I couldn't get him to open up. All he ever said was that he didn't want any more children.

"Then at about thirty-six something came over me. It was almost involuntary. It was cyclical like my menstrual cycle. Periodically I felt drawn to wanting a child. This maternal desire was a feeling so strong. I became anxious, desperate, concerned with my age. I was afraid to mention it to Ethan. I was afraid not to."

Many women, like Clair, are programmed for bearing a child. Career interest may be a sincere lifelong interest, but it does not always stifle the maternal instinct. That maternal seed is biology and chemistry. It can be as natural as any of the natural sciences, as Clair was learning.

"I finally told Ethan that I wanted a child. I told him at my age I hadn't much time to waste. I thought he'd suggest divorce. I was so surprised when he said fine! I knew Ethan had been going through some trauma. His silences and his sufferings over his son were evident but I was afraid to probe him. But now everything's changed. We're closer. We're entering a whole new era about parenting our child and rediscovering his."

Even if your married man doesn't get you in the womb in the beginning, that is not insurance that you are cut out for childlessness. Keep Clair's experience in mind. The maternal seed may be dormant. She was fortunate that Ethan's parenting came of age at the same time.

The final concept to remember with regard to maternity is age. Childbearing for a woman is determined biologically by the clock. We now realize that the time span is larger. A woman can give birth in her thirties, and even in the early forties with risks. However, even with our technology, time is still a factor. When you are wondering whether to mother or not to mother, make sure your indecision doesn't take you too many years. Then time will decide for you. Your career, your new husband, his paternity, his children, there are so many distractions that can take up years of your time. Make sure that you save some time for your maternal decision.

For the mistress who becomes a second wife, maternity can be such a complex decision. Your maternal destiny can be eclipsed by so many things. We've looked at each possibility.

It can even be sabotaged by you, yourself, not knowing your own mind. How can any of us know if we were born to be mothers or not? Can we trust our decision? Can we solve our indecision satisfactorily?

The Triangle Transition can augment much confusion. I can't give each of you the exact answer to the question—to mother or not to mother. But you must somehow exact an answer for yourself.

As a final device to get you through your maternal crisis, I have included a test at the end of this chapter. The test is based on mythology, your own particular mythology about motherhood. The myths that we believe can be revealing. They can even be our values in miniature or a survey of hidden programming. Can your motherhood mythology help you? Take the test and see!

To be or not to be a mother? The decision is awesome. Finding the right solution to your maternal crisis is a once-in-a-lifetime opportunity. It can bring you total joy or total regret. It can make your marriage to that married man richer or ruin it. Your maternity can not be decided without your husband's advice, of course. However, in the end the crisis is still your own. You must indulge yourself in family planning before you go from mistress to wife. Assess your options and make room for choices. His views on your maternity should be heard before the wedding and respected. In the end, though, you are responsible for your own maternal decision, since you will live with the consequences. Childlessness, or maternity, which will it be? Each woman has a choice. Going from mistress to wife, your choosing may be a bit more difficult. Then again if you have the right man, your rewards may be a bit greater too! That is only if you answer correctly . . . To be or not to be a mother?

Were You Born to Conceive?

Is motherhood for you? Women's liberation has definitely freed us from restrictions in innumerable ways. At the same time, it has enslaved us in a complex set of new conflicts. Perhaps the greatest of these conflicts involves the choice of motherhood.

A woman's disposition toward motherhood nowadays can change from decade to decade, depending on how her relationship is going, or how her career is progressing or not progressing. At one point in life a woman can think "never" and yet at another point in the same life she can look longingly at every baby that passes by. Which inclination can you trust? Which desire will make you happy? To remain childless or to mother? To have a new child with him, or to pass with the children you already have?

Since the childbearing years are fixed, even with the modern expanded limits, your decision becomes all the more etched with anxiety. Were you born to conceive? I have designed a test that will help you delve into your value system concerning the concept of motherhood. Perhaps you will learn a bit about your vision and expectations.

Directions: How do you feel about each of the following statements? Circle either "always," "sometimes," or "never" after each to sum up your response. Then we will analyze your responses and see what they say about you in particular.

1. A new baby is a blessing and a joy.   always
                                                 sometimes
                                                 never

2. Motherhood is the fulfillment of   always
   womanhood.   sometimes
                                                 never

3. A baby is the natural outgrowth of two   always
   people's love.   sometimes
                                                 never

4. You never love another child the way   always
   you love one of your own.   sometimes
                                                 never

5. Never giving birth would mean missing   always
   out on one of life's greatest pleasures.   sometimes
                                                 never

6. Working mothers just aren't as good as   always
   the full-time kind.   sometimes
                                                 never

7. If he's anti-baby, it's a temporary feeling. In time it's just natural he'll want a baby with you.

always
sometimes
never

8. You can't live a full life without participating firsthand in molding the next generation.

always
sometimes
never

9. If you opt for childlessness you will regret it someday.

always
sometimes
never

10. Motherhood is a more valid ambition than any other.

always
sometimes
never

To Score:

For every circled "always" answer, give yourself 15 points. For every "sometimes" answer, give yourself 10 points. For every "never" answer, give yourself 5 points. Now add up the number of points for your total.

What does your score mean? Read the evaluation below that relates to your total.

Evaluation:

First let me point out that most of the statements are commonly held beliefs or myths. You may find that debatable, and that is exactly the point. How you react to these statements can be very revealing about your value structure. Sometimes our values are absolute and unchangeable no matter how we try to update ourselves intellectually. And for some people, knowing their values can be the beginning to knowing how and what to change. What are you saying with your score? What are the mothering myths telling you?

50–80 Points: If your total fell in this range, you are a *liberated thinker* with regard to motherhood. Your answers are pregnant with independence and choice with regard to the mothering question. You are not bound by the pressures that say that if you remain childless you will pay with regrets, or that motherhood is the ultimate fulfillment. You don't buy all the saccharine platitudes that can leave a naive, new mother devastated. For instance, a new baby can be a mixed blessing for some. You probably feel that not everyone is suited for parenthood. And that step-parenthood or adopting can be equally rewarding for some parents. Because many of your answers go against the grain of popular opinion, you can probably count on your assertiveness to direct you appropriately. Since you have liberated your thinking from the myths, mothering will be your choice freely and clearly. Is mothering for you? You probably know the answer.

85–115 Points: If your score fell in this range, you are a very *subjective thinker* with regard to motherhood. Your answers are pregnant with maybes, depending on this or that. A subjective orientation can be good. For instance, it's good to realize that some babies are born out of love while others are born out of accidents or strategy, and that not everyone feels motherhood is the ultimate in ambition, or that rearing the next generation is insurance of immortality. Your answers indicate that each person must evaluate parenthood in her or his own way. You probably think that it's the quality of time spent with a child that is more important than the quantity. Therefore working mothers sometimes can be even better mothers. And yet, if you are a subjective thinker, you must also be aware of your tendency when making your own decisions about mothering. Your maternal desires may change depending on life's circumstances from year to year. So be aware of your subjectivity when deciding whether motherhood is for you or not. Knowing how you think is invaluable to the subjective thinker!

120–150 Points: If your score fell in this range, you are a *maternal thinker*. Your answers are pregnant with the myths of motherhood. Regardless of whether you put yourself in the old or the new school of thought, your values are heavily weighted with motherhood. Motherhood as fulfillment, motherhood as ultimate joy, motherhood as natural instinct. For you there is hardly a choice where childlessness is concerned. To choose childlessness would mean choosing regrets, losing one of life's greatest pleasures, and being left out of the future by not being involved with the future generation. Although there is nothing awry about your enthusiasm for mothering, you should not fail to see some dangers. For instance, his feelings about parenthood may be as real as yours. So if he doesn't want children, for him that is natural and may never change. And don't close yourself off to parenting children other than your own flesh and blood. Step-parenting has joys too. And all mothering has disadvantages; don't be too naive about parenting. You were probably born to conceive, so temper your conception of motherhood with a few realities and your experiences will be even better!

In Conclusion:

Is motherhood for you? I hope now you know a little more about your maternal inclinations and conceptions. If you are too subjective or too naive maternally, can you change? If you desperately want motherhood and see that it's impossible, can you ever be happy? Just as these myths are debatable, your ability to change is debatable. Only you can explore your goals. At least now you know what your values are programming you for. That's the beginning in solving the question of maternal choice. Is mothering for you? The question repeats itself to the childless as well as the second wife. To find an answer is difficult sometimes, for some always. Were you born to conceive? The answer is never out of your grasp!

PART IV

Strategies for Coping

CHAPTER 12

Tempering Your Future

Some brides and grooms enter marriage one step ahead of a shower of rice. Chances are if you go from mistress to wife, your shower will include jinxes and summonses along with the more traditional fare. By the time you reach this point in the book, you have some idea of what to expect. This chapter, therefore, is dedicated to helping you cope.

By now you are well aware that your matrimonial transition is not merely that of an ordinary fiancée to newlywed. No, yours is a triangle transition. In going from mistress to marriage, you are not becoming only a wife, but a second wife. In marrying your married man, in all likelihood you are going from mistress to instant stepmother. And in time many of you will become mothers, too, if you are not already. Last, but not least, you are also going from mistress to daughter-in-law. As if those roles weren't enough, add the traditional ones, such as homemaker, lover, friend, confidante, and probably career person too! Demanding, wouldn't you say?

In our society, few of us are prepared extensively for all the roles of marriage. They only prepare us for the rituals. We are taught about ceremony, and etiquette for the gala, and invitations, and silverware patterns. Of what follows the honeymoon, there is a paucity of warning! Since you are no ordinary newlywed if you do marry your married man, I decided that some instruction was absolutely essential.

With regard to coping, the most useful instruction is to focus upon certain traits that will be very beneficial to you in your new married life. We will try to answer a number of questions about disposition. For instance, is there any ideal temperament that will enable a mistress to master the new roles to which marriage will introduce her? Is there any basic philosophy that can serve as a guide? Have you, as a mistress, had any pertinent experience that has equipped you to not only survive but to flourish in your mistress marriage? Are there any special qualities that can help you overcome the disadvantages of a triangle transition? Should you cultivate certain virtues deliberately?

Going from mistress to wife is a unique transition, as you know by now. It involves special joys as well as special demands. And there are no Cana conferences tailored for ex-mistresses! So in order to supplement your knowledge about marriage beforehand, I am going to try and prepare you for your triangle transition.

Success for you as his new wife is often a matter of analyzing your personality and adjusting it. Certain traits are more useful than others. Therefore, if you develop some characteristics and stifle others, you will acquire an edge on coping. By modifying some of your expectations and some of your reactions, you can choose behaviors that will bring you happiness and alleviate stress. Certain tendencies should be rooted out so that you can sidestep some traps inherent in your new position. You will be tampering with your temperament when necessary, because adjusting your personality can temper your future!

We are going to look at different roles that you will be expected to fill and the concomitant challenges of each. Different spheres of your life will pose different demands. There are ways to triumph over the stresses. There are characteristics that will help you and some that can hinder you. With a little tempering and tampering though, love can conquer all! However, we must not underestimate the battles. They can certainly take a lot out of you.

Our Courtship

They say that the first year of marriage is the hardest. Maybe that's true for some newlyweds, but it wasn't true for Jeff and Arizona. For them the year before their marriage was the worst. But the first year of marriage was running a close second!

"I was forty-two when I fell in love with Jeff. I was in love for the first time in my life. I wasn't going to let him go for anything. I deserved this. Jeff was forty-eight and had been married to a miserable creature for nearly twenty years. Damn it! We had earned some happiness. We both told our spouses that we wanted out. To say that all hell broke loose is an understatement. We lived in Tucson at that time. The furor is probably still echoing in the desert!"

In each case a long drawn-out legal battle was launched. Everything that could be fought over, was. Possessions. Custody of children. Suddenly Arizona and Jeff were not just unhappy disenchanted spouses who wanted to purify their lives. They were judged heinous, immoral ingrates who were spewing immorality and filth all over the earth!

"Our courtship was just that, literally a courtship where we were in and out of court. Jeff was almost stripped naked financially. I got practically nothing in the way of material things. I wanted nothing but joint custody of my two children. I got that. Jeff wasn't so fortunate. The divorces became final, but the fighting was far from over. You know how these things can drag on when bitterness prevails.

"We got married at dawn one morning. An old friend of my family's performed the ceremony. We didn't plan any big party. The urge to celebrate publicly was hard to muster. Publicly there was still so much gossip, scandal, and revenge; it was sad. We kept our marriage to ourselves because we were all we needed. We were happy at last. No matter what was ahead, we would face it together."

The first year of their marriage was plagued with harassment of all kinds, from legal to financial to social. They were victimized by character assaults from judges on down to ex-spouses.

"After a while, all the abuse and the injustice rolls off your back. We know who we are. We have clear consciences. We did what was right for us. It is neither Jeff nor I who have been unfair or cruel. We have learned strength and fortitude and to lean on each other."

For Arizona and Jeff, their courtship and their newlywed era was one long trial really. In time they learned to dispense with judges and to ignore juries. Together they decided the verdict, and theirs was the only verdict that mattered. It was "not guilty and very much in love and at peace."

Arizona's courtship is not some rare case. Many mistresses and married men, as you have seen, encounter legal tortures at the hands of our system. Arizona's handling of her courtship is what you should remember. She cited fortitude. Fortitude is one of those biblical virtues. It has an almost archaic sound. When was the last time you heard someone talk about the value of fortitude? What is it exactly?

Fortitude is strength of mind in the face of adversity, and patient and constant courage. Every mistress and married man who face untangling their former marriages and families are facing adversity of the most painful kind. Fortitude is a virtue we should recycle back into the language and back into our lives.

Arizona and Jeff may have been wrong to fall in love. But they were indeed courageous to declare that love honestly and try to change their situations. They could have secretly carried on. They chose not to live hypocrisy. Apparently Arizona and Jeff already had fortitude before the furor. Their character would survive any number of assaults.

Chances are, as you go from mistress to wife, you will encounter trials such as these. That is bad news that has to be broken to you. However, there is good news too. As a mistress you have already been unconsciously developing your fortitude, even if you never labeled it as such. Just think about it.

Mistresses have to be strong. Any woman who manages and finances her own life, solves her problems, and sets her goals, and still is the pillar upon which her married man leans, that is a strong woman! Any woman who holds her love precious and right despite moral outrage doesn't depend on others for her morality or her approval. A mistress has developed her own morality and she adheres to her own conscience. That takes courage beyond measure that cannot be comprehended unless you know well the nature of triangles. There are some marriages that are unholy, immoral, and hypocritical. A mistress understands the subtlety of moral relativity. A mistress understands injustice and patience. All of these components are really aspects of fortitude. Mistresshood has equipped you with this characteristic that will be very valuable in your triangle transition.

As a second wife assaulted by legal injustices, assorted harassments, and fatherhood challenges, you will find some aspects of your mistress personality are indispensible. In a sense you have armor that will protect your character from any attack. As you try to bolster him and bolster your relationship through the hard times, your strength of character will be a great ally. Throughout your affair you had only your convictions and your faith in yourself and in him. In your mistress marriage, that isolation, upon which your self-worth was decided, will be like some moat separating you from social disdain. You have learned to rely on yourself and your married man. As you go from mistress/married man to wife/husband that self-reliance is the best support imaginable. Your perseverance and his is your best coping tool.

Triangle transitions are really rarely smooth. Cultivating fortitude or taking stock of your reserve is a must. Coping, after all is said and done, will be your task. Your strength will help you flourish despite adversity or cause you great stress when it fails.

Learning to handle the trials of becoming a second wife and "partner in crime" is one aspect. Another great challenge will be learning to handle your new husband and his children, together with yours, if such be your case.

Your new role as stepmother will be perhaps the most complicated with which to cope. Your new blended family membership has so many complex conflicts and influences that it is hard to comprehend all its dimensions. And yet understanding must precede developing a strategy for coping. Hopefully, in the chapter on step-parenting we have enlightened you about your new role. Unrealistic expectations were highlighted and possible dilemmas were outlined. The trying aspects of mothering his children were stated as well as the telling rewards in befriending them. Forewarned is forearmed in this aspect of your new family life.

In the following pages we are going to look at step-parenting again, only this time not so much about the experience itself. We are going to get right down to specifics with regard to your qualifications where personality is concerned. Will your own particular disposition make you a natural at stepmothering? Temperament-wise do you have the makings of a good stepparent? If not, what can you do?

First take the following test. Then we will review what traits are best suited for step-parents to cultivate.

Should You Tamper With Your Temperament?

Could you sum up your personality in a few words? If you had to describe yourself in one sentence, what would you say? For most people those questions are anything but simple. Yet we all have a certain tenor to our temperaments. If you look into the question for awhile, you will see what I mean.

There are some temperaments that will find it easier to go from mistress to wife and stepmother. Others will find the transitions harder since they will be vulnerable to more pitfalls. Which category will you fall into? Should you tamper with your temperament?

The purpose of this exercise is to help you identify your temperament. Once you have a picture of your nature, you can see if you are a natural or not at step-parenting. Then you can adapt or adjust to get the most out of your new role.

Directions: This is a multiple choice exercise. Read all the questions and carefully choose one and only one answer. Sometimes that may mean making an educated guess. Try your best. Answer all! Then go on to the scoring and evaluation.

1. What cliché sums you up best? (a) What will be will be. (b) If you don't succeed at first, try try again. (c) Time heals all wounds. (d) If you want something done right, do it yourself.

    1._____

2. When you are in the middle of doing something and you are interrupted, which describes what you would do? (a) You politely state you are busy and ask the intruder to come back later. (b) You put aside your task and tend to the interruption. (c) You take a break from your task, solve the intruder's problem, and then return and finish. (d) You stop and see what the problem is and decide to postpone the least important of the two.

    2._____

3. What do you think is your worst fault? (a) low self-esteem (b) stubbornness (c) disorganization (d) selfishness

    3._____

4. If you could master any of the following qualities, which would you choose? (a) drive (b) patience (c) independence (d) diplomacy

4._____

5. In planning an outing for your new family, which course would you tend to follow? (a) You would design something you know everyone would enjoy, by considering their tastes. (b) You would plan something you think would be perfect. (c) You would let all the family members vote on several ideas. (d) You would select a first, something no one has ever done.

5._____

6. What are your expectations with regard to discipline and stepchildren? (a) You feel you should earn the authority to discipline. (b) For the sake of order you will insist on some discipline rights. (c) You will relegate that chore to Dad. (d) You will incorporate creative distractions, reverse psychology, and persuasion into that area.

6._____

7. Suppose you made a great dinner and his kids refused to eat. What would be your response? (a) You'd laugh and let them cook an alternative, even if it was peanut butter and jelly sandwiches. (b) You would say "fine" and excuse them and not go to any more trouble for a while. (c) You would be hurt and say they should eat out of politeness if nothing else. (d) You would try and conquer their attitude with bribery, humor, or some other ploy.

7._____

8. When things don't go as you plan, how does that usually make you feel? (a) like a failure (b) like you misjudged someone or something (c) like it wasn't meant to be for some reason (d) like rethinking the whole thing and trying again

8._____

9. If his kids ask him if he and Mommy will ever marry again, what will you do? (a) silently resolve to win them over so they won't feel that way (b) counter with a calm

list of your assets in self-defense (c) ask them why they feel that way (d) let it pass and tell yourself it is a normal feeling for them

9._____

10. Second wives rarely feel like newlyweds because they are different from newlyweds. How will you feel about missing the newlywed game? (a) You will realize that neither he, nor his kids, nor yours, if you have them, will feel like newlyweds either. (b) You will concentrate on different values and postpone honeymoon expectations. (c) You will make your own honeymoon anyway. (d) You will dismiss that romantic nonsense and go on to the new challenges of the marriage.

10._____

11. When he gets lonely about his children, how will you try and cope? (a) You will suggest he see a lawyer and try winning custody. (b) You will feel somewhat frustrated because you have no control or power to help him. (c) You will try to soothe him with fond memories and plans. (d) You will assure him that things will change and all bad situations pass.

11._____

12. When your one-big-new-happy-family fantasies fail, how will you feel? (a) disheartened because you tried (b) upset because everyone feels badly (c) driven to try a new battle plan (d) committed to a long term solution

12._____

Scoring:
List your answers in the space provided for them. Then look for the point value given to each answer in the table. Write down the number of points in the space provided. Add up your score for all 12 answers and fill in your total in the space provided.

					Answers	Points
1.	(a) 20	(b) 15	(c) 10	(d) 5	1._____	_____
2.	(a) 5	(b) 10	(c) 15	(d) 20	2._____	_____
3.	(a) 10	(b) 15	(c) 20	(d) 5	3._____	_____

					Answers	Points
4.	(a) 15	(b) 20	(c) 5	(d) 10	4._____	_____
5.	(a) 20	(b) 5	(c) 10	(d) 15	5._____	_____
6.	(a) 15	(b) 5	(c) 20	(d) 10	6._____	_____
7.	(a) 10	(b) 20	(c) 5	(d) 15	7._____	_____
8.	(a) 5	(b) 10	(c) 20	(d) 15	8._____	_____
9.	(a) 15	(b) 5	(c) 10	(d) 20	9._____	_____
10.	(a) 10	(b) 20	(c) 5	(d) 15	10._____	_____
11.	(a) 15	(b) 5	(c) 10	(d) 20	11._____	_____
12.	(a) 5	(b) 10	(c) 15	(d) 20	12._____	_____
					Total_____	

Evaluation:

Your score can range anywhere from 60 to 240 points. Read the paragraph that includes your own score in its range.

60–100 Points: The Independent Temperament. The theme of your nature is independence if you scored in this range. You are self-reliant, self-motivated, and self-sufficient. You like being in control of things. When you aren't, you are likely to feel frustrated. You tend to take things personally, whether they be achievements or failures. While this temperament is admirable in many ways and a help in many goals, it portends trouble in the mistress-to-wife transition. Why? In a nutshell your declaration of independence will lead to mutiny on the bounty. Your step-children will have loyalties, conflicts, and reactions over which you will have no control whatsoever. Your married man will encounter, in all likelihood, crises that you will have to watch standing by his side helplessly. Establishing yourself in your new role will be difficult for you because, the more you assert and try, the more you will see rebellion, anxiety, and failure. Your independence will have to adjust if you are to survive as a new second wife.

105–145 Points: The Altruistic Temperament. The theme of your nature is a collective spirit if you scored in this range. You are very attuned to the needs and the concerns of others. You tend to be selfless, generous, and diplomatic. You are more inclined toward group efforts than you are toward individual achievements. However, while your temperament may seem well suited for the transition from mistress to wife and step-parent, beware! In your sway toward democracy and equality, you could very well be the loser. Giving too much or trying too hard with new roles is a common pitfall for second wives. Your new husband will need time to adjust, as will his children. Your trying to help everyone else will possibly make you feel used, abused, and taken for granted. Giving all the time may make you feel drained. Your collective spirit should be tempered, so that you don't lose sight of your own needs. Aside from being a second wife, you are a person too.

145 – 185 Points: The Challenging Temperament. The theme of your nature is a love for competition and challenge if you scored in this range. There is nothing more stimulating to you than a good problem that needs mastering. You thrive on the excitement of a role to master or a new task to complete. You are characteristically driven and quite ambitious. Chances are you have quite a few successes behind you and you have not begun! You don't see life as consisting of failures and successes but rather of rounds. Perseverance is your forte! While the mistress-to-wife transition may be a more challenging contest than you initially thought, you are well equipped to stick it out. You won't take setbacks and problems in adjustment personally. You are out to conquer all the problems and willing to change strategies all the way down the line. You will resolve to regroup and regroup and regroup until your new role and the roles of everyone else jive well. While your type is not the best suited for the mistress-to-wife change, you are extremely well equipped!

190 – 240 Points: The Patient Temperament. The theme of your nature is patience if you scored in this range. Congratulations! You are best suited and the least likely to need temperament tampering. You have a very easygoing attitude toward life. "What will be will be" and "All things will pass" tend to express your world view. Your temperament is usually a calm one and quite flexible. You aren't in a hurry, or driven to instant successes, or determined to run things your own way. These are the best attitudes to bring into the role of the second wife and step-parent. It will be a new world for you, filled with new pressures, new guilts, new challenges. And sometimes none of them can be alleviated, overcome, or conquered, but merely withstood. Your high tolerance is invaluable. Your time schedule, with its low expectations, will make the adjustment years easier to endure than it would for other more fast-paced temperaments. Yours is the temperament to be emulated. Patience is the asset to be cultivated. As a second wife and step-parent you will probably take life a day at a time and play it by ear. You will strive to survive as best you can and try to relax. That is the best behavior and the best advice anyone can give a prospective second wife.

In Conclusion:
Don't despair!!! None of the temperaments are bad or wrong, per se. Each has its assets and its liabilities. For the Triangle Transitions, though, some temperaments are better emotional equipment. For this imminent stage in your life, you must know yourself thoroughly, so that you can get yourself into condition to go from mistress to step-mother!

The bottom line in this test is the most salient one. You can get yourself into condition. You can identify the best possible characteristics for step-parenting and then incorporate them into your life. The disposition that centered around being patient was the most desirable, because, of all the virtues in the world, patience is the one step-parents need the most.

"The biggest mistake I made in building my relationship with my married man's children was impatience. I was not patient with myself. I expected me to be supermom and his children to adapt to me too quickly. The best of intentions don't work. The only thing that works, which I learned the hard way, is to be tolerant. To be patient with yourself as you try, and succeed, and fail in step-parenting, and to be patient with the children." *(Dalton, Georgia)*

"Patience is the most underrated virtue of all. But the most important. A step-mother can be loving, caring, efficient, unselfish, but if she is not patient, then everything can go wrong all the time." *(Chattanooga, Tennessee)*

The more you learn about step-parenting from stepmothers and soon from your own experience, the more you will agree. Each blended family consists of individuals and their unique complications. And yet the one generalization that holds for every set of families is the need for patience.

A corollary of patience is tolerance and flexibility. While you wait out all the resolving traumas and swirling emotional reactions, both good and bad, you must allow freedom for the children. They must be able to express themselves and so must you! Each must learn tolerance for the other in the new family. Each must try and be flexible about demands and behaviors.

It is a good idea to try to put yourself in their shoes and feel as they must feel. It is also a good idea to ask them to put themselves in your shoes. The point here is a cohesive family only forms when all the components interact and react smoothly. It must be a joint effort and a joint sacrifice. If you are flexible and tolerant it will be a breeze. If you are righteous and rigid, you are in for a stormy ride.

A stepmother has to be a tightrope walker at times, walking a thin line between flexibility and discipline. However, don't worry if you fall; your new husband will catch you. Making mistakes is allowed. Be tolerant with yourself too. Remember forming a blended family is a lifetime venture. There will be decades of family harmony and decades of family turmoil. Think of it as a lifetime venture and all the immediate episodes will be easier to tolerate.

If you are a stepmother and a mother too, that is all the more reason to concentrate on developing these qualities.

Before we leave the subject of parenting and the strategies for coping with it, let's put in a few words for the second wife who is debating about her own maternal desires. Patience, tolerance, and flexibility all imply a certain passivity—letting another person assert himself/herself rather than seeking to dominate. Stepmothers must be careful not to let these virtues run wild. Too much passivity can take its toll. If you go from mistress to second wife and stepmother, don't let that prevent you from going on to mother too!

Stepmothering and being a second wife is demanding and costly in all ways, financially and emotionally. It is so easy for a second wife to delay or to dispel her own maternal desires. We spent an entire chapter delving into your maternal aspirations. Don't stifle your desire to mother, if you are strongly motivated. Don't worry that there won't be enough love or enough time. Don't worry about the conflicts that may arise in your stepchildren or your husband. Motherhood is based on a biological time clock and you must be true to yourself now or it may be too late. Parents often find that their capacity to love children is bottomless, regardless of how many. All children are resilient; their conflicts will disappear as they adapt. A second wife and stepmother must learn when to be self-assertive. Self-assertiveness is different from selfishness. Your own motherhood will not ruin your stepmothering ability. Yet if you deny yourself, you may very well be building resentments that will ruin it later in your life. You must find a balance in your disposition, between passive traits and active traits.

You can adapt to any disadvantage in your triangle transition with the aid of maturity. Maturity. That is definitely one of those catchall, vague words. Some aspects of maturity we have already discussed. Fortitude, flexibility, and patience are under the umbrella of maturity in a sense. However, now we are going to look at the side of maturity that will guide you through innumerable crises. It will give you power to transform negative situations into positive proving grounds. This next story is from my memoirs.

Sticks and Stones

Life is so much like a circle. The older I get, the more I find the rhymes and the rhythms of the past repeating and encircling me, my husband, and my family.

Every once in awhile I hear my stepchildren chanting childhood rhymes. Immediately I am transported back to my childhood. I hear the echos of those exact rhymes that I used to chant jumping rope or playing games.

At another moment in a flash I hear myself give a parental directive. Again I'm whizzed backward as I hear my mother or father say the exact words I am repeating, as if a generation never elapsed.

The past and the present seem like some spinning top.

"Sticks and stones will break your bones, but names will never hurt you."

"Act like a lady."

"This or that will build your character."

"Your dollar is the only friend that will never betray you."

All these little excerpts from the past take on new meanings as I recall them, repeat them, and resurrect them. It's almost as if they add up to one big lesson in life, which of course they do.

They add up to the importance of integrity, personal dignity, and independence. My particular upbringing was a bit scarce at times in the material things in life, but there was never any scarcity of the intangibles. Lessons in character building were heaped upon us, the values of honesty, integrity, and intellectuality. As time passed I realized how valuable these lessons were.

No matter how rich you become, you cannot buy yourself

character like you can a Cadillac. The strength and integrity of your personality are enterprises that no entrepreneur can market.

Although my morality as a mistress will always be debatable by others, the demonstration of my integrity in a trying triangle will never be. Regardless of the stresses and strains I have met, publicly and privately, I have always had this warehouse of character inventory that has inspired me and pulled me through with my dignity and strength intact. People can say anything at all or do anything to you, but no one and nothing can ever take away your integrity. Knowing that makes one strong, and pure, and self-lovable.

I have resurrected those old juvenile chants and parental lectures to emphasize how valuable character and virtues can be to a second-wife candidate. Your temperament should place a premium on these intangibles. Then character assassinations will not affect you. Store a recording of "Sticks and Stones" and its lessons in your mind's recesses, to replay in a trying time.

Your triangle transition will give rise to many obstacles. There will be countless opportunities for bitterness and revenge. There will be opportunities for grudges. There will be times when rage, righteous rage, overtakes you in the face of the system's injustices and life's unfairnesses. There will be harassments and character assaults too. How much of these depends on your own personal circumstances. However, at each obstacle there will be a choice.

You can harass back, avenge yourself. Or you can rise above the temptations. If you fight back, you must be sure you are not stooping to the low levels that human beings can sink to. If you choose integrity and not to stoop, each obstacle will only be a proving ground for you. Each seeming trial and disadvantage will give you added self-affirmation. The catchall is maturity. For every time you do the mature thing, rather than the immature thing, you will be rewarded with knowing you are demonstrating your character not your weaknesses!

Ex-mistresses encounter various trials and tribulations in their new roles in marriage, extended-family living, and blended-family living. Every trial is really an opportunity for you to flourish, to flaunt your character. In this way you are transforming all of life's negatives into life's positives. If there is one basic philosophy to recommend for the second-wife candidate, it would be to eliminate the negatives and accentuate the positives. Make that philosophy the new theme for your mistress marriage.

Although character development is founded in youth, it is never too late to add to your virtues. Becoming a second wife will probably introduce you to many obstacles, and obstacles are what character-building is all about. If you concentrate on your temperament and your disposition and your character, you will not be so vulnerable to stresses. This applies to the oppositions' attempts to bait you and destroy your newfound happiness. It also applies to material sacrifices that mistress marriages so often entail. In cultivating your character, you will also be weeding out items like bitterness and hatred. They are debilitating. They can be a by-product of your triangle transition, if you are not vigilant.

Every behavior pattern is a choice, a deliberate choice that we make. You can control the onslaught of bitterness or the example of maturity that you set. None of us are altogether victims of emotions. The emotions can be tamed and tempered by reason and virtue. Any negatives you encounter can make you a better person, if only you choose to opt for that transformation.

Concentrate on your new marriage and your married man's love. Think about all the new friendships that will in time develop, friendships with his children, with in-laws. Old animosities, forget them, because they are all in the past. Realizing that life is like a circle is a very comforting thought after living through a triangle. If you go from mistress to wife, trade in your triangle for that brass ring instead!

Leave behind all the unpleasantries of triangle living by working on your personality. Be the controller of your destiny by choosing traits that will help you cope and by simply shutting out of your mind thoughts and feelings that upset you. For some it will be easier than for others. Take heart, because none of us is perfect! We all could use a little temperament tampering. But now as you go from mistress to wife, you will have a whole lifetime with the man you love to dabble with your temperament, with his support and love to help you. Your disposition is really one of your greatest potentials in life. Your mistress personality was good training. Now as his wife, dispose yourself to a real happily-ever-after. Old wisdoms can enhance your new life. Temper your future with a few old-fashioned qualities and the quality of your marriage will be wonderful.

CHAPTER 13

I'll Take Romance... Will You?

Mistresses and married men are magicians at creating romance. That is an agreed-upon fact. Romance was cited by mistresses time and time again, when I probed them for advantages to loving a married man. Romanticism seems to come naturally to the lady-in-waiting and her unavailable married man. If you go from mistress to wife, where will romance go? Will it go out the window? Up in smoke? Or will it become a daily part of your diet?

You've probably heard that marriage is hard work. That hardly sounds like a romantic description. And there are those who swear that marriage and romance are mutually exclusive. Either you have a marriage or you have an infatuation. That philosophy contends that marriage provides stability and security, the very things that dampen the passions.

Knowing what you know about the passionate peaks of an affair, and hearing about the institutional confines of marriage, are you worried about the fate of your romance? Can you take that walk down the aisle with your married man and take romance too? Yes.

If you were asked, would you take romance? I'll take romance. Who wouldn't? It is not the impossible dream to be married and still feel romantic. Just because you know couples who have lost the art of romance in their marriage, don't assume that is the standard fate.

Romance is magical. It is spontaneous, chemical, electrical, and exciting. However, romance·has a side that is predictable. It is you and your man who create the climate for romance.

222

You have created that climate in your liaison. You can create that climate in your marriage.

The purpose of this chapter is to give you some advance training in the field of romance. I will insert a few pragmatic lessons in cultivating romance within marriage. We'll take a look at the concept of communication. We will cover some of the necessities for marital bliss. Last of all, some of the dangers of the institution will be highlighted.

Is romance training a bizarre concept to you? It shouldn't be. We are a culture that prizes romance. Our value structure places a premium on passionate experiences. Our entire family structure is based on romance, because we marry for love. If romance is, therefore, a cherished goal and a motivating force, why is it that we don't study it more? Everyone knows how to fall in love. But relatively few know how to sustain that passion over a lifetime. Not much is said about romance and how to keep it fiery over the course of marriage. Romance seems to be attributed to luck. Some couples have it; some don't. It is more than a matter of luck.

In the study of romance, let's look at where it often goes in traditional marital households. The husband and wife start out as lovers. You, as mistress, and your married man qualify as you take your love affair over the threshold. Then all married couples begin adding roles. Workers, parents, housekeepers, garbage-persons, cooks, gardeners, mechanics, educators, psychologists, arbitrators, in-laws, etc. The list is quite long. The times for lovers and friends has to be shared with all those new identities. Often those two most important roles get relegated to the bottom of the list.

Romance must be a priority if you want it in your marriage. Lovers and friends must be high on the list. Not that children, career, and the house should be neglected. It's just that these often preoccupy spouses to the extent that their initial romantic connection is ignored.

All married people have a weekly agenda of chores and responsibilities. Either it is a written reminder or a mental note. Homework supervision, household repairs, bill payments, child care, groceries, laundry, and it goes on. A couple must add "romance" to that list, in the form of an evening out or a lunch together. A shared sporting event. The possibilities are endless. Every couple knows what they would like to do together. The what and where are not as important and the fact of planning "romance."

Before marriage, people date. It is the norm of courtship. Mistresses and married men date, only it is called a rendezvous. Rendezvous may have a more limited span of activities, but the togetherness is still the main ingredient. On these dates or rendezvous, the couple shares hobbies, interests, affection, lovemaking, etc. They go places or do things, fuss over each other, and enjoy.

After marriage, dating patterns are transformed. A new marital lifestyle and schedule is formed. Too many married couples allow the old "date" or "rendezvous" to become an endangered species. Instead of doing the things they enjoyed before marriage, they do new things. Family outings, dinner with in-laws, business functions, mowing the lawn, house projects usually become the only leisure activities. These are fine, especially in the early years of marriage when novelty still prevails. However, as the years go on, these filial, domestic, and business-related functions can become boring. A wife may wonder, "What ever happened to those solitary picnics, the long nature walks?" A husband may wonder, "Why doesn't my wife like to go to a hockey game anymore?"

Marriage adds a new dimension to leisure. However, this too often occurs at the expense of those premarital leisure experiences. Keep dating. Keep rendezvousing. It will keep you and your man happy.

Marriage is a family enterprise. It is a real estate venture. It is a business. The nature of marriage is busy, complex, and everchanging. Sometimes the initial embryo of marriage is forgotten. Marriage happens so that you and your married man can live together, share, love, work toward common goals, and grow. Togetherness is the essence. You, as you become his wife, will run the marriage along with your married man. As you run your lives, toward your goals, and away from obstacles, make sure that love, lust, and fun are there to lubricate this running machine.

The actual physical scheduling of time together is the first necessity that stimulates romance. However, a meeting of the bodies and minds can only run happily if the attitude is in alignment. You can get to the date, but if you lack the right disposition, it can not be fun. This brings us to the concept of communication. The mesh of mind and body works best when a couple is still sharing souls.

Soulmates you are, if you are mistress and married man. Communication isn't one of your problems. How do you keep up the intensity and intimacy of these verbal exchanges after marriage?

Couples that are the happiest over the years are those who still communicate. In fact that word communication is perhaps the most overused word to survive the seventies. Communicating couples can meet challenges, cooperate through hard times, and still manage those fun leisure times. In the early years of married life, communication comes easily. Can that ability be sustained forever?

The knack to keeping the soulmate quality of your relationship is learning about marital stages. Good times elicit closeness. Hard times are the threat to communication and overall happiness.

If one learns to recognize the hard times, which I call "stress times" in a marriage, one can prepare for them. Every marriage has stress times. Sometimes that stress is felt by only one spouse. Sometimes by both. Stress times can be dangerous. They can promote hostility, frustration or withdrawal. However, realizing the stress times and using them can enhance a couple's intimacy. These are times that can provide opportunity for deeper communication, and sharing too.

Here is a list of common stress times, by no means complete or universal. However, you get the gist of the kinds of challenges that create pressure within marriage. Note that stress times are not always bad per se. They are times of change, growth, achievement, and adjustment.

> The birth of a child, especially the first
> The death of a close relative
> An in-law or parent moving in
> A job promotion, loss, or change
> The purchase of a house
> A wife reentering the job market
> A young adult moving out of the nest

These joys or trials can drive a couple apart or closer together. They may trigger depression, elation, insecurity, anger, and many emotional extremes. They can sever communication. They can solidify communication if couples share burdens and joys. Changes such as these should always be discussed openly and dealt with together. In that way a stress time can be an opportunity, not a liability.

The next test will help you ensure good communication

from time to time. It is a tool to help you as a second wife. It can be especially handy during a stress time.

The Communication Quota

Is your relationship measuring up to the Communication Quota? The Communication Quota is a minimal level of shared intimacy. Some relationships far surpass the Communication Quota, while others barely measure up. Which are you and he?

Mistresses and married men tend to excel in the area of communication. Mistresses report to me in vast numbers that they share a unique degree of verbal intimacy with their married man. They all attest to having heard the confessions of their married man. And peak sexual experiences are often testified to, as a reflection of this caliber of communication.

Affairs breed communication more easily than marriages. That may not be fair but it is true. However by keeping your eyes and ears on your own Communication Quota, you can ensure or improve your communication levels.

Keeping close check on your Communication Quota is a good idea whether you are a mistress, a wife, or a second wife. The following test is designed to be a tool in that enterprise.

Directions: Read each of the statements below and respond from among the choices: "always," "sometimes," or "never." Then proceed to the scoring instructions and an assessment of your score.

1. Dialogues often have a way of turning into monologues.

   always
   sometimes
   never

2. There are certain subjects that you just can not broach.

   always
   sometimes
   never

3. You look longingly at couples who are, by their signs of affection, obviously in love, and you regret the passage of that in your life.

   always
   sometimes
   never

4. Changes in behavior don't go unnoticed,   always
   but they are seldom discussed.   sometimes
                                                 never

5. Conflicts among family members are   always
   separate and therefore not topical   sometimes
   between you and him.   never

6. Suspicions are something you keep to   always
   yourself.   sometimes
                                                  never

7. Insecurities are feelings that you hide   always
   and deem silly or weak, certainly not to   sometimes
   be explored with him.   never

8. You know each other's main goals, but   always
   have lost touch with each other's little   sometimes
   goals that make up daily living.   never

9. You have caught yourself staring at him   always
   wishing that you could say something   sometimes
   you can't.   never

10. Your sexual encounters with him are not   always
    highly stimulating as they once were.   sometimes
                                                   never

Scoring:
For every "always" answer, give yourself 15 points. For every
"sometimes" answer, give yourself 10 points. For every
"never" answer, give yourself 5 points. Now total up the number of points you have earned and look below for the category
that includes your total score.

Evaluation:
    120–150 Points: Improper Strangers. This range indicates
that many of your answers were "always." And it makes you
and he strangers, improper strangers because your relationship
should be more intimate than it is. You are not measuring up
to the minimal verbal and sexual intimacy levels. You are not
meeting the Communication Quota. You tend to keep fears as

well as feelings to yourself. Many subjects are out of bounds in your pattern of communication. You may be sharing pleasant news with each other but the mundane and the threatening have been relegated to silence. Verbally you are prone to monologue or he is prone to monologue. The important missing ingredient is a dialogue. Don't panic! There could be simple reasons for this, not necessarily a rotten relationship. Explore those reasons with him. That will be the first step in improving your Communication Quota!

85–115 Points: Partners in Quorum. This range indicates that you do measure up to the Communication Quota. Your intimacy is exhibited enough of the time to give you a quorum, so to speak, on the rule of communication. On the whole you tend to share secret feelings and clandestine conflicts a majority of the time. If you want to see where there is room for improvement communication-wise, go back and look to your "always" answers. There you will find the areas in which you may lack an exchange. A score that results from all "sometimes" answers is spurious indeed. Make sure that you are not being evasive and avoiding the issue. That won't help you or your level of communication! Partners in a quorum are doing fine, but where will you go from here? Relationships rarely remain the same, so just make certain that your Communication Quota goes up and not down.

50–80 Points: Confidante Extraordinaire. This range indicates that you excel in the communication measurements. Congratulations on your confidante status! You are way past the minimums where verbal and sexual intimacy are concerned. Any feeling can be shared, be it positive or negative. No subject is too difficult to approach. You never experience that feeling of dread, that behavior of silence, when you have a problem. Your exchange thrives on honesty and sharing. The challenge for you is not to improve but to sustain this extraordinary level of communication. That will be no easy task. As career and children and changes weave in and out of your life, maintain your confidante role and you should do fine.

In Conclusion:
Your level of communication is ever-changing. If now you excel, then your struggle will be to stay that way. If now you are deficient, then your struggle will be to improve. One of the best methods to check yourself is to give this test to the man in your life. Will he verify or nullify your score?

And remember, if you go from mistress to wife, you have an edge. In all likelihood, you know the joys of good communication. However, don't take anything for granted or you may someday be looking to go from wife to mistress to rediscover the Communication Quota!

That test should be tucked away somewhere so you can pull it out from time to time. It can always serve you as an instant check upon your relationship. Right now you may be steadfast soulmates, but nothing remains the same. As you and your married man go into the realm of marriage, changes will come. However, it is in the best interests of your marriage to be sure those changes don't interfere with your soulmate relationship.

Sometimes a marriage introduces a new era in communication. Before we leave the issue of communication, you should be introduced to a new language—the language of marriage. This new language is the institutional pitfall and by-product of the nuptial lifestyle. Unfortunately it tends to be universal. Every married person picks it up too easily. And worse than the vocabulary of the language itself, is what lies between the lines.

Speak to Me Only

Julie was having her hair done and confessing to the stylist at the same time.

"I don't know why I was so cruel to Grant this morning. I woke up on the wrong side of the bed, I suppose. I snarled at him all through breakfast. Then the phone rang. I was as pleasant as could be to the caller even though it was a wrong number. In an instant I returned to my impatient, grouchy self, as I interrogated Grant about what time he would be home. I was a regular Jekyll and Hyde this morning. Why is it that I reserve the monstrous side for my husband? I wouldn't dare treat a stranger like that!"

The stylist listened patiently. It wasn't often that he heard what his clients were saying. Mostly it was idle chatter. But here was an interesting conversation with a very perceptive individual!

He said, "I guess that's where the saying 'You always hurt the one you love' comes from."

"You know being married gives you the chance to open up about everything. But I think nowadays people are just too honest sometimes. If I'm overly depressed or upset I know I tend to use my husband as a sounding board or a whipping post. I guess he's got to take it because he lives with me. But I'm beginning to wonder, shouldn't we put our best face forward rather than our most neurotic? Maybe all the magazines are wrong. Too much needless hostility and honesty is thrown about nowadays."

Julie suddenly had a flashback that was even too intimate for the stylist to overhear. When she was Grant's mistress, she would never have acted like she had that morning. She only told him the best of her life back then. She saved all her smiles, her pleasantries, and her sensitivities for him back then. Of course the confines weren't good back then, but now she seemed confined to showing him too much of her less gracious side.

"It's human nature," the stylist was saying, "to take each other for granted when you are that close."

"It's marriage too, don't you think? Not all lovers treat each other so mercilessly. No, marriage gives you some rights you shouldn't make use of. I must call Grant and apologize."

Indeed. Indeed. Julie did save her monstrous side for her husband, but that doesn't mean she is any kind of monster. How many husbands and wives are guilty of this peculiar language of marriage? Its grammatical rules are impatience, resentment, cruelty, melancholy, and boredom. It is a method of behavior and a mode of speech that you wouldn't dare pull on a friend or even a stranger. But somehow it is alright to unleash this sullenness or surliness upon your spouse. It happens nearly every day in every marital household in America.

Marriage can breed relationships of boredom, monotony, and inconsideration. And even viciousness. And all these begin with little verbal unpleasantries and digs. It's not nice and it's not fair, but that is one of the by-products of marriage.

Marriage has its "grants" and its "taken for granteds." *Granted*—your roommate is privy to all your moods, your neuroses, and your shortcomings. And *granted*—he/she has vowed for better or worse to stick it out. However, you can abuse those marriage *grants*. When you overdo and overburden your exchanges with depression or nastiness, you are *taking for granted* your spouse. If you take him/her for granted long enough, the marriage *grants* will dissipate into a miserable divorce.

As a mistress you were fun. You were willing. You were

sensitive and considerate. No matter what triangular stresses weighed upon your soul, you still smiled and bared the best of yourself. You aimed to please your married man. Many wives, once married, forget about aiming to please. The same goes for husbands. Your marriage gets into trouble when all the fun, willingness, and sensitivity gets lost in the translation of a new language.

If you go from mistress to wife, be wary of the first words of that marital language that can mean trouble. A wife who is a good troubleshooter obliterates that marital language before it becomes the only tongue spoken in the household. A wife who is a good troubleshooter eliminates the negative behavior implicit in that speech pattern before it becomes the demeanor that demeans all affection. Once again summon your "hindsight/foresight." If you go from mistress to wife, keep in mind your faces. The face of that mistress you were and the face of the wife you become. Speak to him only with love and consideration. Sometimes use silence; it can indeed be golden. Honesty is wonderful, but can be abused. Don't let becoming a spouse narrow you or convert you into some villain. These temptations can befall any spouse, gender aside!

As one second wife so eloquently described:

"The lack of common courtesy and consideration between married people is probably the most real cause of divorce. Sure, some of them are rats, but most are just real people, victims of human nature. A person comes home from a hard day's work, and instead of pleasant companionship, he or she is hit with complaints, demands, or depression. All too often spouses are too busy trying to make someone into what they want. All too often we remove our spouse's individuality by setting limits on them as a person and confining them to routines. We say, 'No new experiences,' and this goes from ballooning to piano lessons or whatever. A wife writes a poem, and instead of praise for her efforts, she gets scolded for skipping some chore. It's as if marriage turns them into different people than they were before it. Husbands and wives seek outside relationships more often to be loved and accepted again." *(Natchez, Mississippi)*

An affair is a cocoon of mutual acceptance. Both of you are cherished by one another, interwoven with love and passion. After marriage, regardless of where you go or what you do, the cocoon should still be maintained. It will always be you and he against the world, so to speak. That world will thrust good and bad at your union. Your cocoon should be weatherproofed. It should envelop you both with warmth, sensitivity, and security.

If there is communication, there will be love. It is the communication that is sometimes difficult. The hard work that marriage requires refers to communication and then compromise. Understanding each other's needs is the beginning. Compromising to accommodate each other is the real test. Talk is cheap, as they say; compromising and cultivating harmony is the burden within marriage.

However, the reward is love and romance. Your marriage contract should highlight methods and motivations to sustain the passions. Don't become a couple whose only "togetherness" time happens at the day's end. Then, with the children finally asleep, the day's work finally finished, there is little energy or incentive to do more than plug into the TV. If you relegate romance to the last priority of every day, your union will be tired and exhausted. If you schedule togetherness, fun, and privacy into your life, into your days and nights, your union will retain sparkle and freshness.

Romance training won't take out the mystery or the spontaneity. Romance training will rather teach you how to maintain passionate peaks over a lifetime. Romance swept you and that married man off your feet. You and he can ground yourselves in marriage and still not lose that romantic feeling. If you want romance, you can have it. Most of us are romantics and we can all take romance.

Handling His Ex...
Woman Vs. Woman

How does a second wife handle her new husband's ex-wife? My initial advice is *she is not your problem; she is his*. Basically the less you have to do with his first wife, the better.

I have always encouraged mistresses, as well as second wives, to concentrate on their relationships with their men and ignore the wife or ex-wife respectively. However, sometimes that becomes impossible!

There is an old saying that it takes two to tangle, but that is not always true. For instance, what does a second wife do if:

his ex-wife persists in invading your neighborhood, making hysterical scenes steeped in slander on your doorstep;

his ex-wife stalks you in your community, confronting you with verbal abuse in the market, on Main Street and anywhere;

his ex-wife begins calling your place of employment, showing up there to confront you, thus impairing your professional status;

his ex-wife continually verbally demeans you in front of your own children and any step-children?

These are only a few examples of the behavior of harassment that is common for many ex-wives. It doesn't take two to tangle in these instances. It takes only one bitter, vengeful, neurotic ex-wife.

I have received countless letters from mistress/second wives who have had problems such as these. They are looking for some strategy. What should they do? How can a second wife handle an unreasonable *woman scorned* as she tries to ruin her ex's new life and marriage?

I wish the answers were as easy to list as the questions. Why aren't they? Is there a strategy that can eliminate this type of harassment? Is society in any way responsible for contributing to this phenomenon? Just how widespread is the problem? These are a few of the questions we will explore in this epilogue.

I have not dealt with all the problems of handling the ex-wife in the meat of this book for several reasons. First of all, many second wives will not encounter this problem in the extreme. For many, this bitterness and harassing behavior may be a temporary phase exhibited and eventually outgrown by the ex-wife. However, a portion of women who go from mistress to wife will encounter a severe case of harassment that becomes debilitating, aggravating, and frustrating.

The blame lies with the ex-wife and with larger society. Although divorcées are no longer treated as lepers, they are still treated in inappropriate ways. Divorced women are seen typically as victims, struggling to raise children alone, unskilled and deserving of empathy and welfare; victims of runaway fathers or vengeful men whose custody desires and visitation attempts are only motivated by revenge. Divorced women are treated as martyrs, victims, and helpless women by the courts, by judges, by lawyers, by case workers in the social services, by relatives and friends, by politicians and even by feminists.

On the other end of the spectrum, divorced men are treated as immoral runarounds, tightwads who don't want to support children, creatures with little if any parental bonding and inclination, potentially violent and jealous people motivated by revenge and spite. When the divorced man marries his former mistress, take all these generalizations and multiply by 1000.

Society's generalizations are narrow, sexist, and unjust. The myths about divorced men and divorced women make the battle lines clear. It is male against female, power against powerless, rich against poor, child molester against mother; the dichotomy is endless in the mythological breakdown.

Where myths are concerned, generalizations are easy to make. Where reality is concerned, generalizations fail to report the truth. Most saliently, generalizations fail to recognize a new, undiscovered victim in all this—the second wife!

In all fairness, some ex-wives are in a bind financially and emotionally. It is equally true that some ex-husbands are in similar binds financially and emotionally. The plight of the divorced man is beginning to surface ever so faintly in society's consciousness. However the plight of the second wife is still unknown.

There are some ex-wives who end a career in marriage only to begin a new career in harassment. Their arenas are the legal system, which affords many of them, free of charge, a tool to legally harass their ex-husbands, as well as his new second wife. The arenas are also the school district, the community, anywhere the two women share common space. Many of these ex-wives receive regular and appropriate child support and alimony. And they chose not to work. Many of these ex-wives have ex-husbands who with their second wives would gladly participate in child care and even day care. Yet these ex-wives want no cooperation; they want only confrontation over the past. These are women who can not let go of their pasts and start a new life. These ex-wives are obsessed and determined to make life miserable for the ex-husband, his new second wife, any and all children involved, and all extended families. It takes only one woman to do this and to do it well. In these cases the second wives are truly victims of a new unacknowledged crime.

Right here and now I am dedicated to two things: one, to suggest some possible strategies and philosophies for second wives, and two, to enlist your support in delineating this problem. I have included this phenomenon in a book geared to women in mistress marriages because these second wives have the hardest time.

The cardinal rule of strategy is to realize the intent of his ex-wife. Her intent is to make your life miserable and ruin your marriage. Therefore cut her opportunities to a minimum. If she bangs on your front door, close the door and call the police. If she harasses you on the telephone, record all threatening conversation. If she damages your job performance by her presence or allegations, call the police. If she tries to engage you in conversations or screaming matches, don't participate. In time, those in the community, the neighborhood, the families, and the congregations will get the picture of a *woman scorned*. Having her behavior on record with the local police is invaluable. Then if your property, or your person is damaged, they will know where to look first. Police verification also comes in handy in the courts. Legal harassment is common to ex-husbands and their second wives. Slander is easy to throw around; having proof of harassment shows the judge whose character is whose.

An equally important corollary is to learn to turn her escapades inside out. Make her behaviors work for you. Look for the silver lining in every cloud. What exactly do I mean by that? Here are a few examples.

If the ex-wife denies visitation and leaves you and your husband with ruined plans for a family outing, reorganize. Use the time to rekindle romance, or do something together that you and he have been wanting to do but haven't had time. In that way her attempts to ruin your day are giving you the opportunity to have a better, more romantic day.

If the ex-wife is bent on letting the bank foreclose on the marital residence to ruin your credit and your husband's investment, buy the house—even if that means going to court to force a sale. Get the house, fix it up, and sell it for a profit. Then she is the only one who loses.

If the ex-wife is continually creating scenes in front of the children—yours, his, or new ones of mutual making—let your homelife without scenes demonstrate the difference. Children will gravitate to the peaceful, secure household.

I haven't the space here to list innumerable examples. Each mistress marriage has unique demands and opportunities, even while harassing techniques are often the same. Expect harassment. You are not the only second wife who is victimized. Expect the children to be used as effective weaponry. Don't let your ex-husband set himself up for wild accusations of rape, child molesting, ex-beating, etc. You can do this by accompanying him at all times he is in his ex's presence. And yet, still she may try these or more creative accusations. This is where having her record with local police really helps.

It is definitely sad that this strategy and advice has to be given at all. But it does. There are second wives out there who know what I mean, who know the exasperation and the humiliation of this harassment. They also know how trying and confusing it can be to deal with the ex and handle her bizarre behavior.

Second wives need help, more help than I can give in so few pages. The best help I can give is to illuminate this problem, to get into print how often second wives and their husbands are a new breed of victim. And so at the end of this epilogue, there is a questionnaire to the second wife, to help her document her problem of harassment.

In matrimonial matters and post-matrimonial matters, the second wife is a person that is overlooked. If the mistress is indeed the scapegoat, the second wife inherits the punishments. Society encourages this fate by its pat stereotypes. Society categorizes post-divorce people by sex, affixing discriminating labels. Many problems in second marriages are problems not of man vs. woman, ex-husband vs. ex-wife, but problems created by first wife, problems of woman vs. woman.

Perhaps when these problems are analyzed without sexist prejudice, society's consciousness will be raised to a higher plane. Issues like harassment, visitation interference, welfare, day care will be seen differently. When this occurs there will be no losers. Ex-wives stripped of eternal sympathy will be forced to abandon spite and start concentrating on a new life. Second wives will be protected from harassment, as will their husbands. Fathers will be saved from deprivation of their children. Children will be saved from emotional child abuse and be allowed to live in peace.

Divorced, remarried men have not been effective in speaking out. Men as a group need promotional assistance. The second wife will be the voice of the future. It is she who will change the system, the government, and the people of America. By enlightening society about harassment, a new picture will emerge—a picture not of poor ex-wife hounded by spiteful ex-husband, but a picture of *woman scorned* victimizing another woman. Villains will not solely be men. Motherhood will not be a convenient armor for spite, because second wives are oftentimes mothers too. When our stereotypes change, society will not tolerate this harassment of the second wife.

Spiteful ex-wives will lose their upper hand in the courts, in custody matters, in financial aid, and in the flagrant disobedience of court orders and laws. Social and judicial procedure will have to change.

If you go from mistress to wife, you may become one of this new breed of victims. Are you ready to accept the burden? Are you prepared to assist in changing society?

We, as second wives, have a responsibility to work for change. Perhaps if we all work together, public opinion and public policy can reflect truth and help only those who need and deserve help. Perhaps, we, as second wives, can raise society's consciousness to that higher plane. Perhaps that higher plane will even embrace justice!

Questionnaire for the Second Wife
Subject: Harassment by His Ex-Wife

Have you been victimized by a spiteful ex-wife? Have you found yourself in some new kind of battle, looking for the bunker? Do you feel like some stunned recruit thrust into a war you didn't know could be launched? Are you defending yourself vigorously without knowing why you should have to in the first place? If the answers are yes, you are a second wife under attack by harassment, perpetuated by his ex-wife.

This is not a new problem for the second wife or for the woman who goes from mistress to wife. However, it is a problem that has gotten little public attention. Help me give this harassment the spotlight it needs. If you are a victim, speak out! If you know a victim, give them this questionnaire! If your husband is a victim give him the questionnaire too!

1. Have you been victimized by pranks? Describe them.

2. Has any of your property been damaged mysteriously? Explain.

3. Has his ex-wife publicly embarrassed you by her screaming, or name-calling? Where?

4. Have you had to call the police for assistance and protection from her hysteria or violence?

5. Do you feel like a prisoner in your own home, afraid of what might happen or of what his ex-wife is capable of doing?

6. Do you fear for the safety of your pets?

7. Have threats been made against you, your property, your pets, or your children?

8. Has your reputation been slandered? Or the reputation of your husband?

9. Has harassment occurred in your neighborhood?

10. Have you been confronted and verbally abused on your property or your doorstep?

11. Has your good name been slandered within the community, or within your religious congregation?

12. Has the school district's record been spiced with lies about you, your husband, and both of your characters?

13. Have you been embarrassed, verbally abused, and called names in front of your own children?

14. Have you been victimized and demeaned in front of your stepchildren?

15. Has this harassing behavior had an effect upon your new marriage? If so, what? Positive as well as negative effects?

16. Has this harassing behavior affected your job performance?

17. Has this harassing burden affected your emotions, your health? The state of your family's health and emotional state?

18. Have you sought help and protection from the legal system? Any results and what kind?

19. Have your extended family members been subjected to harassment too?

20. Do you have any suggestions, remedies, or coping ideas for the rest of the second wife population?

Please let this questionnaire serve as an outline. Answer it, add to it, and use it as a basis to help you describe your story of harassment.

Heretofore this has not been a popular subject. But there comes a time when the affected women have to confront the women who are wrong. There comes a time for second wives when patience runs out, when sympathy runs dry, and when outrage is necessary!

In an era of feminism, it has become unfashionable to criticize women. However, women have come a long way and some women have a long way to go. You can be a true feminist, and work to purify society, even if that means engaging in a suit of woman vs. woman!

If you are a second wife, or a second-wife candidate, this may be part of your destiny.

Mistresses Anonymous Questionnaire

This questionnaire is designed to collect the real facts about women who are involved with married men. The myths will continue so long as mistresses are afraid to tell the truth about themselves. Please answer these questions and feel free to add anything you desire. I guarantee that you will remain anonymous. No signature is necessary. And I guarantee you will be helping women everywhere.

Thank you.

1. Where do you live? _____
2. How would you characterize your location—small town, big city, etc.? _____
3. How old are you? _____
4. Are you single, married, separated, divorced, widowed? _____
5. What religion, if any, are you? If you practice one, how? _____
6. What is your occupation, if any? _____
7. Do you consider yourself liberated? In what way? _____
_____
8. Do you consider yourself a mistress? _____
9. How old is your married man? _____
10. What is his occupation? _____
11. How did you meet him (at work, socially, or whatever)? _____

12. Was the first date your idea or his?   _____

13. Was he the first married man you dated?   _____

14. Why did you choose to date a married
    man?   _____

15. Did you know he was married first off?   _____

16. How long have you been seeing him?
    Or how long did the relationship last?   _____

17. If he didn't tell you right from the start
    he was married, when did you find out?
    And how?   _____

          _____

          _____

18. How did his being married make you
    feel?   _____

19. How often did you meet?   _____

20. In what kinds of places?   _____

21. What did your meetings consist of?   _____

22. Could you see him whenever you
    wanted?   _____

23. When did sex enter into the relationship?
    From the start? If not, when?   _____

24. How important was the sexual aspect?   _____

25. Was your sex life with him rewarding?
    More rewarding than with other lovers
    before him?   _____

26. If he was still sleeping with his wife, did
    his infidelity with her inhibit you? How?   _____

27. Was he still having relations with his
    wife?   _____

28. Did you have sexual relations each time
    you met?   _____

29. Describe if you wish any aspects of your
    sex life that you think would shed light
    on this subject.   _____

    _____

    _____

    _____

30. Did he complain that his sex life with
    his wife was unsatisfying for him?   _____

31. Are you or were you in love with your
    married man? How do you know?
    _____
    _____

32. What do you think is the main reason for
    your relationship (sex, friendship,
    business, or any other)?
    _____

33. Did you ever ask him to get a divorce?
    _____

34. Or did he promise divorce?
    _____

35. After how long in the course of the
    relationship did either of the above
    occur?
    _____

36. If you asked him to divorce, how did he
    respond?
    _____

37. Did divorce become an ongoing
    question, struggle, argument (which or
    all)?
    _____

38. Do you think his wife knew about your
    affair? If so, how? What makes you
    think she knew?
    _____
    _____
    _____

39. Did you ever have contact with his wife?
    How (a coincidence, business, a
    confrontation)?
    _____
    _____
    _____

40. If his wife found out, did it end the
    affair? Did it change the affair and how?
    _____

41. Did your married man give you any
    money? For what (rent, expenses, etc.)?
    _____

42. Did you want him to give you money or
    gifts?
    _____

43. Did you refuse to take money or gifts?
    Why?
    _____

44. Did he have children? How many?
    _____

45. Did you meet his children? How?
    _____

46. How do you feel about his children?
    _____

47. Would you marry your married man if
    he divorced?
    _____

48. Why do you think your married man
    hasn't divorced?
    _____

49. Do you think he will divorce? What
    makes you think so?
    _____
    _____

50. Did you date other men during your relationship? _____

51. Did you have sexual relations with other men? _____

52. How did you feel about this? _____

53. How did he feel about your dating or having relations with other men? _____

54. Whom did you tell about this affair? _____

55. Did you tell your mother? _____

56. Did you make new friends because of him? _____

57. Did you lose friends because of him? _____

58. How did he change your life (your job _____ or friendships, social life, emotional _____ state, etc.)?

59. Have you ended the relationship, or has he? Why and how? _____

_____

60. Is he or was he the first married man with whom you became involved? _____

61. Are you glad you met him? _____

62. Are you sorry you met him? _____

63. Would you ever date a married man again? _____

64. What did you like about being a mistress? _____

65. What didn't you like about being a mistress?

66. Do you have any children? How old? _____

67. Do they know of your affair? _____

68. Have they met your married man and in what circumstances? _____

_____

69. Do they approve? Disapprove? _____

70. How do you feel your being a mistress affects your children, if at all? _____

Thank you for answering. Since this is anonymous, may I quote you? _____

Return this questionnaire and any comments or questions to me at:

Melissa Sands/Mistresses Anonymous, Inc.
Publisher of the Triangle Tabloid P.O. Box 151
Islip, N.Y. 11751

Questionnaire for the Married Man

This questionnaire is designed to collect the real facts about married men involved in the triangle. The stereotypes will reign so long as men remain silent. Married men have needs and feelings that deserve to be aired and understood. Please answer all the questions and add to any with your views. I guarantee that you will remain anonymous. No signature is required. I also guarantee that your answers will benefit hundreds of thousands of men and women.

This questionnaire was developed by Melissa Sands and Michael Sands, respectively, President and Executive Vice President of Mistresses Anonymous, Inc.

1. Where do you live? _____
2. Characterize your locale—city, rural, suburb, etc. _____
3. What is your age? _____
4. What is your race? _____
5. What is your religion? _____
6. In what ways do you practice your religion? _____
7. What is your occupation? _____
8. What is your educational training? _____
9. How would you rate your physical appearance? _____
10. Why did you get involved with another woman? _____
11. Where did you meet this other woman? _____
12. How do you feel about the word "mistress"? _____

13. Did she initially know you were married? _____
14. Where do you meet with your mistress? _____
15. Of what do the meetings consist? _____
16. How old is your mistress? _____
17. What is her marital status? _____
18. Do you finance her in any way? Explain. _____
19. How would you describe your sex life with your mistress? _____
20. Do you expect fidelity from your mistress? _____
21. Is this your first affair? _____
22. Are you in love with your mistress? How do you know? _____
23. Will you divorce? _____
24. How long has this relationship been going on? _____
25. How has it affected you as a person? _____
26. How has it affected your work? _____
27. How has it affected your family life? _____
28. How long have you been married? _____
29. Characterize your marriage (happy, unhappy, etc.). _____
30. Is this your first marriage? _____
31. How old is your wife? _____
32. Do you have children? How many? _____
33. How is your sex life at home? _____
34. Do you and your wife communicate? Explain. _____
35. Does your wife know you are having an affair? _____
36. If your wife learns of the affair, what will happen? _____
37. Do affairs have a "price"? _____
38. What would you do if your wife had an affair? _____
39. Do you believe in monogamy? _____
40. Who is your best friend? _____
41. Having a wife and a mistress, do you have time for yourself? _____
42. Is this your last affair? _____

Thank you for answering.
Please send this to:

Mistresses Anonymous
P.O. Box 151
Islip, N.Y. 11751